War Magic

WAR MAGIC
Religion, Sorcery, and Performance

Edited by

D. S. Farrer

berghahn
NEW YORK · OXFORD
www.berghahnbooks.com

First published in 2016 by

Berghahn Books

www.berghahnbooks.com

© 2016 Berghahn Books

Originally published as a special issue of *Social Analysis*, volume 58, issue 1.

Cover: Self-mortification to earn karma for her devotees. Joyce Phoon, Singapore, 2007. Figure 1.6, this volume. Photograph © Melvin Hodder.

All rights reserved.
Except for the quotation of short passages for the purposes of criticism and review, no part of this book may be reproduced in any form or by any means, electronic or mechanical, including photocopying, recording, or any information storage and retrieval system now known or to be invented, without written permission of the publisher.

Library of Congress Cataloging-in-Publication Data

Names: Farrer, D. S., editor.
Title: War magic : religion, sorcery, and performance /
  edited by D. S. Farrer.
Description: New York : Berghahn Books, 2016. | "Originally published as a
  special issue of Social Analysis, volume 58, issue 1." | Includes
  bibliographical references and index.
Identifiers: LCCN 2016017637 (print) | LCCN 2016031229 (ebook) |
  ISBN 9781785333293 (pbk. : alk. paper) | ISBN 9781785333309 (ebook)
Subjects: LCSH: War and society. | War—Religious aspects. | Magic. |
  Shamanism.
Classification: LCC GN497 .W284 2016 (print) | LCC GN497 (ebook) |
  DDC 306–dc23
LC record available at https://lccn.loc.gov/2016017637

British Library Cataloguing in Publication Data

A catalogue record for this book is available from the British Library.

ISBN 978-1-78533-329-3 (paperback)
ISBN 978-1-78533-330-9 (ebook)

Dedicated to Muriel Jean Playsted and Sheila Martin

Contents

List of Illustrations	ix
Introduction	
War Magic: Religion, Sorcery, and Performance	1
D. S. Farrer	
Chapter 1	
Tangki War Magic: Spirit Warfare in Singapore	25
Margaret Chan	
Chapter 2	
Javanese Ritual Initiation: Invulnerability, Authority, and Spiritual Improvement	47
Jean-Marc de Grave	
Chapter 3	
Discourse of Decline: Sumatran Perspectives on Black Magic	67
J. David Neidel	
Chapter 4	
Tamil Tiger Ritual, War, and Mystical Empowerment	88
Michael Roberts	
Chapter 5	
Shamanic Battleground in Venezuela	107
Željko Jokić	

Chapter 6
Chants of Re-enchantment: Chamorro Spiritual Resistance to 127
   Colonial Domination
      D. S. Farrer and James D. Sellmann

Chapter 7
War Magic and Just War in Indian Tantric Buddhism 149
      Iain Sinclair

Index 165

Illustrations

Figures

0.1	Victory from the ruins: St. Leonard's Parish Church, VE Day 1945	6
1.1	*Or leng* or black command flag, replete with esoteric meanings of thunder and war	34
1.2	*Or leng* legend	35
1.3	A Singaporean *tangki* pierced with rods topped with the godheads of the Generals of the Five Directions	36
1.4	The hooks will be used when the *tangki* later drags a heavy carriage behind him	37
1.5	A Singaporean *tangki* cuts his tongue to produce blood to make a talisman	39
1.6	Self-mortification to earn karma for her devotees. Joyce Phoon, Singapore, 2007	41
1.7	A Thai *tangki* performing in Singapore	42
2.1	Mbah simulating the *windu kencana* initiation rite of the *keris*, Yogyakarta, 2005	53
3.1	A student of *ilmu kebal* being tested with a machete	73
3.2	Entranced dancer performing on a board of nails	75
4.1	Young Tiger fighter with holy ash on his forehead heads for the battlefield in the late 1980s	89
4.2	Photographs of female *māvīrar* surrounded by tropes of abundance at a *māvīrar* shed in Velvittathurai, November 2004	97
5.1	A *shapori* transformed into the ancestral jaguar Irariwë	112
5.2	A candidate receives the crown of light (*watoshe*) during a shamanic initiation	113
5.3	A *shapori* engaged in protective, integrative activities in his own community	115
5.4	Transformed into a moon *hekura*, the *shapori* searches for a victim outside a *shapono*	116
6.1	I Fanlalai'an, Solomon Islands FestPac, 2012	139

Tables

2.1 The generic mantra for all *aji* invocations   54

Maps

3.1 Central Sumatra   70
5.1 Research area in the Upper Orinoco River region   111

Introduction
War Magic: Religion, Sorcery, and Performance

D. S. Farrer

War magic is violence, orchestrated or defended against through magic, used alternately to harm or to heal.[1] Compelling the investigator to navigate complex webs of definition in 'religion' and 'magic', war magic appears multi-sided, with porous conceptual boundaries incorporating various particular historical contexts. Janus-like offense and defense inevitably form a dualistic central pole around which webs of meaning arise, to wit, 'black' and 'white' magic, spells to harm and protect, and talismans to unleash or ward off the murderous and sickening powers of unseen enemies, supernatural entities, gods, demons, and the dead. Taking a performative, ethnographic, embodied approach to war magic—otherwise referred to as assault sorcery, magical death, and warrior religion—reveals that war magic is located in specific sites of cultural performance, where people evoke and enact supernatural, liminal, or divine power, on the one hand, to perpetuate violence and, on the other, to resist harm. Here we ask not so much what magic means as what magic does, not if magic is rational or illogical, but in what circumstances it is presumed necessary and effective. Battles of ideas are resolved in bloodshed in the permanent global theater of war.

Whether a belief held is 'true' or 'false' from some particular or universal cultural parameter hardly matters when a hijacked aircraft is about to explode. In the post-9/11 era, the relationship of religion and magic to violence and

Notes for this section begin on page 21.

warfare requires urgent investigation. Prior to the leveling of the World Trade Center brought to pass by al-Qaeda suicide attacks, the sociology of religion ignored Islam. Questions of violence and religion were drawn behind a liberal veil of supposed 'ethnocentrism'. Discussing Islam in the frame of warrior religion became politically incorrect. Thus, a key insight of the great sociologist Max Weber was ignored, and an original avenue of inquiry was closed down, resulting in an eclipse of war magic and warrior religion. Only recently have researchers started to address this. Of course, questions of violence, war magic, and religion cannot be relegated solely to Islam, and all this needs to be understood in relation to centuries of colonial exploitation, slavery, and capitalist oppression, a scenario in which anthropology itself is sorely implicated. Meanwhile, a rich literature is emerging that examines even supposedly pacifist religions such as Buddhism in the context of religious violence.

Bruce Kapferer (2003), himself following the legacy of Evans-Pritchard [1937] (1977), resituates sorcery firmly at the epistemological core of anthropological discourse. War magic is hereby added to the mix, located both as malevolent black magic and as votive protection from such dark forces. Neil Whitehead's (2002) ground-breaking book *Dark Shamans* and (edited with Sverker Finnström) *Virtual War and Magical Death* (2013) provided a nuanced understanding of localized and international technologies of terror emerging from the anthropological study of assault sorcery in South America. Whitehead (2002: 2) commenced his research with the notion of 'semiotics' consisting of "the formal properties of signs, symbols, and rituals," to which he contrasted 'poetics' or "how those signs are used performatively through time." A decade later, 'virtual warfare' is where 'magico-primitivism' meets the 'techno-modern', reiterating Kapferer's (1997: 287) original insight that "[p]ower has the shape of sorcery." In other words, sorcery has become war; in effect, sorcery *is* war (Whitehead and Finnström 2013: 2). Such technologies of terror operate, for example, through remote assassination by computer-operated drones flown by stealth at night, locating targets with covertly obtained intelligence from smart phones, in deadly attacks launched from operational bases thousands of miles away. Technological destruction rains down as if fated by the gods.

While the terms 'war magic' and 'dark shamanism' appear interchangeable, war magic may be pitted against assault sorcery in a socially sanctioned response to attacks. Jokić (chap. 5) shows how the war magician and the dark shaman are one and the same person: "[T]he same practitioner who can cure and protect his or her kin with the help of assistant spirits can also use those spirits for the purpose of inflicting harm and death to others." *War Magic* approaches the problem of sorcery, power, and defense via 'the mastery of souls' by combining theoretical insights from phenomenological and psychological anthropology together with the anthropology of performance, read alongside careful ethnographic observations and historical interpretations. Myths, signs, symbols, perceptions, and beliefs—the reasoning accompanying magical violence—here fall under the umbrella term 'cognition' (including recognition). To this is added 'performance', the release of mystical forces via rituals performed and enacted for the purposes of harming others or defending the community, where liminal rites of passage suspend the 'normal' everyday rules of being to facilitate extraordinary circumstances, amazing occurrences, and dramatic uncanny meetings. Finally, perspectives from 'embodiment', "an existential condition in which the body is the subjective source or intersubjective ground of experience" (Csordas 1999: 143), lock the body to the development of identity, including self or other, friend or foe, freedom fighter or terrorist. Performance literally gets under the skin (chap. 1), becoming part of the person's experience and comprehension of the world.

The re-evaluation of shamanism, sorcery, religion, and magic presented in *War Magic* refers to actual experiences of colonial violence, alongside fears of violence, and the resulting misfortunes, sickness, and death (Clastres [1980] 2010). The chapters travel through Singapore, Java, Sumatra, Sri Lanka, India, Guam, and Venezuela. War magic and warrior religion are considered as symbolic, performative, and embodied practices concerned with innovation and the revitalization of tradition, tempered historically by colonial and postcolonial trajectories in societies undergoing rapid social transformation. Each chapter investigates indigenous philosophies among expert practitioners. The scope of this book incorporates Chinese exorcists (*tangki*s), Javanese spirit siblings, Sumatran black magic, Tamil Tiger suicide bombers, Chamorro spiritual re-enchantment, and Yanomami dark shamans. Taken together, the chapters blaze a trail through the tangled literature and myriad social practices connecting numinosity to violence and spirituality to warfare, contributing to global debates concerning contemporary spiritual innovation, revival, and revitalization.

Discourses specifically concerning war magic have arisen primarily from anthropological studies of Papua New Guinea, Southeast Asia, and Polynesia (Farrer 2009; Reay 1987; Shaw 1976). Historical accounts of war magic in Southeast Asia, such as Anthony Reid's (1988) tour de force, *Southeast Asia in the Age of Commerce*, document the critical importance of magic in matters of warfare, politics, and legal process. There is, of course, considerable overlap in the vast literature on magic and sorcery—especially where they relate to organized violence and death—and to some degree the terms are interchangeable. As an analytical concept, warrior religion was largely confined to sociology (Levtzion 1999; B. Turner 1998; Weber [1922] 1991). Subsequent studies of dark shamanism, shamanic warfare, and shamanic assault have emerged from South America (Whitehead 2002; Whitehead and Wright 2004).[2] Contemporary studies in anthropology, archaeology, history, sociology, folklore, and mythology demonstrate that warrior religion and war magic are ubiquitous social phenomena that have arisen across the globe in a diverse range of cultures. Ancient Icelandic sagas testify to the violent power of the priest-chiefs whose "influence depended on such things as physical strength, personal fame, and skill at arms, just as much as on birth and inherited wealth" (V. Turner 1985: 86). Druids worshipping the Celtic war goddess Morrighan called down lightning like rain to eradicate armies with fire and, pointing one finger, hopped around the enemy camp to cast death spells (Ross 2004: 113). Legends relate how the warrior druid, also serving as poet and king, used cunning and courage to overcome mighty foes.

Whether cowardly or courageous, cunning and trickery are integral elements of war magic that operate through framing, reframing, and misframing (Goffman 1974). During World War II, while the Nazi Party sought an 'unholy alliance' (Levenda 2002) with demonic forces and embraced its 'occult roots' (Goodrick-Clarke 1992), and the Catholic Church turned a blind eye to the persecution of the Jews, the British Army experimented with the 'dirty tricks' of war magic, including illusion, misdirection, and deception (Fisher [1983] 2004). Stage magic became war magic to outwit the 'Desert Fox', Rommel, between 1941 and 1945. Jasper Maskelyne, a professional stage magician, disguised tanks as supply vehicles, used strobe lights to make the Suez Canal disappear, and tricked the Germans into bombing a false harbor for three nights by switching around the regional lights (ibid.). The dirty tricks of war magic are the basic ingredients of modern intelligence and espionage. In many cultures, however, as in antiquity, there is a fine line between the religious virtuoso, sorcerer, healer, stage magician, and trickster. Possibly the greatest magician ever to have lived, Jesus of Nazareth "cured lunatics, paralytics, lepers, the dumb, the blind, the withered, the woman with the issue of blood and those afflicted with demoniacal possession" (Butler [1948] 1993: 73) and accomplished the most difficult magical feat of all: he raised the dead, including himself.

The pejorative use of the word 'magic' and its cognates must be recognized. During the Middle Ages, the Catholic Church in Europe developed a discourse in which 'magic', 'sorcery', and 'witchcraft' became demonizing labels to justify social exclusion, persecution, torture, tribunals, and execution. Magic, so the creed went, stood in the way of the conversion of savages, heathens, and idolaters to the true path of the righteous, which was necessary to rid the world of sin and guarantee salvation in everlasting life. In their doctrines, Victorian scholars—such as Sir James Frazer, Sir Edward Tylor, Auguste Comte, Herbert Spencer, and subsequently Emile Durkheim and Max Weber—echoed this 'civilizing' prejudice that magic was a lower form of rationality in the evolution of thought, which supposedly developed through magic and religion to culminate in the scientific worldview. The Weberian notion that the world was entering a final rational phase of disenchantment was, however, short-lived. Yet the claim that the present era is one of re-enchantment giving witness to the rise of 'occult economies', that is, the real or imagined deployment of magical means for material ends (Comaroff and Comaroff 1999), or conversely that we have entered an era of terminal decline (the Kali Yuga), begs the question. What is apparent is the ability of people everywhere to engage simultaneously with enchanted, disenchanted, and re-enchanted modes of thinking (notwithstanding cognitive dissonance), where a "discourse of decline" (Neidel, chap. 3) or of amplification through the onset of a burgeoning transnational "New Age culture" (Hutton 1999: 111) may suggest changes in culture as some traditional functions atrophy and others develop.

Religious thought has forever thrived in the jaws of contradiction, and this is reflected in religious practice where the management of liminality pays the rent.

Christianity, like the other "great world religions" institutionalizes liminality (V. Turner 1969: 107), that is, rituals of birth, marriage, and death. The modern church, reeling under countless corroborated incidents of child abuse, nevertheless provides a source of comfort to bereaved family members in the cold industry of death. In England, bombed-out churches, the ruins of victory in World War II, are poignant reminders of a time when priests faced the awkward task of rationalizing the mass slaughter of innocents in terms of God's will. Figure 0.1 shows the ruins of St. Leonard's Parish Church on VE Day, with church-goers holding signs reading "Thank God," "Victory," and "We've Won."

In their social application, religion, sorcery, and magic are nebulous polyvalent concepts that overlap and interpenetrate in complex ways. Generally speaking, magic + malice = sorcery/witchcraft. War sorcery here refers to the organization of ritual practices to harness magical, spiritual, and social-psychological forces that result in an opponent's misfortune, disease, destruction, or death. War magic is an umbrella term that includes war sorcery but also encompasses the various measures used to counter malign sorcerous forces, such as invulnerability magic, and the use of special formulas and amulets designed or utilized for spiritual protection. Warrior religion denotes the social organization of the means of destruction where religion provides a dividing line between 'us and them'. Given the so-called war on terror and the widespread confusion and hostility surrounding the key ideological differential of the modern world order—that being the divide between those with and those without religious 'faith'—a new understanding of religion, secularism, and organized violence is vital.

Warfare refers to "a planned and organised armed dispute between political units" (Keith Otterbein, cited in T. Otto 2006: 23; see also Haas 1990). Warfare comprises the whole spectrum of organized violence within and outside of states, including violent encounters between individuals and small groups of people and (depending on the numbers, organization, and resources) violent antagonisms between different sets of people within communities, genocide, full-scale war between nation-states, and world war. Warfare affects every aspect of the wider society and creates high levels of personal anxiety. Long after the bloodletting desists, the reverberations of political violence are embedded in social organization, health care, education, family narrative, and life history. The large-scale militarization and mobilization of whole populations during wartime is facilitated by a dramatic increase in the rate of workforce exploitation. Military attitudes, discipline, and factory organization spread throughout the social structures of the twentieth century. The non-military workplace was bureaucratized while the family bore the brunt of wartime shock, trauma, stress, and upheaval, repercussions of which were passed down through mental illness across the generations.

Warfare became 'total' by the end of World War I (Virilio 2004: 204), involving trench, naval, and aerial fighting between nation-states that culminated in clear victory or defeat, reparation, rebuilding, and national restructuring. The explosions, however, of the Twin Towers in New York City by the unconventional means of hijacked commercial aircraft obliterated more than

FIGURE 0.1 Victory from the ruins: St. Leonard's Parish Church, VE Day 1945

Source: D. S. Farrer, private collection

prime real estate and thousands of human lives. As counter *"information bombs"* (ibid.), the 9/11 explosions disrupted almost a century of understandings of war that had evolved following World War I. It was acknowledged that the leadership and organizational configuration of Islamic religious groups was different from their bureaucratic Western counterparts and could better be described as 'galactic' (Tambiah 1976), like stars clustered in galaxies, or, more cynically, as 'Medussan', where to chop off one snake head only results in another hundred sprouting forth to replace it. The destruction of 9/11 provoked, or justified, the United States and the United Kingdom to undertake a 'war of manoeuvre' (Gramsci 1971) in Afghanistan and Iraq. Because so-called Islamic terrorists exist beyond nation-states and territories as demarcated by the Western powers, the Bush administration, in the 2001 Patriot Act, immediately redefined 'terrorism' from a criminal activity to an act of war, thus redefining war itself.

Therefore, despite all the ink spilt on religion, magic, and warfare over the past century, we find ourselves at an academic ground zero, if not exactly *illa terra virgo nondum pluviis irrigata* (lit., 'virgin earth not yet watered by the rains'). Christianity is represented as some kind of 'social preservative' to 'save' culture, tradition, and the 'American way of life'. Religion, then, provides a better justification to wage war than 'weapons of mass destruction' that have gone missing or the need for oil to navigate overpowered SUVs through endless, snarled corridors of traffic. World War II is not yet over for the United States, the world's self-appointed police officer and superpower defender of 'liberty, freedom, and democracy'. The result is a society in a perpetual state of military mobilization. Trotsky's cry of permanent revolution was trumped by one of permanent war.

Navigating Webs of Definition

What, then, is the substance of religions worth their weight in blood, oil, and gold? The thorny problem of adequately defining or 'setting bounds' to magic and religion has bedeviled anthropology and leaves us with the problem of navigating elaborate webs of definition. After decades of research, Brian Morris (2006: 1) suggests a "working definition" of religion as "essentially a *social phenomenon*," as opposed to Geertz's 'symbolic system', Tambiah's 'awareness of the transcendent', or Rudolf Otto's 'feeling of the numinous'. Melford Spiro (1987: 197) defines religion as "an institution consisting of culturally patterned interaction with culturally postulated superhuman beings." Among other factors, 'superhuman' could be read as 'supernatural', 'occult', or 'numinous.' Morris (2006: 2–13) immediately doffs his cap to the main theoretical contenders, including intellectualist, emotionalist, cognitive, structuralist, phenomenological, and sociological approaches, to emphasize the continued importance of anthropology in bridging humanist and naturalist accounts. Implicitly following Weber, the institutional aspect of religion is an important definitional tool, vis-à-vis rituals, ethics, doctrines, scriptures, beliefs, congregation and church (or their equivalents), hierarchy, and emotional ethos. All of these terms, however, are problematic, and each draws us further into a seemingly endless web of definition where the centrally bound definitional point remains elusive.

The Resurgence of Warrior Religion

Religion exerts a powerful influence upon social behavior. Following Nietzsche (2000), Max Weber developed a sophisticated perspective that maintained the agency of religion as a counterpoint to theories that relegate religion to the status of epiphenomenon, illusion, or opiate. Weber's ([1905] 2002) insights concerning religion led him to theorize how sets of calculative Protestant attitudes had the unintended consequence of spawning modern 'rational' capitalist development in the West. While recognizing the rationality of Islam, and noting the great historic trading routes from the Middle East, Weber (1978: 265, 444, 474–475, 623–627) regarded Islam primarily as a 'warrior religion'. In this view, Islam prepares its followers psychologically for battle by reconciling the believers to death and the afterlife. More importantly, in Weber's opinion, the organization of Islamic ritual and worship tightly knit the community (*ummah*) and prepare the believers to obey orders given by the leader of the prayer. For Weber, standard organizational definitions regard religion as a group activity in which divine or supernatural entities are entreated or supplicated for the greater good, that is, for the benefit of an ethical project or community. By comparison, magic is considered a way to power employed by self-serving individuals, and sorcery is seen as magic proceeding via demonic intervention.

Weber's views concerning Islam as a warrior religion came under fire from Bryan Turner (1998) in *Weber and Islam*. For Turner, the Orientalism and Eurocentrism of the colonial era infected Weber's 'ideal type' of Islam. In a more subtle approach, both for and against Weber, who clearly endorses the views of the fourteenth-century sociologist Ibn Khaldun, Nehemia Levtzion (1999: 160) suggests that as long as the role of jurists, clerics, and Sufis is recognized in the expansion of Islam, the idea of Islam as a warrior religion may be appropriate under particular historical or social conditions and at particular phase of Islam's development, notably the early period of Islamic expansion during which nomadic tribes supported the charismatic leadership of the Prophet Muhammad. While warrior religion is well illustrated in Islam, it operates under many guises in most societies at different points in time (see, e.g., Elliott 1998; Farrer 2011; Shahar 2008). During my fieldwork in Malaysia, a Muslim martial artist complained to me after prayers in the Zawiyah that clerics are "religious nerds" who do nothing but loaf about the mosque all day (Farrer 2009: 164). To follow the oral tradition (*haddith*) of the Prophet properly, he said, Muslims should practice archery, horseback riding, and wrestling. Nowadays, of course, this *haddith* extends to firearms, automobiles, and mixed martial arts. Combined with a conviction that there is nothing to fear in this world, not even death, such attitudes sustain tenacious warriors. Although de Grave and Neidel (this volume) point out that the influence of so-called modernist Islam encourages Indonesians to abandon their magical beliefs and practices, the danger of a decline in war magic is a pendulum swing in the direction of warrior religion, further evidenced by the murder and persecution of Sufis at the hands of ISIL, so-called Islamic State fighters.

Beyond Primitive Religion

Contemporary scholars who have relinquished the study of 'primitive religion' as an interesting, if misguided, enterprise are no closer to a final definition than their forebears (Sørensen 2007; Stein and Stein 2008). For some anthropologists, the rejection of a grand theory, fanned by the pre-fin-de-siècle postmodern turn, rendered any universal definition of magic or religion impossible. Klass and Weisgrau (1999), for example, claimed that studies in primitive religion were abandoned once it was realized that labeling the other as 'savage', 'barbarian', or 'primitive' is basically a subjective exercise, leading to the conclusion that questions of religion should be left for the individual to decide. Anthropologists could then approach depth psychology for insights concerning ritual and religious symbolism, set in terms of the individual's quest toward personal transformation (Morris 1987: 163–181; V. Turner 1961, 1967, 1975). Citing Rudolf Otto, Carl Jung (1969: 7) borrowed the notion of the *numinosum* to define religion as an experience of something beyond, as a "dynamic agency or effect not caused by an arbitrary act of will … that seizes control of the human subject," who is always cast as victim rather than creator. This notion places the 'mystical experience' of the invaded victim at the core of religious sensibility. It is an experience that may be subsequently manipulated by charisma, magic, and ritual. The emphasis on mystical experience, however, neglects those for whom religion is merely a set of mundane rituals, or those for whom religion is a loosely accepted set of practices that are enacted at moments of crisis or celebration and are otherwise left hung out to dry.

Dramatic shifts in the understanding of violence and warfare correspond with wider shifts in the meaning of culture and religion. Drawing inspiration from Weber, Evans-Pritchard, Kapferer, and Whitehead, this collection seeks to address war magic and warrior religion through the grounded particularities of their embodied ritual practice and performance. Provided that the researcher is willing and able to suspend or bracket (*epoché*) her cultural conceptual divisions, issues of magic and religion may emerge as specific social phenomena, leaving universal definitions for sociological exercise—at which Weber's ([1922] 1991) *The Sociology of Religion* remains unsurpassed. Nevertheless, whereas dark shamanism is a strategy to inflict harm, war magic operates to cure ills. As Chan (chap. 1) points out, the ancient Chinese ideograph 毉 (*yi*, physician) is comprised of an arrow in a quiver at the top left, a hand drawing a bowstring at the top right, and two dancing wu 巫 female shamans or sorcerers below. Akin to the *pharmakon* (remedy/poison), therefore, the central themes of war magic include violence and healing, brought about through ritual and performance, with the goal of unleashing or controlling the power of gods, ghosts, demons, and the dead (Farrer 2008; Kapferer 2004; Taussig 1987).

War magic refers to an attribute, power, or practice, whereas war magician is a (possibly hereditary) social status—that is, it is institutional (and thereby religious). Terms used to address the war magician include 'war sorcerer', 'witch', 'warrior shaman', 'war wizard', 'warrior druid', 'warrior priest', and, perhaps less commonly, 'guru', 'shaman', Shaiva, and Sufi (Mauss [1902] 2001; Winstedt [1925] 1993). While these terms reflect religious or political sensitivities, depending on circumstance, culture, and situation, they also indicate problems with the commonly employed analytical boundaries drawn between magic, sorcery, shamanism, and religion. In anthropology texts, magic is typically defined as the ability to influence others or events through supernatural intervention or agency.[3] Magic is regarded as an individual enterprise that serves particular ends rather than benefiting the community at large, in contrast to religion, which serves ethical ends directed toward the wider community or society. Sorcery and witchcraft are often defined in much the same way as magic, with interstitial boundaries left arbitrary or unclear, although there is some predilection to relegate sorcery and witchcraft to malevolent, murderous, or harmful magic. Sometimes the sorcery-witchcraft distinction reflects historical European differences drawn between sorcery and witchcraft, with sorcery being looked on as a primitive and possibly rather innocuous type of magic that later evolved into maleficent witchcraft, typified in times of medieval Christianity by accusations of keeping familiars, summoning demons, and worshipping Satan (Russell and Alexander [1980] 2007).

Shamanism is deemed the earliest known form of religion, with practitioners entering into trances or altered states of consciousness in order to commune with spirits and supplicate them for the ethical community ends of healing the sick or staving off misfortune (Eliade 1972; Lewis [1971] 2003). Sorcery, in contrast, may be defined antithetically to shamanism as a ritual practice to summon or compel—not supplicate—ancestral, demonic, or nature spirits into this realm to carry out the individual and possibly unethical bidding of the sorcerer, diviner, or necromancer. This definition is, of course, almost interchangeable with the definition of witchcraft given above.

Anthropological accounts have tended to neglect war magic and warrior religion despite the fact that the discipline emerged during the most violent century of recorded human history. Similarly, apart from a few exceptions, contemporary sociological theory has dismissed the notion of Islam as a warrior religion, viewing it as merely a reflection of Weber's Orientalism fueled by Western fears of 'conversion by the sword'. In social and cultural anthropology, war magic and warrior religion make only the occasional ethnographic guest appearance, usually being relegated to parentheses, a footnote, or an aside. War magic and warrior religion have predominantly been placed in the margins of studies that focus on artwork, area studies, cults, curiosities, curatives, dance, ghosts, hunting, jewelry, legal culture, the occult, performance, poisons, power objects, possession, religion, ritual, scarification, secret societies, sorcery, the supernatural, tattoos, trance, weapons, witchcraft, and violence. In contrast, this book resituates the cross-cultural problematic of war magic and warrior religion in its rightful place at the epistemological core of anthropological discourse.

The Eclipse of War Magic

The eclipse of war magic in anthropology dates back to the time of Bronislaw Malinowski, who considered in depth almost every conceivable type of magic *except* war magic, which was relegated to tantalizing asides on uncut groves or *boma* (Malinowski [1935] 1965: 87). The film *Bronislaw Malinowski: Off the Veranda* (Singer 1985) points out that, during his Trobriand fieldwork, Malinowski lived right next door to the magician for his own protection. Another ethnographic film, *Trobriand Cricket* (Leach 1976), provides an intriguing glimpse of Trobriand war magic and, in the process, advances an implicit critique of Malinowski. Here war magic is shown transposed onto cricket, a game introduced by missionaries to inculcate discipline and rule-governed competitive behavior as an alternative to internecine village revenge attacks. In the Trobriand adaptation of cricket, the wicket posts had to be situated closer together than in the Western game and the pitch made considerably longer due to the Trobrianders' accuracy in throwing the ball—an ability honed by hurling spears. The resounding chant "PK," intended to make the catcher's hands stick like glue, sounds amusing amid the dance of tribesmen marching like soldiers and stretching out their arms to mimic airplanes landing. However, sticking, catching, holding, and seizing are key aspects in combat, sorcery, and witchcraft alike. For Malinowski (1948: 14), the function of religion is to help the community tackle the universal and inescapable social fact of death, whereas magic functions as insurance against uncertainty. As far as 'uncertain situations' go, few can be more precarious than modern violence and warfare, with their threat of impending sudden death. Despite his copious field notes on the subject, Malinowski's neglect of war magic is indicative of his wider ethnographic aim to debunk the colonial myth of the violent, primitive 'savage'.

'Data' provided by the Trobriand war magician Kanukubusi led Malinowski ([1922] 2013: 409) to the important discovery that "magic rests in the belly." Although Malinowski made a great advance in considering magic from the unified perspective of the spell, the ritual performer, and the performance, he overemphasized the spell at the expense of the embodied practice of magic. Colonial ethnography experienced difficulties in conceiving of embodied magic. Instead, it emphasized the importance of spells, the holy word, or incantations over the embodied ritual practice or performance of magic and religion (Farrer 2009). In Southeast Asia, however, Islamic utterances or prayers introduce, close, or may utterly displace so-called animist spells in ritual performances of supernatural phenomena. Here, contra-Malinowski, the importance of the spell is secondary to magical performance (see also Tambiah 1968, 1985, 1990). Such performances include war dances, martial arts displays, walking on fire, eating broken glass, climbing barefoot up a ladder of knives, and dipping one's hands into cauldrons of scalding water, boiling oil, or molten tin (Farrer 2009: 232–243; Waterson 1995: 94). In Asia, sorcery, mysticism, shamanism, and magic may all blur into religion. Consequently, a focus on war magic and warrior religion problematizes and destabilizes taken-for-granted Western conceptual boundaries between magic and religion, body and soul, real and unreal, now and the hereafter.

The Mastery of Souls

Returning to the web of definitions for sorcery, magic, and witchcraft, the most well-known ethnographic definitions derive from the Africanist model espoused by Evans-Pritchard ([1937] 1977). Evans-Pritchard configured the witch as the unsuspecting individual holder of a witchcraft substance contained within the belly, in contrast to the sorcerer who is the knowing member of a secret society. The description of the viscous witchcraft substance in the belly of the Zande witch is strongly reminiscent of that alluded to by Malinowski years earlier.[4] Localized ethnographic definitions and distinctions, however, floundered once they were applied to other ethnographic regions, where foreign regional divisions between sorcery, witchcraft, shamanism, and magic proved inadequate. In this connection, contributions to Michele Stephen's (1987b) edited volume *Sorcerer and Witch in Melanesia* reveal that Evans-Pritchard's model fails to apply in New Guinea and more widely across Southeast Asia, where specialists in ritual, religion, and magic are better characterized by their 'mastery of souls' (see Stephen 1987a). The capability to affect the destiny of souls, or in Sufi terms 'to knock someone's leaf from the tree of life' in order to cause misfortune, suffering, and death, betrays an ability harbored in war magic. According to Reay (1987: 89–91), however, war sorcery involves manipulating objects belonging to the victim, as opposed to war magic proper, which proceeds through ritual and incantation—a somewhat arbitrary distinction between magic and sorcery that need not detain us here. A more useful concept is that of war magic employed as a form of 'defensive magic' (often emphasizing protection, invulnerability, or invincibility) against 'offensive magic' (consisting of hostile supernatural acts of witchcraft or sorcery), whether or not the latter may be considered subjective or objective, passive or aggressive, intentional or denuded of agency.

A paternalistic mission of representation in advocate anthropology previously meant that the 'dark' or 'evil' side of informants and their social doings was glossed over or ignored by anthropologists seeking to promote their informants' culture in a positive way, especially against racist colonial and imperialist powers. Moving toward a post-colonial era in which the actions of political elites are increasingly distanced from their historical antecedents means that a space has opened for ethnography to recognize that 'they lie, we lie' (Metcalf 2002) and that anthropology has gained ground to become grittier and more subtle, relevant, and realistic. It is not surprising that the notion of 'dark shamanism' emerged from Amazonia, where the liberal trope of the heroic anthropologist—supposedly representing impoverished downtrodden people who were otherwise left without a voice—was made irrelevant by the poisoning of Neil Whitehead, himself a victim of shamanic malevolence (Whitehead and Wright 2004; see also Whitehead 2013).

While religion purports to be engaged in the ethical project of becoming-human, to make people live decent and civilized lives, for Deleuze and Guattari ([1987] 2004) the warrior tends toward 'becoming-intense', 'becoming-animal'. Following Dumézil (1970), Deleuze and Guattari ([1987] 2004: 232–309) note that the war machine entails all kinds of 'becomings-animal', insofar as the warrior remains a liminal and transgressive figure, exterior to the state even if subordinated to it. Becoming-animal involves the fighters of the war machine undergoing intense ritual ordeals, possibly enduring bodily alteration through tattooing or scarification as well as psychological trials of privation, torment, and intimidation. Outside of the conditions of war, hunting, shamanic trance, drumming, dance, yoga, and martial arts provide opportunities for becoming-intense, becoming-animal (Farrer 2013). Intense animal becomings, for example, are suggested in the practice of hatha yoga (Farrer 2009: 124–127), with adepts adopting animal postures such as 'the crow' and 'the cobra' and other stances known as 'warrior poses'. Or consider another example from martial arts. In the Javanese martial art of the 'evil tiger' (*silat siluman harimau*) (Farrer 2006: 41; 2009: 268–269), becoming-animal to summon an ancestral spirit of a tiger or crocodile, as a spirit-helper, is the culmination of a ritual practice where the martial artist lies in an open grave for eight consecutive nights (Farrer 2009: 255–256, 269).

Becoming-animal may also illustrate more sinister practices. In Guyana, *kanaimà* shamans, for example, operate in small packs to assault victims (often vulnerable women or children), whom they seize from behind in order to dislocate the victims' shoulder or fingers. This is followed by a subsequent attack, taking place up to a year or two later, in which the victims are forced to their knees so that a poisonous snake can bite their tongues, and they are then made to lie face down. The victim's anus is penetrated with the rough tail of an iguana or armadillo that is vibrated to destroy the anal wall. The anal sphincter is then slit and the enlarged wound prized open with a flexed twig so that the target's rectum can be stuffed deeply with bags of astringent herbs. After the victim's agonizing death (usually by dehydration), the *kanaimà* practitioners attend the victim's grave and slide a stick into the corpse so that they can taste the *maba* (honey-like) "juices of putrefaction" (Whitehead 2002: 14–15). A climate of fear, terror, and revenge is perpetuated by such revolting and offensive practices.

From another angle, Kapferer (1991, 1997, 2003) points out that sorcery exists to attain power. Ideology, politics, and warfare—and religion, sorcery, and magic—are familiar bedfellows. Each set of ideas exists as interlinked, interwoven, multiplicitous social phenomena that can only be artificially teased apart from the others in the set for the purposes of definition and description. In *The Unabridged Devil's Dictionary*, Ambrose Bierce ([1881] 2000: 216) perceived sorcery as the "ancient prototype and forerunner of political influence." Bierce defines politics as a "strife of interests masquerading as a contest of principles" where public affairs are conducted "for private advantage" (ibid.: 184). To the skeptical unbeliever, political demonstrations of religiosity appear to be epiphenomenon, subsidiary posturing, hypocrisy, or ideological gloss to the war for oil and control of the planet's resources. Nevertheless, religion must be regarded as a central actor in the theater of war. Whether Islamic, Buddhist, Judaic, or Christian, revitalized religions can provide the moral switch to activate war machines and terror networks in the service of apparent global, human, and divine interests in order to secure, symbolic, cultural, social and economic capital.

Introduction to the Chapters

The chapters presented in this book discuss demon-killing exorcists in the Singapore Chinese diaspora (Margaret Chan), Javanese secret society initiations (Jean-Marc de Grave), black magic in Sumatra (J. David Neidel), Tamil Tiger ritual, war, and assassination in Sri Lanka (Michael Roberts), Chamorro re-enchantment on Guam (D. S. Farrer and James D. Sellmann), Yanomami shamans in Venezuela (Željko Jokić), and tantric Buddhist war magic in India (Iain Sinclair). The methods employed are predominantly ethnographic—Chan, de Grave, Farrer, Neidel, and Jokić are ethnographers. The chapters engage with an interdisciplinary literature, including social anthropology (de Grave, Farrer, Jokić, and Neidel), theater studies (Chan), religious studies (Sinclair), and history (Sellmann and Roberts).

In chapter 1, "*Tangki* War Magic: Spirit Warfare in Singapore," Margaret Chan explores exorcist war magic in *tangki* Chinese spirit-medium worship. Within the communities of the Hokkien diaspora in Taiwan and Southeast Asia, *tangki* worship—whose origin stretches back to pre-Sinic tribal rituals performed five thousand years ago—remains active. In *tangki* worship, warrior gods become incarnate through spirit-possession in order to kill evil spirits. *Tangki*s are thus spirit-mediums operating as the exorcist protectors of their communities. Devotees consult *tangki*s to cure illness, change their luck, or solicit oracles. The entranced *tangki* cures by vanquishing disease-causing malevolent demons, brings good luck by driving away the spirits of ill fortune, and advises on metaphysical strategy through oracles.

Tangki Chinese spirit-medium worship has no liturgical canon but instead emphasizes the performance of war magic ritual. It is a ritual theater of spirit-possessed mediums believed to be warrior gods incarnate: beyond representation, *tangki*s provide a virtual "interactive magic." Bloody acts of self-mortification present the inherent violence of war. Self-mortification, piercing the flesh with rods, or injuring the body with swords or mace-like weapons is the hallmark of *tangki* performances in which the *tangki* opposes evil demons. *Tangki*s pierce their bodies with swords and rods in order to take on the spirit-power imbued in these weapons. Driven into the flesh, the weapons supercharge the *tangki* with spirit-power. Adopting Buddhist concepts of self-mortification, contemporary acolytes pierce themselves with ceiling fans and fluorescent tube lights, and in 2007 a woman poked a modified bicycle frame through her face. Given the virtuality of *tangki* war magic, ritual theater is made relevant to a new generation of devotees, who are assured by spirit-warriors that their everyday life will be "an actuality of *pingan* (peace and safety)."

In chapter 2, "Javanese Ritual Initiation: Invulnerability, Authority, and Spiritual Improvement," Jean-Marc de Grave probes *kanuragan*, a secretive Javanese initiation ritual linked to the cult devoted to a person's four sibling spirits. For de Grave, *kanuragan* develops the process involved in the mystical acquisition of authority. His chapter describes the process of transmission, the people involved in such practices, and the role that *kanuragan* plays in Javanese society for security, warfare, and healing. A fundamental use of *kanuragan* is to "gain strength and invulnerability," a purpose that may be served by "external entities called *aji*" that are transmitted by the master. Soldiers, fighters, politicians, and the police obtain mantras to render them invulnerable to blades, spears, and bullets. Other powers include invisibility (*aji siluman*), the destruction of evil ghosts, invulnerability to wild animals, and protection against poisonous animals. De Grave illustrates his chapter with ethnographic data provided by Mbah, a *kanuragan* master, who describes war magic being used against the Dutch forces in the anti-colonial war of 1945–1949.

The Javanese employ their sibling spirits as a self-help source for a range of issues related to health and welfare. De Grave shows that *kanuragan* is regularly used in Java for warlike and health purposes and ties this to Javanese mythology, cosmology, and Sufism. From the traditional Javanese perspective, *kanuragan* is a valuable cultural activity; however, the Indonesian state and modernist Islamic clerics regard it as a primitive and dangerous pre-Islamic cultural trait that should be excised. From the standpoint of modernist, orthodox, and radical Islam, *kanuragan* includes black magic, such as the declared ability of Rama Hari to transform himself into a black panther. Despite contemporary Islamic marginalization, *kanuragan* continues to attract adherents in secret, especially functionaries of the state. De Grave concludes that "[t]he development of radical Islam after the fall of Suharto in 1998 ... has given birth to another form of warrior religion." Whether this trend is more threatening toward Javanese war magic than modernist Islam or secularism remains to be seen.

In chapter 3, "Discourse of Decline: Sumatran Perspectives on Black Magic," J. David Neidel examines magic and sorcery in Jambi, Sumatra. Highland villagers are feared by many people in the neighboring lowlands due to their reputation for black magic. Drawing on two years of ethnographic research in highland Jambi, Neidel's chapter foregrounds emic perspectives to reveal local conceptions of supernatural powers. The ability to cause sickness or death in a distant target is the form of magic most often discussed by outsiders, but this is only one of a large repertoire of supernatural abilities recognized and/or practiced by highland peoples. These powers tend to "focus on killing or disabling an enemy or, conversely, on providing protection from attacks by humans, wild animals, or supernatural beings" and thus constitute a form of war magic. Relying on first- and third-person accounts, Neidel describes the various pathways through which supernatural abilities are acquired and the types of people—including lowlanders—who seek out such powers. In doing so, his discussion draws links between the beliefs and practices surrounding sorcery, ancestral worship, spirit-possession, and shamanism.

Neidel asserts that "[i]t would appear to be widely held in highland Jambi that the potency of magical powers has declined over time. Village ancestors, whose exploits are recorded in village histories and legends (*tambo*), are widely believed to have engaged in truly amazing feats of magical prowess, such as flying to the island of Java, raising the dead, or creating new stream channels overnight." Such deeds are now believed to be beyond the abilities of present-day practitioners. Neidel discusses various reasons for this perceived "decline in potency," attributing reasons to developments in education, better medicine and health-care facilities, improvements in transport and communications, and changes in political representation that have marginalized the necessity for supernatural intervention. He reports a colleague's view that, due to the increase in economic living standards, "people in the region have become *malas membunuh orang* (lazy to kill people)." Neidel concludes that because of "the influence of modernist Islam," people in highland Jambi have abandoned their magical beliefs and practices "on the grounds that magic is immoral or no longer needed, not that it is irrational or illogical." The notion that magic adapts to modernity is, of course, well explored by many authors, following the Comaroffs (1999). Neidel's "discourse of decline" provides a new twist on the theme, whereby narratives of decline that do not attribute the decline to Western modernity offer protection against the subversive nature of modern, secular materialism.[5]

Michael Roberts, in chapter 4, titled "Tamil Tiger Ritual, War, and Mystical Empowerment," explains the defensive/violent origin of symbolic and iconic representations where "supra-mundane forces" act as guiding principles for social action. For Roberts, the LTTE was "one of the most innovative insurgencies in the history of insurrection" whose personnel extended and adapted the available cosmologies. To grasp the "enchanted practices" of the Tamil Tigers, Roberts works through a series of "interpretative leap[s]" based upon journalists' reports, personal communications, photographs, and his own travels in Sri Lanka.

Roberts spurns the demonizing language of terrorism applied to the Tamil Tigers in his discussion of the *kuppi*, a vial of cyanide that the Tamil Tigers bite upon to commit suicide rather than be captured. *Uyirayutham*, one of the fundamental principles of the LTTE, "refers to the gifting of one's life as a weapon." In this way, defensive suicidal action acts as a gift of the self. Thus, Tiger identity was one of "selfless zeal" embodied in the *kuppi* cyanide capsule. Roberts reveals that the *kuppi* and *thāli* are similar in appearance: "In its original form, the *thāli* was a turmeric-stained string ... placed around a woman's neck by her spouse at the rite finalizing their marriage," signifying a "permanent bond." Other "rites of encompassing protection" include sacred rings and chains, *kolam* designs drawn by women daily upon the threshold, the *nūl kaddu* charmed string worn around the waist of boys, rites of *pradakshina* (collective circumambulation of the village)—all of which bespeak "the power of encirclement."

Tantric rites and amulets thus provide examples of what Roberts refers to as "encompassment in Hindu practices," where "protection [is] sought through ... 'astrological alignment', a form of parallelism or 'analogue magic'." Cosmic encirclement shows that the "devotee seeks to disembody him- or herself in the process of embodying the divine figure that he or she is propitiating" in an attempt to 'fuse' with the chosen deity, given that deities can alternate between benevolent protection and malevolent cruelty. According to Roberts, "[s]uch practices are facets of the generalized technology of 'beguilement', a modern form of enchantment that works within and through the psychology of instrumental rationality."

Drawing upon two years of ethnographic fieldwork in South America, Željko Jokić reflects upon Yanomami combative, predatory, assault, and defensive shamanism in chapter 5, "Shamanic Battleground in Venezuela." His research challenges New Age and other one-sided misrepresentations of shamanism that deny cultural differences and consequently misplace the subject. Jokić argues that the exclusion of malign practices misrepresents other life-worlds to reproduce "colonial ways of knowing." He indicates that "[d]estructive aspects of Yanomami shamanism and sorcery still persist in a contemporary post-contact situation of culture change." Jokić discusses assault shamanism from the victim's standpoint and from the perspective of the predator *shapori* (shaman). Yanomami shamans and their spirit-helpers (*hekura*) engage in hostile acts to inflict misery and death on shamans and others from distant villages. Victims are primarily children. Hostile magical assaults are motivated by competition for power and prestige, jealousy, and vengeance.

Whereas the principal motive for magical assaults is retribution for past deaths, the *shapori* utilize their *hekura* to attack and kill their enemies and to cure their own people. Sensitive to the "moral ambiguity" of the *shapori*, Jokić distinguishes offensive from defensive shamanistic activities, stating: "While a *shapori* can save life, he can also take life. He is responsible for order but can also create disorder. He becomes both protector and defender of the community, shielding his people from the intrusions of the outside *hekura* and enemy shamans." In Jokić's view, the categories of shaman and sorcerer overlap, with the exception of *ōka* sorcery, "a technique of covert war magic that can sometimes trigger a real war." *Ōka* sorcery involves poisonous powder made from the *aroari* plant: the sorcerer blows the powder "in the direction of a passer-by on the forest path, either from a distance or nearby through a blowpipe or from the palm of his hand." Even the *shapori* may not prevent the resulting agonizing death.

For Jokić, "magical practices and the accompanying social experience of violence, sickness, and death are first and foremost embodied practices." To paraphrase Jokić, the *shapori* employ their *hekura* to access human bodies during healing and killing sessions: they either occupy the victim directly or detect and extract an object of witchcraft or other invading *hekura*. Via the work of his *hekura*, the *shapori* discovers the "body fault" or spirit-intruder in a victim or personally intrudes into another's body. Jokić emphasizes that the *shapori*'s malevolent activity or "supernatural warfare" must take into account non-human acts driven by the "cannibalistic nature" of the *hekura* spirits, demanding to be fed human flesh. Occasionally, *shapori* must kill in order to appease the spirits and spare the lives of their own relations. Finally, Yanomami *shapori* who intentionally engage in predatory acts are fully endowed with the cannibalistic characteristics of malevolent spirit-beings—chief of whom is Irariwë (Jaguar)—during ecstatic trances fueled by dance, trance, and psychotropic snuff.

In chapter 6, "Chants of Re-enchantment: Chamorro Spiritual Resistance to Colonial Domination," D. S. Farrer and James D. Sellmann fuse Farrer's three-year ethnographic case study of a Chamorro chant group with findings from Sellmann's investigations into ancient Chamorro philosophy. Aside from the considerable American diaspora, the Chamorro people live predominantly on Guam, a remote island in the Pacific referred to as 'the tip of the spear' due to its occupation as a vital military base for the American global superpower. Hence, in this chapter war magic and warrior religion are conceptualized as "embodied cultural positions that reflect and respond to economic, military, and colonial conditions," providing a lens to study "cognitive, embodied, and practice-based forms of resistance to domination." The chapter commences with an action that may be perceived as a gesture of indigenous defiance to colonial domination—or alternatively as a drug-induced momentary lapse of reason—when Leonard Z. Iriarte, a territorial conservation officer, shot down a B-52 bomber with an automatic rifle. This action must be understood in terms of the legacies of Spanish and American colonial occupation and the resurgence of belief in the supernatural powers of ancestral ghosts.

Farrer and Sellmann contend that the 'ancient Chamorro' cosmology and worldview are exemplified by the use of ancestral skulls in warfare, where skulls were used to line trenches in magical battle formations against the Spanish. When the skulls were trampled underfoot in 1700 after a 30-year war, "[t]he Chamorros did not merely surrender to the Spanish; they surrendered to their ancestors." In the process of Spanish colonial conversion, the Chamorro substituted the ritual use of human skulls for the worship of a crucified god, and, as a result, the Chamorro "deathscape has shifted from skulls and sharpened leg bones to a respectful fear of spirits, ghosts, and *taotao mo'na* [ancestral ghosts]." War magic and warrior religion are thus parallel forces in conflict. Sixteenth-century priests destroyed the power of the skulls in favor of religious conversion, procession, and confession, which were used as ideological weapons in the battle for human souls. Although the Spanish colonizers decimated the Chamorros and attempted to eradicate their culture, including dance and chant, the Chamorro language survived, providing the rudimentary elements for the revival of ritual chant (*lålai*). Stripping away the Spanish loan words, I Fanlalai'an, a contemporary Chamorro chant group led by Iriarte, "re-creates ritual context using arcane but vital indigenous words." The chant is a form of Chamorro artistic expression to facilitate the respectful remembrance and invocation of the ancestors, through the chant compositions and the act of chanting itself. The *taotao mo'na*, feared and revered on Guam, thus provide the basis for the emergence of a new religion, Chamorro spiritualism, practiced by I Fanlalai'an, whose self-professed mission is "to define Chamorro culture."

Iain Sinclair in chapter 7, "War Magic and Just War in Indian Tantric Buddhism," contemplates Buddhist war magic. Recent scholarship has lifted the doctrinal evasion of violence in Buddhism to permit subtle and realistic accounts that discuss war magic, albeit denying specifically Buddhist war or Buddhist violence. Sinclair deciphers Buddhist texts, written in the original Sanskrit in the seventh to the thirteenth centuries, to outline and discuss defensive magic, invocatory magic, yogic magic, and black magic for "paralyzing armies," read alongside the justifications for war magic developed in tantric Buddhist communities. While tantric Buddhist scripture execrated killing, people living in classical India were inevitably exposed to war. Sinclair emphasizes that "[t]he preservation of life in war is ... regarded as paramount, even—especially—in a last-ditch battle to preserve non-violent Buddhist ideals." Defensive war magic was pacifist in nature and aimed to halt or disperse armies before they had the opportunity to engage combatants or spill blood. Yet destructive war magic also developed. Hence, although war magic was predominantly directed at avoidance to nullify a threat or to stop an advancing military force, an "immobilized army" might not just suddenly fall silent but be "frozen to death in a magically summoned blizzard."

Sinclair explains that 'invocatory' war magic was used to coax "a powerful deity to intervene on the practitioner's behalf" and was employed to "infuse the swords, maces, and soldiers' armor with the mantras." Some techniques were more fanciful, such as "the tantric master [riding] naked on an elephant to the enemy encampment, holding a skull bowl 'full of excreta, phlegm, and so on.' which he imbibes and spits in their direction." Sinclair contrasts such practices with the "war magic of the yogin," which relied upon "direct personal identification with the deity." Meditations included "Stunning All Armies" by "visualizing mountain-sized forms dropped upon the enemy's head." Other forms discussed include the "possibility of killing with a thought." As Sinclair notes, such "magical slaying, along with other transgressive acts enjoined in the higher tantras, can be sanctioned insofar as it is a manifestation of transcendence."

War-magical operations prescribed in liturgy and incantations give directions "to invoke the protective powers of a spirit, bodhisattva, or other such Buddhist object of worship" through the repetitive recitation of mantras at appropriate times and in appropriate places, utilizing magic circles and talismans. Sinclair notes: "Magic provided a means for Buddhists to wage war without engaging in hand-to-hand combat, which was out of the question for the monastic class and most laypeople." In conclusion, Sinclair's chapter shows that Indian Buddhists turned their attention to war, but they did not resort to 'holy war'. Fundamentally, for Sinclair, tantric war magic emerged as a response to the inevitability of war, eventually becoming consolidated in a system that produced "a clear definition of a just war—one that was defensive, unavoidable, dispassionate, and minimally harmful, waged against a systemically violent opponent."

Each of these chapters contributes to the contemporary debate on religious revitalization and innovation. With the omission of occult ethnography in Africa,[6] our coverage cannot profess to be global or comprehensive, yet the book does provide in-depth accounts of particular practices located in contemporary Asia, the Pacific, and South America. War magic and warrior religion suggest and invite research into the revival of indigenous spirituality that strives toward embodied empowerment, anti-colonialism, and the re-enchantment of the world, often through the development of occult abilities or enhanced supernatural potency. In places where magic is shown to be in decline, this may be due to the onslaught of religious fervor. Magical, spiritual, or religious attributes fuel charismatic leadership and add legitimacy to groups and organizations struggling to revive, redefine, transform, or maintain cultures threatened by rapid social change and instability. Invulnerability, exorcism, and sacred magical cures provide comfort by reinforcing cultural continuity despite the fact that some of these ritual practices may be modern innovations rather than relics from the distant past.

Foregrounding embodiment and performance in war magic and warrior religion collapses the mind-body dualism that has resulted in an interminable inquiry into magic (whether read as 'primitive mentality' or the 'savage mind') versus rationality, to highlight social action historically pursued through embodied practice and performance. This has provided a method to re-evaluate religion and magic from the perspective of the practitioner's and the victim's embodiment in their experiential life-world. War magic and warrior religion promote dance, trance, hallucinogens, the self-infliction of pain, suicide, poisoning, and murderous revenge attacks. Yet poison inevitably appears alongside remedy, where war magic operates as an antidote for assault sorcery, colonial occupation, political oppression, and threats from enemy invasion.

Acknowledgments

This research project commenced in 2003 and follows up my doctoral research, which was subsequently published in 2009 as *Shadows of the Prophet*. Throughout this period, John Whalen-Bridge was a source of encouragement and constructive criticism. Roxana Waterson and Syed Farid Alatas played important roles in the development of my thought. I am especially grateful to Ellis Finkelstein for many years of epigrammatic encouragement. Thanks to Knut Rio, Tom Mountjoy, and Shawn Kendrick for editing the book. The authors featured in this volume deserve my special thanks. Aside from her own chapter, Margaret Chan critically reviewed the introduction and my co-authored contribution. Željko Jokić provided technical support when all else failed. J. David Neidel patiently endorsed the project from the outset, James D. Sellmann joined halfway through, and Iain Sinclair swiftly entered toward the end. Michael Roberts initiated me to *Social Analysis* through the special issue on "Noble Death." Jean-Marc de Grave reviewed the introduction and provided insightful comments. Initially, Neil Whitehead agreed to contribute to this project, although he subsequently withdrew. It is with regret that this book is being published after his death.

D. S. Farrer is Associate Professor of Anthropology at the University of Guam. He is the author of *Shadows of the Prophet: Martial Arts and Sufi Mysticism* (2009), and co-editor (with John Whalen-Bridge) of *Martial Arts as Embodied Knowledge: Asian Traditions in a Transnational World* (2011). His research interests include martial arts, performance, visual anthropology, and the anthropology of art with a regional focus toward Southeast Asia and the Pacific.

Notes

1. An earlier version of this manuscript was published in 2014 in *Social Analysis: The International Journal of Social and Cultural Practice* 58, no. 1, under the title "War Magic and Warrior Religion: Sorcery, Cognition, and Embodiment." In this final, definitive version, significant albeit subtle aspects of text and style have been modified, including revised, succinct titles (except chaps. 6 and 7), the elimination of keywords and abstracts, revised transliterations, and updated references.
2. Some anthropologists now replace the term 'shaman' with 'medium' (see, e.g., Benjamin 2010: 3). To avoid the proliferation of terms, however, 'shaman' is preferred here; otherwise, the addition of terms such as 'assault medium' and 'dark medium' would be required.
3. See Klass (1995) for a critique of the notion of the 'supernatural'. See also Gell (1998).
4. Compare this to the remarkable, deep-gray blob that Edith Turner et al. (1992: 14) said emerged from the back of a patient during the *ilhamba*, a shamanic operation, in Zambia.
5. I am indebted to the manuscript reviewer for this observation.
6. On African occults, see Kiernan (2006).

References

Benjamin, Geoffrey. 2014. *Temiar Religion 1964–2012: Enchantment, Disenchantment, and Re-enchantment in Malaysia's Uplands*. Singapore: NUS Press.

Bierce, Ambrose. [1881] 2000. *The Unabridged Devil's Dictionary*. Ed. David E. Schultz, and S. T. Joshi. Athens: University of Georgia Press.

Butler, E. M. [1948] 1993. *The Myth of the Magus*. Cambridge: Cambridge University Press.

Clastres, Pierre. [1980] 2010. *Archeology of Violence*. Trans. Jeanine Herman. Los Angeles, CA: Semiotext(e).

Comaroff, Jean, and John L. Comaroff. 1999. "Occult Economies and the Violence of Abstraction: Notes from the South African Postcolony." *American Ethnologist* 26, no. 2: 279–303.

Csordas, Thomas J. 1999. "Embodiment and Cultural Phenomenology." Pp. 143–162 in *Perspectives on Embodiment: The Intersections of Nature and Culture*, ed. Gail Weiss and Honi Fern Haber. New York: Routledge.

Deleuze, Gilles, and Félix Guattari. [1987] 2004. *A Thousand Plateaus: Capitalism and Schizophrenia*. Trans. Brian Massumi. London: Continuum. Originally published in 1980 as *Mille plateaux*, vol. 2 of *Capitalisme et schizophrénie*.

Dumézil, Georges. 1970. *The Destiny of the Warrior*. Trans. Alf Hilterbeitel. Chicago: University of Chicago Press.
Eliade, Mircea. 1972. *Shamanism: Archaic Techniques of Ecstasy*. Trans. Willard R. Trask. Princeton, NJ: Princeton University Press.
Elliott, Paul. 1998. *Warrior Cults: A History of Magical, Mystical and Murderous Organizations*. London: Blandford Press.
Evans-Pritchard, E. E. [1937] 1977. *Witchcraft, Oracles and Magic Among the Azande*. Oxford: Clarendon Press.
Farrer, D. S. 2006. "'Deathscapes' of the Malay Martial Artist." *Social Analysis* 50, no. 1: 25–50.
Farrer, D. S. 2008. "The Healing Arts of the Malay Mystic." *Visual Anthropological Review* 24, no. 1: 29–46.
Farrer, D. S. 2009. *Shadows of the Prophet: Martial Arts and Sufi Mysticism*. Dordrecht: Springer.
Farrer, D. S. 2011. "Coffee-Shop Gods: Chinese Martial Arts of the Singapore Diaspora." Pp. 203–237 in *Martial Arts as Embodied Knowledge: Asian Traditions in a Transnational World*, ed. D. S. Farrer and John Whalen-Bridge. New York: SUNY.
Farrer, D. S. 2013. "Becoming-animal in the Chinese Martial Arts." Pp 215–246 in *Living Beings: Perspectives on Interspecies Engagements*, ed. Penny Dransart. ASA Monographs No. 50. London: Bloomsbury.
Fisher, David. [1983] 2004. *The War Magician: The Man Who Conjured Victory in the Desert*. London: Weidenfeld & Nicolson.
Gell, Alfred. 1998. *Art and Agency: An Anthropological Theory*. Oxford: Oxford University Press.
Goffman, Erving. 1974. *Frame Analysis: An Essay on the Organization of Experience*. Boston: Northeastern University Press.
Goodrick-Clarke, Nicholas. 1992. *The Occult Roots of Nazism: Secret Aryan Cults and Their Influence on Nazi Ideology*. New York: New York University Press.
Gramsci, Antonio. 1971. *Selections from the Prison Notebooks*. Ed. and trans. Quintin Hoare and Geoffrey Nowell Smith. London: Lawrence and Wishart.
Haas, Jonathan, ed. 1990. *The Anthropology of War*. Cambridge: Cambridge University Press.
Hutton, Ronald. 1999. *The Triumph of the Moon: A History of Modern Pagan Witchcraft*. Oxford: Oxford University Press.
Jung, C. G. 1969. *The Collected Works of C. G. Jung*. Vol. 11: *Psychology and Religion: West and East*. Ed. and trans. Gerhard Adler and R. F. C. Hull. 2nd ed. Princeton, NJ: Princeton University Press.
Kapferer, Bruce. 1991. *A Celebration of Demons: Exorcism and the Aesthetics of Healing in Sri Lanka*. 2nd ed. Bloomington: Indiana University Press.
Kapferer, Bruce. 1997. *The Feast of the Sorcerer*. Chicago: University of Chicago Press.
Kapferer, Bruce, ed. 2003. *Beyond Rationalism: Rethinking Magic, Witchcraft and Sorcery*. New York: Berghahn Books.
Kapferer, Bruce. 2004. "Ritual Dynamics and Virtual Practice: Beyond Representation and Meaning." *Social Analysis* 48, no. 2: 35–54.
Kiernan, James, ed. 2006. *Modernity and Belonging*. Vol. 4: *The Power of the Occult in Modern Africa: Continuity and Innovation in the Renewal of African Cosmologies*. Berlin: LIT Verlag.
Leach, Jerry, dir. 1976. *Trobriand Cricket: An Ingenious Response to Colonialism*. 50 min. Documentary film. Produced by Gary Kildea and Jerry Leach.
Klass, Morton. 1995. *Ordered Universes: Approaches to the Anthropology of Religion*. Boulder, CO: Westview Press.

Klass, Morton, and Maxine K. Weisgrau. 1999. "Introduction." Pp. 1–6 in *Across the Boundaries of Belief: Contemporary Issues in the Anthropology of Religion*, ed. Morton Klass and Maxine K. Weissgrau. Boulder, CO: Westview Press.

Levenda, Peter. 2002. *Unholy Alliance: A History of Nazi Involvement with the Occult.* 2nd ed. London: Continuum.

Levtzion, Nehemia. 1999. "Aspects of Islamization: Weber's Observations on Islam Reconsidered." Pp. 153–161 in *Max Weber and Islam*, ed. Toby E. Huff and Wolfgang Schluchter. New Brunswick, NJ: Transaction Publishers.

Lewis, I. S. [1971] 2003. *Ecstatic Religion: An Anthropological Study of Spirit Possession and Shamanism.* 3rd ed. London: Routledge.

Malinowski, Bronislaw. [1922] 2013. *Argonauts of the Western Pacific: An Account of Native Enterprise and Adventure in the Archipelagoes of Melanesian New Guinea.* Long Grove, IL: Waveland Press.

Malinowski, Bronislaw. [1935] 1965. *Coral Gardens and Their Magic: The Language of Magic and Gardening.* Vol. 2. Bloomington: Indiana University Press.

Malinowski, Bronislaw. 1948. *Magic, Science and Religion, and Other Essays.* New York: Doubleday.

Mauss, Marcel. [1902] 2001. *A General Theory of Magic.* Trans. Robert Brain. London: Routledge.

Metcalf, Peter. 2002. *They Lie, We Lie: Getting on with Anthropology.* London: Routledge.

Morris, Brian. 1987. *Anthropological Studies of Religion.* Cambridge: Cambridge University Press.

Morris, Brian. 2006. *Religion and Anthropology: A Critical Introduction.* Cambridge: Cambridge University Press.

Nietzsche, Friedrich. 2000. "On the Genealogy of Morals." Pp. 437–600 in *Basic Writings of Nietzsche*, ed. Walter A. Kaufmann. New York: Random House.

Otto, Ton. 2006. "Conceptions of Warfare in Western Thought and Research: An Introduction." Pp. 23–28 in *Warfare and Society: Archaeological and Social Anthropological Perspectives*, ed. Ton Otto, Henrik Thrane, and Helle Vandkilde. Aarhus: Aarhus University Press.

Reay, Marie. 1987. "The Magico-Religious Foundations of New Guinea Highlands Warfare." Pp. 83–120 in Stephen 1987b.

Reid, Anthony. 1988. *Southeast Asia in the Age of Commerce, 1450–1680.* Vol. 1: *The Lands Below the Winds.* New Haven, CT: Yale University Press.

Ross, Anne. 2004. *Druids: Preachers of Immortality.* Gloucestershire: Tempus.

Russell, Jeffrey B., and Brooks Alexander. [1980] 2007. *A History of Witchcraft: Sorcerers, Heretics and Pagans.* 2nd ed. New York: Thames & Hudson.

Shahar, Meir. 2008. *The Shaolin Monastery: History, Religion, and the Chinese Martial Arts.* Honolulu: University of Hawai'i Press.

Shaw, William. 1976. *Aspects of Malayan Magic.* Kuala Lumpur: Yau Seng Press.

Singer, Andre, dir. 1985. *Bronislaw Malinowski: Off the Veranda.* 52 min. Documentary film in the series "Strangers Abroad: Pioneers of Social Anthropology." Distributed by Films for the Humanities and Sciences.

Sørensen, Jesper. 2007. *A Cognitive Theory of Magic.* Lanham, MD: AltaMira Press.

Spiro, Melford E. 1987. *Culture and Human Nature.* Chicago: University of Chicago Press.

Stein, Rebecca L., and Philip L. Stein. 2008. *The Anthropology of Religion, Magic, and Witchcraft.* 2nd ed. Boston: Pearson Education.

Stephen, Michele. 1987a. "Master of Souls: The Mekeo Sorcerer." Pp. 41–80 in Stephen 1987b.

Stephen, Michele, ed. 1987b. *Sorcerer and Witch in Melanesia.* New Brunswick, NJ: Rutgers University Press.

Tambiah, Stanley J. 1968. "The Magical Power of Words." *Man* (n.s.) 3, no. 2: 175–208.
Tambiah, Stanley J. 1976. *World Conqueror and World Renouncer: A Study of Buddhism and Polity in Thailand against a Historical Background*. Cambridge: Cambridge University Press.
Tambiah, Stanley J. 1985. "A Performative Approach to Ritual." Pp. 123–166 in *Culture, Thought, and Social Action: An Anthropological Perspective*. Cambridge, MA: Harvard University Press.
Tambiah, Stanley J. 1990. *Magic, Science, Religion, and the Scope of Rationality*. Cambridge: Cambridge University Press.
Taussig, Michael. 1987. *Shamanism, Colonialism, and the Wild Man: A Study in Terror and Healing*. Chicago: University of Chicago Press.
Turner, Bryan S. 1998. *Weber and Islam*. London: Routledge.
Turner, Edith, with William Blodgett, Singleton Kahona, and Fideli Benwa. 1992. *Experiencing Ritual: A New Interpretation of African Healing*. Philadelphia: University of Pennsylvania Press.
Turner, Victor W. 1961. *Ndembu Divination: Its Symbolism and Techniques*. Manchester: Rhodes-Livingstone Institute, Manchester University Press.
Turner, Victor W. 1967. *The Forest of Symbols: Aspects of Ndembu Ritual*. Ithaca, NY: Cornell University Press.
Turner, Victor W. 1969. *The Ritual Process: Structure and Anti-Structure*. Chicago: Aldine Publishing.
Turner, Victor W. 1975. *Revelation and Divination in Ndembu Ritual*. Ithaca, NY: Cornell University Press.
Turner, Victor W. 1985. "An Anthropological Approach to the Icelandic Saga." Pp. 71–93 in *On the Edge of the Bush: Anthropology as Experience*, ed. Edith L. B. Turner. Tucson: University of Arizona Press.
Virilio, Paul. 2004. *The Paul Virilio Reader*. Ed. Steve Redhead. New York: Columbia University Press.
Waterson, Roxana. 1995. "Entertaining a Dangerous Guest: Sacrifice and Play in the *Ma'pakorong* Ritual of the Sa'dan Toraja." *Oceania* 66, no. 2: 81–102.
Weber, Max. [1905] 2002. *The Protestant Ethic and the "Spirit" of Capitalism and Other Writings*. Ed. and trans. Peter Baehr and Gordon C. Wells. New York: Penguin Books.
Weber, Max. [1922] 1991. *The Sociology of Religion*. Trans. Ephraim Fischoff. Boston: Beacon Press.
Weber, Max. 1978. *Economy and Society: An Outline of an Interpretive Sociology*. 2 vols. Ed. Guenther Roth and Claus Wittich. Berkeley: University of California Press.
Whitehead, Neil L. 2002. *Dark Shamans: Kanaimà and the Poetics of Violent Death*. Durham, NC: Duke University Press.
Whitehead, Neil L. 2013. "Ethnography, Knowledge, Torture, and Silence." Pp. 26–45 in Whitehead and Finnström 2013.
Whitehead Neil L., and Sverker Finnström, eds. 2013. *Virtual War and Magical Death: Technologies and Imaginaries for Terror and Killing*. Durham, NC: Duke University Press.
Whitehead, Neil L., and Robin Wright, eds. 2004. *In Darkness and Secrecy: The Anthropology of Assault Sorcery and Witchcraft in Amazonia*. Durham, NC: Duke University Press.
Winstedt, Richard. [1925] 1993. *The Malay Magician: Being Shaman, Saiva and Sufi*. Oxford: Oxford University Press.

Chapter 1

TANGKI WAR MAGIC
Spirit Warfare in Singapore

Margaret Chan

Tangki spirit-medium performances are not for the faint-hearted. To the beating of drums and gongs, the *tangki*, head shaking and eyes rolling, dances in a deep trance. Some *tangki*s cut themselves with knives or hit their bodies with spike-balls to spill sacred blood. Others pierce themselves through a cheek with rods that can be as long as six *chiok* (about six feet) and one *choon* (about one inch) thick,[1] or they drive needles and swords into the flesh of their arms and back. Bristling like a human pincushion, the *tangki* dances energetically in an awe-inspiring performance. The performance, however, is less about spectacle than it is about exorcist war magic.

Tangki worship is a signifying practice of the Minnan (southern Min) people of Hokkien (Fujian) province, which is located on the southeast coast of mainland China. The Hokkiens form the vast majority of the Chinese of Taiwan and a major proportion of the Chinese communities in Southeast Asia (Pan 1998: 31). *Tangki* worship has also spread to Teochew (Chaozhou) and Hainan with the migration of Minnan people to these regions.

Notes for this chapter begin on page 44.

The roots of *Tangki* worship extend back to pre-Chinese tribal folk cultures five thousand years ago (Chan 2006, 2015). The practice consists of congeries of independent sects that share a loose ritual tradition. The worship does not have an ecclesiastical canon and does not feature chanting or the recitation of prayers. The *tangki*'s techne is war magic—a ritual theater in which the protagonists are spirit-possessed mediums believed to be warrior gods incarnate. The *tangki*'s magic is not the witchcraft or sorcery defined by Ellen (1993: 8) as "the use of supernatural agency by persons to harm other persons." It is a magic that may be described, in Kapferer's (2005a) terms, as the 'virtuality' of war between gods and demons.

Virtuality and Actuality in Ritual and Theater

Kapferer (2005b: 157–159) writes of the role of theater in Suniyama exorcism, but he resists the use of the theater paradigm, which can reduce ritual to mere representation. Ritual, he argues, is a dynamic within which meanings are made, so that if the theater analogy has to be used, then ritual would more appropriately be likened to "what goes on behind the scenes" rather than "what is overtly presented" (Kapferer 2005a: 50–51). Approaching from an epistemological perspective that regards the ontology of theater as interactive magic and not as representation, I argue that *tangki* war magic is ritual theater. I point to reader-response theories, which argue that the reader participates in the making of meaning. I will postpone this deliberation until the next section in order to continue my discussion of the concept of virtuality.

Kapferer (2005a) defines virtuality against the actuality of lived life. Lived reality is a chaos within which the virtuality of ritual offers respite by "slowing down" or "holding in abeyance or suspension" some of the exertions of living (ibid.: 48). Norton (1972) offers another perspective with his examination of virtuality and actuality as 'things'. Suppose, says Norton, that only 9 out of 10 members of a committee turn up for a meeting. The meeting is held since virtually all are present. A virtual committee has now been created. Norton notes that virtuality implies the "admission that something is not the case in fact. But something else *is* the case" (ibid.: 499; original emphasis). How much 'in effect' is a virtual thing? Norton answers that it should be "enough (and no less) in order to be able to persuade the observer that the reality is present and that it is operative" (ibid.). Norton also argues that virtuality can be stretched and tested. Would the presence of 5 key members also suffice to constitute the virtuality of the actuality of a 10-member committee?

But virtuality has to be 'enough'. If virtually nobody turned up, we would have the actuality of a non-actual committee, even if three members had in fact turned up (Norton 1972: 500). Virtuality, Norton points out, is actuated out of actuality, whereupon the virtuality would transcend the referred actuality: "Virtuality is housed within the actual but over against it as well; and it is over against the actual that the virtual immediately objectifies its identity and its difference" (ibid.: 500–501). This notion of an objectified identity ties in with

Kapferer's (2005a: 47) proposition of virtuality as an "existential reality" that is as fully lived as ordinary life. Further, we note that Norton's discussion of virtuality employs concepts of spatiality, and this links with Kapferer's arguments about the "phantasmagoric space of ritual virtuality" (ibid.). The virtuality of ritual can thus be depicted as a means of escape from the everyday through a transcendental experience, but there is always the return to actuality, which is likely to be a new actuality.

Tangki War Magic as Ritual Theater

Returning to my proposition that *tangki* war magic is ritual theater, I would agree with Kapferer that the use of theater as an analytical tool in the examination of ritual can reduce ritual to mere representation. I am especially concerned with the conventions of theater as entertainment. Against this worry of the concept of theater as facsimile, I would point out that, in the Asian tradition, ritual is theater and theater is ritual. As in my book, *Ritual Is Theatre, Theatre Is Ritual* (Chan 2006), I argue here that theater constitutes the magic of *tangki* worship.

Traditional Asian theater pieces are performances of ritual. For example, Chinese Nuo, featuring masked performers (see below), is exorcist theater and is the root of Chinese painted face opera and Japanese Noh (Tian 2003–2004).² The Ramnagar Ramlila, an epic re-enactment of the life of the Hindu deity Rama at the city of Varanasi in India, is a site of pilgrimage (Sax 1990). Malaysian, Thai, and Indonesian shadow puppetry concerns the restoration of cosmic balance (Wong and Lysloff 1991; Yousof 2010), and the Sinhala Suniyama is dramatized ritual healing (Kapferer 2005b).

In *tangki* spirit-medium worship, the instance of possession, when the spirit of the mortal steps aside to allow the spirit of the god to take its place, is the magical moment of the transmogrification of a mortal into a god, and this transformation is enacted theatrically with the possessed medium behaving in a manner that the audience of devotees would expect of the role. Hence, a medium possessed by the Monkey God would perform suitably simian gestures drawn largely from the Chinese staged shows of the legend of the Monkey God.

Although—and this bears repeating—I am not discussing a performance of representation, the concept of the double-of-theater articulated in Western theater theory is most helpful to my discussion of *tangki* war magic. Laurence Olivier performing Hamlet was Olivier and also Hamlet at the same time. This double-of-theater, I have argued (Chan 2012), constitutes the essential magic of Chinese ritual theater. It is this double nature—one that 'is and also is' (the possessed medium enacting a spirit-warrior, the statue that is likewise a god, the anthropomorphic puppet who is also a performing deity)—that makes the image the magical doorway into the virtuality of ritual (Chan 2006: 133–149; 2012). The Chinese character for puppet and ancient masked actor is 傀 (*kui*), an ideograph that clearly illustrates the ontology of the exorcist as a 'double-nature-being', for it combines the 亻 (*ren*) human radical with that of 鬼 (*gui*), ghost or spirit. The emotive music of drums and cymbals and the synesthesia derived from watching the cruel spectacle of *tangki* self-mortification invite participants to enter into the virtuality of *tangki* theater.

The techne of the *tangki* is the staging of the phantasmagoria of war. As with the phantasmagoria theater of eighteenth- and nineteenth-century Europe, there is the equivalent of magic lantern projections of ghouls and specters upon the screen of the imagination, for *tangki* phantasmagoria must, as Norton points out, be 'enough' to persuade the observer that the reality is present and that it is operative. The actuality, within which the virtuality of *tangki* war magic is actuated, is a mythic world that is founded upon a shared body of knowledge involving a tradition of warrior god exorcisms that go back five thousand years, as well as a belief in demons affirmed in the corpus of demonology.

Devotees who enter into the *tangki* ritual theater are not passive spectators. Reader response theories that have come from literature and now prevail in theater analysis see the reader as an active participant in the dynamic process of making meaning. Rosenblatt ([1938] 1995) proposes that reading is 'transactional'. Dow (1986: 60–61) writes that 'magical healing' (within which category he includes Western psychotherapy) takes place in a shared, socio-culturally informed mythic world. Healers make this world become real for patients, with healing seen as a process of negotiations of meaning between healer and patient. In a psychiatric study of *tangki* healing in Singapore, Lee et al. (2010: 77) report that success depends on the healer's ability to enact a shared mythic world and then to persuade patients to attach themselves emotionally to transactional symbols presented in the enactment. For healing to take place, patients need to reframe ideas enacted by the *tangki* to be consistent with their own explanatory models (ibid.: 74). In common with the discourses of Dow, Kapferer, and Lee et al., this chapter acknowledges the place of theater in ritual healing.

The Mythic World of Tangki *War Magic*

Tangki worship is a Hokkien tradition, but the *tangki*'s mythic world is founded within a Chinese universality. Hsu (1997) argues that the ancient Chinese identity was that of 'culturalism', which involved a shared body of ideas. Culture, according to Hsu, is very much a product of social process, as indeed is *tangki* war magic. In the last sections of this chapter, I discuss how the virtuality of *tangki* theater has stretched to accommodate new societal norms.[3]

Returning to Hsu (1997), we understand that the word 'China' was coined by Central Asians with reference to Ch'in (Qin 221–206 BCE), the first imperial dynasty that unified China.[4] The Chinese, however, did not use this name until the nineteenth century, when notions of the nation-state emerged. Beginning in the Zhou era (1027–221 BCE), the Chinese regarded themselves as subjects of the emperor who ruled over 'the world under heaven' (*tianxia*). Thus, for the Chinese, their country was their universe, and a Chinese identity based on cultural universalism emerged.

By the Warring States period (476–256 BCE), Chinese cultural universality had united all peoples within the boundaries of the empire. Chinese and non-Chinese states did not dispute the idea of cultural unification; instead, they fought each other to win the mandate to rule over the united empire. Hsu (1997) proposes that the Qin unification of China in the third century BCE was inevitable, owing to Chinese cultural universalism.

Chinese cultural universalism is the subtext (to use the vocabulary of theater) for the enactment of the *tangki*'s mythic world within which the virtuality of *tangki* war magic is actuated. We shall see how the plot, which features spirit-general protagonists battling against demonic antagonists, can be traced directly back to Zhou times and the proto-Chinese dynasties.

Ancient Nuo *Exorcism: The Template for* Tangki *War Magic*

The religious procession through a precinct that is intended to drive out evil has a central place in Chinese religious rituals. The practice goes back to the *nuo* exorcisms of the first proto-Chinese Xia dynasty (2205-1806 BCE) (Tian 2003-2004: 344). From as early as this time, *nuo*s were performed as collective exorcist rituals presented as attacks against evil spirits. By the Zhou era, the *nuo* was institutionalized, and the emperor himself presided over the more important state *nuo*s.

Nuo rituals were processional and always led by a warrior exorcist, known as the *fangxiangshi*, who has been variously named 'the warrior of the four directions' or 'the manic general who clears the way'. The *Zhouli* (*Rites of Zhou*) describes the *fangxiangshi* as an exorcist who wears a grotesque bearskin mask, is armed with a lance and shield, and dances wildly (Bodde 1975: 77-83; de Groot 1910: 974-982).

The Zhou *nuo* exorcisms were violent performances during which sacrificial animals were torn apart. At the Da Nuo (Grand Exorcism), staged annually in winter, soldiers were commanded by the emperor to drive out evil spirits fiercely by "ripping open victims on every side ... [a]ttacking birds are stern and swift" (*Lü Shi Chun Qiu* [The Annals of Lü Buwei], cited in Tian 2003-2004: 344-345). Always at the head of these rampaging processions was the *fangxiangshi*, brandishing a lance and carrying a shield while "leading one hundred slaves into houses and tombs to chase away pestilences, ghosts and spirits" (ibid.: 345). The tradition of the state *nuo* exorcism continued until the Ming period (1368-1644), with a hiatus during the Mongolian Yuan dynasty (1279-1368). State *nuo* rituals were no longer practiced in the Manchu Qing era (1644-1911), but folk *nuo* exorcism continues up to the present as masked drama (ibid.: 348).

The Modern Tangki *as Heir to the* Fangxiangshi

These descriptions of ancient *nuo* exorcism almost fit contemporary spirit-medium parades of the Thai Vegetarian Festival in Phuket (see Cohen 2001: 88-94), or the Capgomeh (fifteenth day of the first lunar month) procession in Singkawang, West Kalimantan (Chan 2009), or the *yiukeng* (demon-expelling tours)[5] conducted by Singaporean *tangki*s (Chan 2006: 102-103). All are processions featuring entranced *tangki*s wielding, or pierced by, weapons. The spirit-mediums walk a route through the community, clearing the neighborhood of evil spirits. The link between ancient *nuo* exorcism and the development of the *nuo* masked drama of southwest China is well-documented (see, e.g., Chongqing et al. 1989; Riley 1997), but I am not aware of scholarship on the historical development of the *tangki* role, which includes links to the *fangxiang-shi*, other than that set out in my writings on Chinese spirit-mediums (Chan 2006: 20-41). Yet the evidence is compelling, for the *tangki* clearly performs the ancient ritual role of the warrior exorcist.

Tangki *as Warrior Hero of Folklore and Theater*

In medieval times, theater and storytelling were the most important sources of entertainment for villagers, who were largely illiterate. The storytellers' dramatized readings developed into street opera and puppet shows. Performers used iconic gestures and a code of props, costumes, and make-up as markers to identify the cast of gods. Chinese woodblock printing ensured that the images of the gods were widely disseminated, and gradually these portrayals of gods and demons—their appearance, dress, and behavior—concretized in the minds of the people as an internalized body of knowledge that constitutes the habitus of the *tangki*. This embodied knowledge, "beyond the grasp of consciousness... values given body, *made* body... by the hidden persuasion of an implicit pedagogy" (Bourdieu 1977: 94; original emphasis), can inform trance behavior. A psychiatric report of patients in a Singapore mental hospital who were susceptible to trance demonstrated a clear cultural connection. Of the 29 Chinese patients studied, 55 percent portrayed Buddhist and Daoist deities, while 31 percent presented themselves as possessed by ghosts and spirits. The Malays largely enacted deceased ancestors or animal spirits or legendary Malay warrior heroes, and the Indian patients mostly drew from the Hindu pantheon (Ng 2000: 571).

The unconsciously acquired somatic knowledge in turn produced what might be considered the 'canon' of *tangki* worship—a doxa of beliefs, unanimously held, unspoken but understood by all, "the aggregate of the 'choices' whose subject is everyone and no one because the questions they answer cannot be explicitly asked ... [an] absolute form of recognition of legitimacy through misrecognition of arbitrariness, since it is unaware of the very question of legitimacy" (Bourdieu 1977: 168). When in a trance, *tangki*s perform the theatrical images of their habitus, and devotees judge the authenticity of *tangki* possessions against a doxa yardstick. For example, if the *tangki* of the Monkey God performs like an opera actor in the role, this meets the 'gold standard' of true possession by the god. New knowledge is also incorporated into the doxa, so we now see *tangki*s dressed in the image of the gods portrayed on television shows. *Tangki*s have also learned new methods of self-mortification, such as thrusting an electric fan through a cheek. What would constitute orthopraxy and what would be heterodoxy? Between what should-be and what should-not-be lies the gray area of the *tangki*'s doxa, which, as we will learn later, is a flexible virtuality.

The Antagonist: Ghosts in the Chinese Imagination

War magic and the warrior exorcist are responses to the deep-held Chinese belief in the existence of ghosts. The notion of ghosts is endemic in the Chinese mythic world as evidenced by the "staggering amount of materials" on the subject in traditional Chinese literature and "some 200 words still in use" that are related to the radical *gui* 鬼, which is commonly translated as 'ghost' (A. Yu 1987: 397–398). Ghosts feature in the major works of Chinese history, including the *Zuo Zhuan* (The Chronicles of Zuo, covering the period from 722–468 BCE), one of the oldest Chinese works of narrative history, and the *Shiji* (*Records of the Grand Historian*), written from 109 BCE to 91 BCE. Ghost stories are found in virtually all periods of Chinese popular tales; thus, "to study this topic is to engage in a survey of the history of traditional Chinese fiction" (ibid.: 399–401).

Popular *zhiguai* (demon tales) and *chuanqi* (traditional tales of the marvelous) formed part of the repertoire of wandering balladeers and storytellers. These stories supplied the images of ghouls and specters for the phantasmagoria of *tangki* ritual theater. A corpus of Chinese demonology has developed, and since *tangki* war magic often deals with healing, I shall set out some ideas from traditional Chinese medicine. For the sake of variety, the following discussion uses different terms—demons, evil spirits, ghosts—which generically represent the malevolent spirits that have to be repelled by war magic.

Demonology

Schiffeler (1976: 19) writes of the Neolithic belief that illness was the result of ghostly *gui* attacks, which caused the *hun* ethereal soul to leave the body, thus leaving the *po* carnal soul vulnerable. Cure was effected by sorcerer-physicians who would drive out the *gui*. Waley ([1934] 1968) reports that during the Shang dynasty (1557–1027 BCE) the attitude toward religion was 'auguristic-sacrificial', evincing a belief in magic rather than heavenly rewards for good behavior. Omens and good fortune were obtained by specific performances of ritual sacrifice. The Zhou dynasty, which followed the Shang, was the age of Confucius, who would not speak of "extraordinary things, feats of strength, disorder, and spiritual beings" (Legge [1861] 2012: book 7). Yet at *nuo* exorcisms, "[w]hen the villagers were going through their ceremonies to drive away pestilential influences, he put on his court robes and stood on the eastern steps" (ibid.: book 10). Confucius was a rationalist. Although he did not believe in spirits, the *nuo* exorcisms were important state events, and he "sacrificed to the spirits, as if the spirits were present" (ibid: book 3). Confucian rationalism prevailed among the elite. The wizards and witches of the Shang courts were dismissed, and the educated began rejecting notions of the occult. The villagers, however, continued to believe in spirits.

The change in attitude is apparent in the shift away from the demonological paradigm in ancient Chinese medicine to a more systematic approach to cures. Schiffeler (1976: 26) demonstrates how the new idea was reflected in the changed etymology for the Chinese ideograph for *yi* (physician). The ancient character 毉 comprises three ideas: an arrow in a quiver at top left, a hand drawing a bowstring at top right, and two dancing *wu* 巫 female shamans or sorcerers below. The contemporary character is 醫, where the shamans are replaced by the symbol 酉 representing the medical amphora, with its two handles and narrow neck. This ideographic change is suggestive of the displacement of the shaman curer by the secular herbalist-physician.

The present-day simplified character for physician, *yi* 医, retains the notion of an arrow in a quiver and is a visual legacy of ancient medical beliefs in healing as a war upon demons. Up to Han times (206 BCE to AD 220), it was held that demon attacks had to be repelled with arrows shot from a bow made of peach wood. Such a spell is prescribed in the *zhiguai* demonography recovered from a third-century BCE tomb at Shuihudi, Hupei, and also in the *Baize tu* (Diagrams of White Marsh), a manual of demon lore, dating perhaps to the Six Dynasties (AD 220–589), in which Baize, a divine beast, tells the Yellow Emperor about the supernatural creatures in the world and describes ways to counter their attacks (Harper 1985: 491–493).

Demonological Paradigm in Early Medical Texts

Scholars are of the opinion that the belief that evils spirits caused illness only began to wane after the Han period, and then only among the educated (Barend 2000: 132). All the pre-modern medical texts have a shamanistic base. The third-century BCE *Wushier Bingfang* (Prescriptions for 52 Ailments) is held to be the earliest extant text of Chinese medical lore. Discovered in the Mawangdui archaeological site located in Changsha (tomb 3, burial date 168 BCE), this treatise prescribes magical cures, including "[m]alediction, archery, flagellation, magical entrapment, and demon inquisition," to treat ailments such as "bites, warts and swellings" (Harper 1985: 494). The *Wushier* provides clear proof of the shamanistic history of Chinese medicine.

The discovery of the Mawangdui corpus has put to question the romantic notion of the mythic origins of two other ancient books. Dismissing earlier suggestions that these works were written at the mythic dawn of Chinese civilization, scholars now argue that the *Shen Nong Ben Cao Jing* (Shen Nong's Materia Medica Classic), considered the most ancient text on Chinese herbalism, and the *Huangdi Neijing* (*The Yellow Emperor's Classic of Internal Medicine*), which sets out the principal ideas of systematic medicine and acupuncture, were probably written after the Mawangdui burial date.

One of the arguments proffered for the later dates of publication is the nascent move away, in the *Shen Nong* and *Neijing*, from the purely magical prescriptions of the *Wushier*. Notwithstanding this shift toward rationalism, demonology and the magic correspondence theories are still present in the two later texts. For example, in the *Shen Nong* the efficacy of herbal medicine is discussed in terms of demon slaying: "Tao Hua ... kills malign demonic influx ... Tao Xiao ... kills hundreds of ghosts and spiritual matters" (Kim 2001: 111).[6] In the *Neijing*, the wind is described as an evil that attacks the veins and the five viscera, causing sickness (ibid.).

Folk Medicine to Counter Demon Attacks

Schiffeler (1976: 33) writes of the social distance between folk medicine and treatments based on learned medical treatises. The nobility had the services of well-read doctors, but the ordinary people still largely relied on religious healing. Benedict (1988: 140-142), in her discussion of the bubonic epidemic that raged through China in the nineteenth century, notes the popular belief that the plague was caused by the displeasure of gods or by witchcraft or ghostly magic. In descriptions reminiscent of the ancient *nuo* exorcism discussed earlier in this chapter, Benedict describes processions in Yunnan in which villagers rang bells, beat on gongs and drums, and discharged firearms to scare off demons. In Kunming, soldiers marched through the streets while striking at invisible demons with their swords. In Mengzi, soldiers assembled in front of the local *yamen* (government office) every evening to "fire salvos in all directions to scare away the evil spirits" (ibid.: 142). The firing of guns recalls the ancient sorcerer-physician as a shaman shooting arrows at demons.

Daoist Magic as Violent Confrontations with Demons

War magic is hence the strategy for curing ills, according to Chinese folk belief. To this day, spirit-mediums use swords to behead demons, spells to summon spirit-soldiers, and charms to issue death threats to the demonic enemy. Writing about religious rituals in contemporary Taiwan, Boretz (1995: 93) notes that although the symbols of war magic "may seem quaint survivals of the imperial past, the weapons and blood are nevertheless real, the passion and violence tangible." A Han *nuo* incantation set out in the fifth-century *Hou Han Shu* (Book of Later Han), contains this malediction (Harper 1987: 263-264):

> Let all twelve spirits be charged to pursue the foul and baleful.
> Scorch your carcass.
> Pull apart your trunk and joints.
> Cut away your flesh.
> Rip out your lungs and guts.
> If you do not quickly depart, those who remain will be fodder.

The brutal self-mortification practiced by *tangki*s follows in this violent tradition. Spirits may be insubstantial beings by Western conventions, but in Chinese popular imagination they have a real presence, and war against them is unflinchingly gory. Illustrations of the Chinese hell testify to this idea: sinners have their limbs cut off or their bodies sawed in half or flayed. Anthony Yu (1987: 409) remarks: "Not only do the damned spirits or ghosts suffer as if they had bodies, but the instruments of their affliction are of material substance." The *tangki* has therefore to be a most indomitable spirit-general.

Tangki *Spirit-Generals in the Heavenly Emperor's Army*

The *tangki* is a warrior in the armies of Tiangong (the Heavenly Emperor). Initiation rituals include reporting at a Tiangong temple to enlist in the celestial army. The temple-keeper presents the *tangki* initiate with a registration certificate, a copy of which must be burned to dispatch it to heaven. The *tangki* is then given the regalia of office: a flag of command (*ling qi*), a seal of office (*gong yin*), and a ritual sword in a scabbard (*bao jian*, the Precious Sword), which symbolizes the *tangki*'s license to kill demons.

The *tangki* does not operate as a lone knight errant; he is a general at the head of spirit-armies. The parish of a temple is protected by the 36 celestial armies under the command of Bei Ji Shangdi (the North Pole Emperor, also known as the Emperor of the Dark Heavens). The spirit-power of Bei Ji Shangdi's command is imbued in the *or leng*, a large black flag that is emblazoned with the eight trigrams and other esoteric symbols. The black flag (see figs. 1.1 and 1.2) is not a mere symbol illustrating ideas of the 'black command'. It is held to be the very energy source of Bei Ji Shangdi, and offerings are made to it. The *tangki* has a covenant with Bei Ji Shangdi and his celestial armies and can call upon the assistance of the 'black command'. An *or leng* planted outside a shrine or temple is a sure sign that a *tangki* works within.

The *or leng* must not be confused with other black flags. In the battle against the forces of evil, the *tangki* also calls upon the help of the 72 terrestrial spirit-armies under the command of the Wu Fang Wu Se Shen Ling (Five Directions and Five Colors Spirit-Powers) who are represented by five colored

FIGURE 1.1 *Or leng* or black command flag, replete with esoteric meanings of thunder and war

Photograph © Patrick Choo

FIGURE 1.2 *Or leng* legend

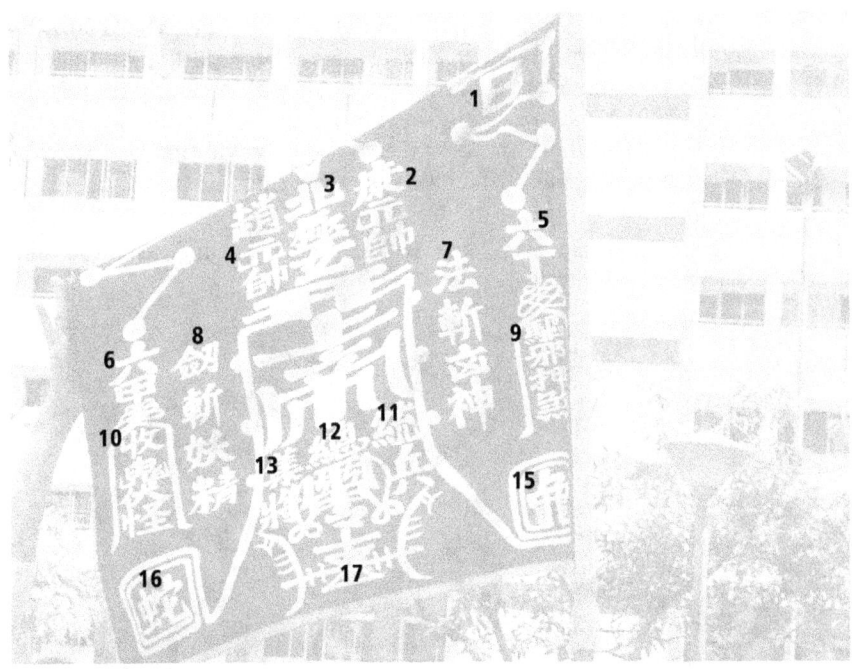

1. *Sun ri* (日) on the top left corner (right of viewer) and moon *yue* 月 on the top right corner, which is hidden from view because the flag is not fully unfurled (*Note:* The moon and the sun together represent *yin-yang* 阴阳.)
2. Marshal Kang
3. Dark Emperor of the North Pole (*Note:* The character *xuan* 玄 for dark appears like the *nu* 女 female radical. Deliberate calligraphic mistakes are often made in talismanic script in order to mislead the uninitiated.)
4. Marshal Zhao
5. Six Ding spirit-generals
6. Six Jia spirit-generals
7. Magic beheads fiends (*Note:* The *xiong* 凶 radical has been written with an additional head radical, 亠.)
8. The Sword beheads demonic spirits (*Note:* The *jing* 精 radical for goblin spirit has been written incorrectly.)
9. Dispel evil, detain malignant deities (*Note:* The hidden character is *sha* 煞, malignant deities.)
10. Arrest ghosts, subdue demons
11. Unite soldiers
12. Chief
13. Gather spirit-generals
14. Thunder command
15. Tortoise (totem animal of Bei Ji Shangdi)
16. Snake (totem animal of Bei Ji Shangdi)
17. This spindle-shaped motif represents the guts (符胆 *fu dan*) of the talisman, which is its focus and source of power (*Note:* The *fu dan* on this flag is embellished with weapon-shaped symbols.)

Interpretation and translation by Raymond Goh, Patrick Choo, and Margaret Chan. Digital mark-up by Barbara Tan.

flags. The black flag (not to be confused with the *or leng*) represents the army of the north. The red flag is that of the southern army, the green flag that of the eastern army, and the white flag that of the western army. The yellow flag represents the central army under Nezha. The *tangki* invokes the Wu Fang Wu Se Shen Ling in ceremonies through the performance of sacred choreographies (occasionally with the help of a troupe of youthful dancers), while waving five color-coded flags. The *tangki* may also pierce his body with rods topped with the godheads of the Generals of the Five Directions (figs. 1.3 and 1.4).

FIGURE 1.3 A Singaporean *tangki* pierced with rods topped with the godheads of the Generals of the Five Directions

Photograph © Victor Yue

FIGURE 1.4 The hooks will be used when the *tangki* later drags a heavy carriage behind him

Photograph © Victor Yue

Weapons Replete with Spirit-Power

Jimmy Yu (2012) writes of self-inflicted violence as a part of the mores of sixteenth- and seventeenth-century China. These performances were essentially about the negotiation of subjectivity and sanctity. As Yu explains: "Performers engaged in self-inflicted violence to exercise power and to affect people, events, and the environment. It enabled them to graphically and viscerally demonstrate moral values, reinstitute order, forge new social relations, and secure boundaries against the threat of moral ambiguity" (ibid.: 3). Since a *tangki* is regarded as a god incarnate, *tangki* self-mortification has been described as an act to demonstrate the invulnerability of the *tangkis* (see, e.g., Schipper [1982] 1993: 47; 1985: 31). Although the elements of bravado and spectacle do enter into a *tangki* performance, the underlying motive has a theological basis. *Tangkis* pierce their bodies with swords and rods in order to take on the spirit-power imbued in these weapons: driven into the flesh, the weapons supercharge the *tangkis* with spirit-power. *Tangkis* also spill their own blood to make talismans. For this, the *tangki* will strike his head or back with a sword, axe, or mace. More often, the tongue will be cut (fig. 1.5) so that the oozing blood can be smeared on strips of yellow-colored paper. These talismans effect cures, acting not so much as medicines but as commands to disease-causing demons to leave the patient.

Thunder Magic

Chinese talismans often relate to the power of thunder. The Chinese hold that thunder, not lightning, is the punishment that heaven metes out to evil-doers. The swirling and often jagged strokes with which talismanic ideographs of thunder are written might suggest the images caused by the natural phenomena known as Lichtenberg figures, which are feathering, fernlike, or treelike displays that appear on a body that has been struck by an electrical discharge (Hammond 1994: 490). Thus, the writing on *tangki* talismans is less a lettered tradition and more a martial act, which possibly explains why many *tangki* talismanic scripts are barely legible scrawls.

The punitive force of thunder is under the command of people who know the secrets of *lei fa* (thunder magic). The formulas for thunder magic found in manuals such as the twelfth-century *Wang Wenqing Leishuo* (The Thunder Discourse by Wang Wenqing) are all performance-based. As with all Daoist rituals, this involves dancing esoteric choreographies to music and incantations: the performer controls his breath in a specific manner and uses magical hand and finger gestures. The efficacy of thunder magic is clearly martial. In a spell set out in the *Wang Wenqing Leishuo* (cited in Reiter 2004: 227), the correct ritual performance summons the "rumbling emissaries of the thunders," the one million spirit-soldiers under the fire-bell generals, the stalwarts of the three heavens. The legions are armed with "crystallized halberds and battle axes." Evil spirits are smote by thunder to "cut their heads innumerable times and slice endlessly their bodies." Those evil-doers who obey the orders of the ritualist will be spared, but those who refuse to disperse will die (ibid.).

The Big Dipper is the single most important element of thunder magic and other Daoist lore. Accordingly, many Daoist religious props, including the *tangki*'s sword, are marked with the sign of the Seven Stars Constellation, the source of thunder magic. This comprises a series of dots joined by zigzag lines. Great magic is invoked when choreography, following the pattern of the Seven Stars, is danced using the limping *yubu* or *yu* step.

The Dance of Yu

Tangkis dance the *yubu* as a side-to-side stagger punctuated by a hopping on one leg. The heel-toe, heel-toe shuffle takes the *tangki* forward in a zigzag line. The magic properties of the *yubu* were formalized as early as the fourth century in the *Baopuzi* (*The Master Who Embraces Simplicity*), the earliest extant document on Daoist magic. The *yubu* imitates the limping steps of Da Yu (Yu the

FIGURE 1.5 A Singaporean *tangki* cuts his tongue to produce blood to make a talisman

Photographs © Victor Yue

Great), the legendary founder of the Xia dynasty, who, according to myth, saved China from a great flood through magic (Chan 2006: 85–86). It has also been recorded in the sixth-century BCE *Shangshu* (The Esteemed Documents), also known as the *Shujing* (Classic of History), that Da Yu subdued the Miao tribes with his magical dance, allowing for the establishment of the proto-Chinese Xia dynasty (McCurley 2005: 141–142).

That a sacred dance can mount a military campaign is also proposed by a second example: the Tang general Pei Min routed invading Turkic tribes by standing on top of his horse and performing the sword dance, "an art as appropriate to magicians as to warriors" (Teiser 1988: 442). Sacred choreographies as rituals of exorcism constitute the signifying feature of the performances of *jiajiang* (infernal spirit-generals) in Taiwan (see Sutton 1996, 2003).

Thus, every performance element in the *tangki* repertoire is an act of war magic. The martial spirit may be overt in the bloody acts of self-mortification, but even by blowing out sprays of imbibed lustral water, the *tangki* is fighting off demonic attacks with *qi* (energy).

Contemporary *Tangki* Ritual Theater: Reflecting a Diverse Society

Contemporary *tangki* war magic in Thailand has absorbed Buddhist ideas of karma, manifested in 'bizarre' types of self-mortification that use instruments such as fluorescent light tubes, ceiling fans, and rods fixed with satellite dishes. These spectacular ideas have spread to other countries. In April 2007, a female *tangki* in Singapore, possessed by Nezha, pierced a bicycle through her face (fig. 1.6). Nezha is the central commander of the spirit-armies of the five directions, so his *tangkis* often perform the 'fiercest' self-mortification. The bicycle, however, cannot be explained in terms of Chinese popular religion or war magic lore, which decrees that weapons, not a utilitarian object like a bicycle, should be pierced into the body.

A clue as to the provenance of this 'bizarre' self-mortification is that it was performed under the guidance of a Thai ritualist. Thai *tangkis* also took part in the same celebrations. One of them weighed down a rod pierced through his cheek with a ladder, the flags of the five spirit-armies, two banners, and other decorations (fig. 1.7).

Reporting on *tangki* performances in Taiwan, Schipper (1985: 31) describes the *tangki* as the *ti shen* (replacement body) who "spills his blood in order that the village may live in peace." A finer point can be made by analyzing the 'bizarre' *tangki* self-mortification of the Thai vegetarian festival in terms of the Buddhist doctrine of karma.

'Bizarre' Self-Mortification and Buddhist Self-Sacrifice

Benn (2007: 1–18) writes of a remarkable Chinese history of self-immolation. Beginning in the fourth century, there have been accounts of several hundred monks, nuns, and laypeople who made offerings of their bodies for a variety of

FIGURE 1.6 Self-mortification to earn karma for her devotees. Joyce Phoon, Singapore, 2007

Photograph © Melvin Hodder

FIGURE 1.7 A Thai *tangki* performing in Singapore

Photograph © Melvin Hodder

reasons. Benn includes within the scope of self-immolation a variety of practices, such as offering the body to be fed upon by insects, slicing the flesh, burning incense upon the body, starving oneself, and auto-cremation (ibid.: 9–10).

Benn (2007: 9) sees in the Chinese concept of *sheshen* (the abandoning of the body) a somatic strategy for the attainment of Buddhahood that he suggests is inspired by the *Lotus Sutra*. This doctrine of Mahayana Buddhism proposes that the carnal body is an impediment to enlightenment. Self-immolation in these terms is therefore "not aberrant, heterodox, or anomalous, but part of a serious attempt to make bodhisattvas on Chinese soil" (ibid.: 11). In this regard, I note the Sinicized legend of Guanyin, a woman who attained nirvana after she sacrificed her hand and eyes to help cure her sick father.

Newlin (2008) considers the Chinese concept of abandoning the body to be culturally salient to an analysis of the rash of self-immolation by fire that took place in Vietnam between 1963 and 1975. Newlin's discourse brings the Chinese Buddhist idea of self-sacrifice to contemporary Indochina. These arguments can be used to understand recent self-immolation events in Tibet.

Writing on the 'philosophy of social charity' in Thai Buddhism, Kumar (2001: 70, 74) asserts that Thai Buddhism is focused on the notions of karma and rebirth and that it regards the practice of charity as the best way to live the religious life. Although Thai Buddhism derives from the Theravada school,

Kumar notes the influence of Mahayana Buddhism. One Mahayana theory concerns the 'transfer of merit'. Bodhisattvas have an infinite store of merit, "acquired through many lives of heroic self-sacrifice," which can be drawn upon to short-circuit an unworthy individual's karmic path to rebirth in paradise (ibid.: 70–71). Kumar also writes that giving to others can redound to the credit of the donor. The greater the use that donees can derive from the gift, the more merit, in karmic terms, is earned by the donor. This principle, notes Kumar, has led to extreme acts of self-sacrifice (ibid.: 68–76).

Conclusion: *Tangki* War Magic—Real and Relevant

Although it is secondary to ideas of karma or the acquisition of spirit-power, the notion of performances of invulnerability is useful in an analysis of modern *tangki* self-mortification. We recall Norton's arguments of virtuality as needing to be 'enough' to move the audience to believe in the existence of an actuality. Lee et al. (2010: 56) write how contemporary society is now "culturally more diversified due to globalization and immigration." Health belief systems are also now multi-dimensional with the co-existence of biomedical and alternative healing therapies. In such a situation, they note, healers and patients may live in different local worlds. For healing to take place, there must be a meeting of the two parties in a common mythic world.

In order to ensure that their war magic remains an existential reality, *tangki*s have had to adapt their ritual theater to make it relevant to a new generation of devotees. The doxa, which has been extended to include Buddhist ideas and contemporary instruments of self-mortification such as LED lights and satellite dishes, is now suitably contemporary. Singaporean *tangki*s have broadened their ritual theater to incorporate modern notions of medicine. Besides driving away demons of pestilence with weapons and magical flags, they also prescribe herbs, perform acupuncture and massage, and, as a matter of routine, refer patients to medical doctors.

The *tangki*'s war magic comprises the staging of a ritual theater of war between spirit-warriors and malevolent demons. The ritual is a phantasmagoric space that the *tangki* and his devotees choose to enter in order to make meaning. The virtuality of *tangki* war magic, which presents spirit-warriors fighting for the community, assures devotees that their real, everyday life will be an actuality of *pingan* (peace and safety).

Acknowledgments

This research was supported by the Singapore Ministry of Education (MOE) Academic Research Fund (AcRF) Tier 1 grant. I thank Patrick Choo, Victor Yue, and Melvin Hodder for the use of their photographs. I am grateful to Raymond Goh for help with translations, Taoist priest Jave Wu for sharing his knowledge of Taoist rituals, and Lee Su Yin and Timothy Pwee for their assistance in editing and proofreading. I am indebted to the anonymous reviewers of this chapter for their kind and very useful suggestions.

Margaret Chan is Associate Professor of Theater and Performance Studies (Practice) in the School of Social Sciences, Singapore Management University. She received her PhD from the University of London in 2002. Her research areas include creative thinking, theater anthropology, performance studies, Asian ritual theater, and Chinese spirit-medium worship. She is the author of *Ritual Is Theatre, Theatre Is Ritual: Tang-ki Chinese Spirit Medium Worship* (2006).

Notes

1. This refers to Chinese linear measurement. The lengths varied in different periods and regions, but the contemporary *chiok* measures approximately 33 centimeters. The *choon* is one-tenth of a *chiok*, the *hoon* one-tenth of a *choon*. For more on Chinese weights and measures, see Wilkinson (2000: 234–242).
2. The word *nuo* was an ancient malediction, a curse shouted at ghosts and other evil spirits to drive them away.
3. See Barth (1970) for a discussion of culture as a dynamic social process.
4. Historical dates going back thousands of years can only be notional, but they are included to give a sense of the time frame involved.
5. The Hokkien phrase *yiukeng siew suat* translates as an 'exorcist tour of the parish to drive away evil spirits'. In the community, this phrase is shortened to *yiukeng*, meaning 'tour of parish'.
6. Tao Hua is Flos Pruni Persicae (flower of the peach tree), and Tao Xiao is old Fructus Pruni Persicae (aged and more dehydrated peach fruit).

References

Barend, J. ter Haar. 2000. "Rethinking 'Violence' in Chinese Culture." Pp. 123–140 in *Meanings of Violence: A Cross Cultural Perspective*, ed. Göran Aijmer and Jon Abbink. Oxford: Berg.

Barth, Fredrik. 1970. "Introduction." Pp. 9–38 in *Ethnic Groups and Boundaries: The Social Organization of Culture Difference*, ed. Fredrik Barth. London: George Allen & Unwin.

Benedict, Carol. 1988. "Bubonic Plague in Nineteenth-Century China." *Modern China* 14, no. 2: 107–155.

Benn, James A. 2007. *Burning for the Buddha: Self-Immolation in Chinese Buddhism.* Honolulu: Kuroda Institute.

Bodde, Derk. 1975. *Festivals in Classical China: New Year and Other Annual Observances during the Han Dynasty, 206 B.C.–A.D. 220*. Princeton, NJ: Princeton University Press.

Boretz, Avron A. 1995. "Martial Gods and Magic Swords: Identity, Myth, and Violence in Chinese Popular Religion." *Journal of Popular Culture* 29, no. 1: 93–109.

Bourdieu, Pierre. 1977. *Outline of a Theory of Practice*. Trans. Richard Nice. Cambridge: Cambridge University Press.

Chan, Margaret. 2006. *Ritual Is Theatre, Theatre Is Ritual: Tang-Ki Chinese Spirit Medium Worship*. Singapore: Wee Kim Wee Center, Singapore Management University and SNP Reference.

Chan, Margaret. 2009. "Chinese New Year in West Kalimantan: Ritual Theatre and Political Circus." *Chinese Southern Diaspora Studies* 3: 106–142.

Chan, Margaret. 2012. "Bodies for the Gods: Image Worship in Chinese Popular Religion." Pp. 197–215 in *The Spirit of Things: Materiality and Religious Diversity in Southeast Asia*, ed. Julius Bautista. Ithaca, NY: Cornell Southeast Asia Program Publications.

Chan, Margaret. 2015. "Contemporary Daoist Tangki Practice." Pp. 1–19 in *Oxford Handbooks Online*. New York: Oxford University Press.

Chongqing, Huangpu, Cao Lusheng, and Richard Schechner. 1989. "Nuo Theatre in Guizhou Province." *TDR: The Drama Review* 33, no. 3: 113–121.

Cohen, Erik. 2001. *The Chinese Vegetarian Festival in Phuket: Religion, Ethnicity and Tourism on a Southern Thai Island*. Bangkok: White Lotus.

de Groot, Jan J. M. 1910. *The Religious System of China: Its Ancient Forms, Evolution, History and Present Aspect, Manners, Customs and Social Institutions Connected Therewith*. Vol. 6, book 2. Leyden: E. J. Brill.

Dow, James. 1986. "Universal Aspects of Symbolic Healing: A Theoretical Synthesis." *American Anthropologist* (n.s.) 88, no. 1: 56–69.

Ellen, Roy. 1993. "Introduction." Pp. 1–25 in *Understanding Witchcraft and Sorcery in Southeast Asia*, ed. C. W. Watson and Roy Ellen. Honolulu: University of Hawai'i Press.

Hammond, Charles E. 1994. "The Interpretation of Thunder." *Journal of Asian Studies* 53, no. 2: 487–503.

Harper, Donald. 1985. "A Chinese Demonography of the Third Century B.C." *Harvard Journal of Asiatic Studies* 45, no. 2: 459–498.

Harper, Donald. 1987. "Wang Yen-shou's Nightmare Poem." *Harvard Journal of Asiatic Studies* 47, no. 1: 239–283.

Hsu, Cho-yun. 1997. "Cultural and Lineage Roots of the Chinese Dual Identities." National Humanities Center. http://nationalhumanitiescenter.org/publications/hongkong/cho.htm (accessed 12 April 2012).

Kapferer, Bruce. 2005a. "Ritual Dynamics and Virtual Practice: Beyond Representation and Meaning." Pp. 35–54 in *Ritual in Its Own Right: Exploring the Dynamics of Transformation*, ed. Don Handelman and Galina Lindquist. New York: Berghahn Books.

Kapferer, Bruce. 2005b. "Sorcery and the Beautiful: A Discourse on the Aesthetics of Ritual." Pp. 129–160 in *Aesthetics in Performance: Formations of Symbolic Construction and Experience*, ed. Angela Hobart and Bruce Kapferer. New York: Berghahn Books.

Kim, Jong-Young. 2001. "Oriental Medicine as a Heterogeneous Ensemble." *Korean Journal of Medical History* 10, no. 2: 103–123.

Kumar, Bachchan. 2001. "Philosophy of Social Charity in Thai Buddhism." Pp. 65–81 in *Spiritual Value of Social Charity*, ed. Wazir Singh and N. K. Singh. Delhi: Global Vision Publishing House.

Lee, Boon-Ooi, Laurence J. Kirmayer, and Danielle Groleau. 2010. "Therapeutic Processes and Perceived Helpfulness of Dang-Ki (Chinese Shamanism) from the Symbolic Healing Perspective." *Culture, Medicine, and Psychiatry* 34, no. 1: 56–105.

Legge, James, trans. [1861] 2012. *The Analects of Confucius*. Adelaide: University of Adelaide Library. http://ebooks.adelaide.edu.au/c/confucius/c748a (accessed 11 April 2013).
McCurley, Dallas. 2005. "Performing Patterns: Numinous Relations in Shang and Zhou China." *TDR: The Drama Review* 49, no. 3: 135–156.
Newlin, Aura. 2008. "Fiery Self-Sacrifice: Transience and Illusions in the Phenomenon of Modern Self-Immolation." *Graduate Discourse* 4, no. 1: 16–37.
Ng, Beng-Yeong. 2000. "Phenomenology of Trance States Seen at a Psychiatric Hospital in Singapore: A Cross-Cultural Perspective." *Transcultural Psychiatry* 37, no. 4: 560–579.
Norton, Richard. 1972. "What Is Virtuality?" *Journal of Aesthetics and Art Criticism* 30, no. 4: 499–505.
Pan, Lynn, ed. 1998. *The Encyclopedia of the Chinese Overseas*. Singapore: Archipelago Press and Landmark Books.
Reiter, Florian C. 2004. "'The Discourse on the Thunders' by the Taoist Wang Wen-ch'ing (1093–1153)." *Journal of the Royal Asiatic Society* (3rd series) 14, no. 3: 207–229.
Riley, Jo. 1997. *Chinese Theatre and the Actor in Performance*. Cambridge: Cambridge University Press.
Rosenblatt, Louise M. [1938] 1995. *Literature as Exploration*. 5th ed. New York: Modern Language Association of America.
Sax, William S. 1990. "The Ramnagar Ramlila: Text, Performance, Pilgrimage." *History of Religions* 30, no. 2: 129–153.
Schiffeler, John W. 1976. "The Origin of Chinese Folk Medicine." *Asian Folklore Studies* 35, no. 1: 17–35.
Schipper, Kristofer. [1982] 1993. *The Taoist Body*. Trans. Karen C. Duval. Berkeley: University of California Press.
Schipper, Kristofer. 1985. "Vernacular and Classical Ritual in Taoism." *Journal of Asian Studies* 45, no. 1: 21–57.
Sutton, Donald S. 1996. "Transmission in Popular Religion: The Jiajiang Festival Troupe of Southern Taiwan." Pp. 212–249 in *Unruly Gods: Divinity and Society in China*, ed. Meir Shahar and Robert P. Weller. Honolulu: University of Hawai'i Press.
Sutton, Donald S. 2003. *Steps of Perfection: Exorcistic Performers and Chinese Religion in Twentieth-Century Taiwan*. Cambridge, MA: Harvard University Asia Center.
Teiser, Stephen F. 1988. "'Having Once Died and Returned to Life': Representations of Hell in Medieval China." *Harvard Journal of Asiatic Studies* 48, no. 2: 433–464.
Tian, Min. 2003–2004. "Chinese Nuo and Japanese Noh: Nuo's Role in the Origination and Formation of Noh." *Comparative Drama* 37, no. 3–4: 343–360.
Waley, Arthur. [1934] 1968. *The Way and Its Power: A Study of the Tao Te Ching and Its Place in Chinese Thought*. London: George Allen & Unwin.
Wilkinson, Endymion. 2000. *Chinese History: A Manual*. Cambridge, MA: Harvard University Asia Center.
Wong, Deborah, and René T. A. Lysloff. 1991. "Threshold to the Sacred: The Overture in Thai and Javanese Ritual Performance." *Ethnomusicology* 35, no. 3: 315–348.
Yousof, Ghulam-Sarwar. 2010. "Islamic Elements in Traditional Indonesian and Malay Theatre." *Kajian Malaysia* 28, no. 1: 83–101.
Yu, Anthony C. 1987. "'Rest, Rest, Perturbed Spirit!' Ghosts in Traditional Chinese Prose Fiction." *Harvard Journal of Asiatic Studies* 47, no. 2: 397–434.
Yu, Jimmy. 2012. *Sanctity and Self-Inflicted Violence in Chinese Religions, 1500–1700*. New York: Oxford University Press.

Chapter 2

JAVANESE RITUAL INITIATION
Invulnerability, Authority, and Spiritual Improvement

Jean-Marc de Grave

In this chapter I review a special activity that every Javanese knows about and has often practiced in his life in one way or another.[1] It is called *kanuragan*—a secret ritual initiation based upon the teaching of a master concerning local cosmological knowledge, cults, and practices to gain strength and invulnerability on the basic level and to acquire wisdom and spiritual improvement on the advanced level. From the Javanese point of view, *kanuragan* presents itself as an educational process for youths. The fact that we find it in the non-Islamized context of Bali (Hooykaas 1974: 110, 122, 124) seems to indicate that the practice preceded the spread of Islam to Java in the fifteenth century. Other elements, notably tied to conceptions of birth, suggest that its earliest forms may even be anterior to the Indianization of Java and could possibly be tied to headhunting (Berthe 1968).

Research concerning *kanuragan* activity appears to have been broadly ignored by the academic world. I have underlined in previous research (de Grave 2001:

Notes for this chapter begin on page 64.

7; 2008) that the Leiden School—and Koji Miyazaki (1979, 1988) in the continuation of its work—noticed the importance of warfare authority in Javanese systems of representation and that Pemberton (1994) indirectly found it in the *rebutan* rituals of communal ceremonies, including the Javanese New Year's Eve as described here.[2] In light of these works, *kanuragan* activity appears as a missing link that concretely shows how such representational rituals and epics are effectively anchored in socio-cultural activity and morphology. Other researchers working on Java have failed to take this activity into consideration and may not even have noticed its presence, since it is taught under the auspices of secrecy.[3]

Whatever the case, a modern version exists alongside the traditional form of *kanuragan*. As I have shown previously (de Grave 2001), the modern version can be found in local martial arts schools that incorporate body techniques of the so-called Asian martial arts, including strikes, kicks, holds, locks, and evasions, where integration is also initiatory and requires the progressive acquisition of deeply embodied social and cultural knowledge. Approximately tens of millions of practitioners have attended such schools in Indonesia. The cadres and protectors of these schools are also usually national figures in ritual, religious, political, and economic domains, and they are often practitioners themselves.

Here I address the most ritualized traditional form of *kanuragan* that I have encountered in Java. Although the people involved are numerically less significant than those in modern *kanuragan* schools, they are much more important on the scale of Javanese social values. The main point, from the perspective of this book, is that *kanuragan* is also more closely tied to the general subject of war magic.

As will be shown in this chapter, *kanuragan* appears to have played an important role in the Indonesian War of Independence (1945–1949), long before which the Dutch colonial government had issued a general, but not exhaustive, interdict against martial activities such as *kanuragan* and local martial arts. This prohibition endures into the present due to the Indonesian government's goal of reducing physical violence via the ongoing interdict against bearing weapons or fighting in public. An effective way to actualize the prohibition was realized through the 'sportization' of martial arts activities, understood as a kind of rationalization of violence. This approach is largely supported by the Indonesian government through the national federation of the Ikatan Pencak Silat Indonesia (IPSI, Pencak Silat Association of Indonesia), the leading organization of martial arts.

The sportization of martial arts is not specific to Indonesia. It can be linked to the general trend of pacification underlined by Norbert Elias (2008)—that is, the pacifying influence of sports on social contexts. An example is the introduction of cricket in Trobriand society in an attempt to eliminate village revenge attacks, as D. S. Farrer illustrates in the introduction to this book. For Indonesia, it should be noted that religious institutions such as Muslim schools and Sufi brotherhoods have played an important role in the adaptation of *kanuragan* to an Islamized social context before it enters the secular process of sportization.

Thus, Javanese *kanuragan* has to face both secular martial arts sport and the hegemonic tendency of Islam to contest what Muslim ideology considers to be 'subaltern cults', such as the 'sibling spirits' of the human being in Javanese conceptions. In the process, Islam and sport become part of a broader modernizing process that induces specific conceptions and embodied practices, both Muslim and secular, but also Christian, Chinese, Japanese, and European.[4]

In this sense, I would like to argue that the particular role of war magic can be understood as a way that different social institutions—in the broad meaning that Mary Douglas (1987) assigns to this term—are complementary or enter in competition with each other. In this instance, such networks include nationalist versus colonial networks, sport networks, formal religious networks, or government networks versus *kanuragan* networks. In my view, this perspective encompasses technical aspects, embodiment and transmission, and apprenticeship as the main basis—even as 'the' main basis in certain cases—for the constitution of social values.

This approach is in accordance with Farrer's important observation (this volume) that anthropological accounts "have tended to neglect war magic and warrior religion." The key reason, I think, is that war magic did not figure in the ethical conceptions of researchers of an older generation, who likely had no access to the techniques concerned or simply ignored them. Here, by referring to different groups or communities, I would like to illuminate a specific aspect of traditional *kanuragan* to show how it can be conceived as a highly valued activity from the Javanese point of view, yet also as a simple or dangerous Javanese cultural trait from the perspective of the state or of Islamic ideology.

First, I discuss the main concepts and techniques used in traditional *kanuragan*, which I initially researched during a year of participant observation in 1995. Then I endeavor to describe traditional *kanuragan* activities and their direct link to war and to the Javanese concept of authority. Doing so sheds light on the similarities and differences between magic and religion according to different perspectives (e.g., religion viewed as a principle or as a social network) that are themselves tied to diverse, culturally marked categorizations. This helps to determine what local practices can teach us with regard to other perspectives and categorizations.

What Is Traditional *Kanuragan*?

The *kanuragan* initiation ritual is characterized by two elements in its foundation. The first is linked to the cycle of life and particularly to birth. According to Javanese conceptions, when a human being comes to earth, four sibling spirits accompany him (see de Grave 2001). Among them are especially an 'elder brother' (*kakang*), coming from the 'amniotic fluid' (*kawah*), and, even more valued, a 'younger brother' (*adhik*), coming from the 'placenta' (*ari-ari*). The *kanuragan* practice aims to use the power of these four sibling spirits. The second element of the ritual consists in the acquisition of external entities called *aji*, each of which has specific characteristics.

In the following paragraphs, I first introduce the *kanuragan* school discussed in this chapter and its teachings. Next, I describe basic-level *aji* that serve to obtain different kinds of invulnerability or possession by an animal spirit. Subsequently, I detail some aspects of advanced-level practice: healing patients, going on pilgrimages, and improving meditation techniques with the aim of increasing one's potential for spiritual authority. I then present different warfare or conflict situations in which these *aji* are put into practice empirically and indicate the representational system attached to them.

The Trah Gondosuman School

The teaching of the Trah Gondosuman (TG) *kanuragan* group takes place near the royal palace in the city of Yogyakarta, Central Java, under the direction of a *sesepuh* (old experienced person) named Mbah. The basic level of teaching—referred to as *kaenoman*, a substantive form of the adjective *enom* (young)—addresses young people. First, the practitioner recognizes the master, or guru, as his father and the group as his family. He is then given the basic 'formula' by which he can seek help from his 'four [spirit] siblings' (*sadulur papat*) in order to interpret the teachings of the master.

The basic level of the teaching is composed of five principal forms of knowledge (*ngèlmu*) that one must obtain in order to succeed in mastering one's emotions (*rasa*)—especially fear and anger—and one's attachments. Through mastery of the emotions, the practitioner obtains confidence in himself. The practice sequence is similar for all of these forms of knowledge: observing a period of fast (*pasa*) after the corresponding accession ceremony, learning the right spells (mantra) and prayers (*dunga*), and offering a ritual meal (*rasulan*).

Each form or *ngèlmu* helps the practitioner attain a specific state of invulnerability (*kedhotan*). For every *ngèlmu* practiced, there exists a specific offering (*sarat*). This consists of a food that is ingested at the moment of the accession rite but must not be ingested afterward, in order to preserve the capacity enabled by the *aji*. The food varies according to the transmitted form. Mbah, the schoolmaster, calls this food a 'key' (*kunci*). Its purpose is to rid oneself of the *aji* if this proves to be necessary at the moment of dying, for example, in case possessing such a capacity should perturb the natural process of death.[5]

The *aji* has its own existence. It can be transmitted from person to person or can be acquired by establishing a particular relation with the spirit world. The word *aji* also designates the special spells by which one obtains or invokes an *aji*. In both cases, the *aji* is supposed to be an emanation of the divine world.

The Basic Level

To give an indication of the technical, social, and representational aspects of the *aji*'s teaching, we will review the transmission process of two different forms: *windu kencana aji* and *pangèlmunan*, as well as their respective basic-level specificities. I will also discuss a supplementary *aji* related to spirit-possession to provide additional information about Sufi influences and the teaching as a whole.

The Windu Kencana Aji

The term *windu* designates an eight-year Javanese period or cycle, while the word *kencana* means 'in gold' or 'gilded' (see more on this below). This form introduces the practitioner to the general teaching. Under this title, the ceremony is accompanied by the oath of fidelity that the new members pronounce in the presence of the *sesepuh* and the advanced members. With this oath, the students confirm their wish to receive the teaching, to use it with dignity, and to remain faithful to the master and to the more elderly members, "as a child toward his father and his eldest brothers."

After this special phase that initiates the candidate to the teaching, the transmission of the *windu kencana aji* aims to render the student invulnerable (*kedhot*) to blows caused by pointed weapons. This transmission can be divided into three principal parts: first, the candidate meets the master, who tells him the conditions for carrying out the transmission; second, the master dictates the kind of fast to be made; and, third, the master fixes the date on which the initiation ceremony will be organized. For this *aji*, the fast is spread out over a period of seven days and seven nights, during which time the acolyte must avoid adding any salt or sugar to his food. Meat is also forbidden. The master designates this form of fast by the word *mutih*.[6] The student chooses the period of fasting himself, according to his activities and to his state of concentration; the only stipulation is that this period must start and end at sunset, around 6:00 PM, and that it must take place before the date fixed for the initiation ceremony.

During the period of fasting, according to Mbah, it is necessary to avoid getting angry and, especially, to fight or to have sexual relations. Equally important is the need to avoid the emotional disharmony provoked by the unbalanced use of the senses. It is thus a requirement to strive to keep united (*manunggal*) the senses of hearing, seeing, smelling, tasting, and feeling (*sukma rasa*). The sense of touch is in fact included in the *sukma rasa* (on this point, see de Grave 2011; Hellman 2009). Fasting is therefore not only an issue of food; it concerns all the senses, including the inner feeling (*rasa pangrasa*). The practitioner must reproduce the concentration developed during the period of fasting at the moment of the initiation ceremony. He knows what to expect and must not be overwhelmed by any feeling of fear.

The initiation ceremony described here took place on the evening of 25 May 1995, a sacred night known as Friday *Kliwon*. This night, which is calculated by the confluence of the seven-day week and the five-day week of the Javanese calendar,[7] returns every 35 days and is thus considered propitious for ceremonial activities. The eight young people who were expected all arrived at 8:00 PM, some having traveled a distance of 20 kilometers. Aged from 20 to 30, their social origins and occupations were varied, with some employed as farmers, workers, students, and teachers. Everyone sat on mats placed on the floor in the living room, facing Mbah. Gradually, the other members of the TG cadre also arrived, notably, a bespectacled young law student, Mas Bambang, and a 45-year-old chief building worker. Both of them, along with the latter's son, assisted the master.[8]

When everyone had arrived, Mbah began to speak in Javanese.[9] He declared first of all that the group had managed to collect only 700,000 rupiah to prepare the Javanese New Year's Eve activities—half of the sum that was needed. Then he announced the evening's program. Previously, the *sesepuh* (the members of the superior or *kasepuhan* level) had opened the session with ritual prayers and performed a collective consecration of water with specific spells aimed at healing a sick person. Next, the necessary ingredients for the accession rites were prepared and consecrated by prayers. Then, the ritual tests took place. Finally, the ritual meal of *rasulan* offered by the students was eaten. What follows is a more detailed description of the ceremony.

After the opening therapeutic ceremonial, which had been carried out by Mbah and the six 'elders' (men typically aged from 35 to 50 years old), dishes of food were brought out: a plate with two small cones of rice (*tumpeng*) on it; a plate of peanut sauce (*bumbu pecel*), soy (*kedhelé*) cooked with coconut palm sugar (*gula jawa*), and soybean sprouts (*kecambah*); a plate of raw cabbage (*kobis*) cut in strips; and two big, young black roosters, boiled, spiced, and flavored (*ayam ingkung*).

Once the food was blessed by Mbah, a flower water glass that had been consecrated at the beginning of the meeting was placed in front of the guru. On his instructions, one of the assistants filled another glass three-fourths full with water from a bottle prepared in advance. The master took an envelope made of banana leaves held closed by a small pointed bamboo stick. He opened the envelope, which was full of flower petals, and took out two kinds: jasmine (*mlathi*) and champak (*kanthil*), both of which are white. Ignoring the red rose petals, he then put the white flowers in the second glass of water, which was placed next to the first one that had been blessed. The benzoic resin (*menyan*) that had been lit at the time of the therapeutic ceremony was revived, and three sticks of incense were lit and put in the small vase where the three preceding ones were now nearly burned out. During these preparations, four big enameled basins containing flower water were brought into the room and placed close to the glasses and the incense in an east-west axis (food, incense, glasses, basins).

Mbah again recited the opening and basic prayer, the *keblat papat kalima pancer*, which had been used at the beginning of the therapeutic ritual. Next, the eight participants moved to another room. Now bare-chested, each in turn drank three sips of flower water from the two prepared glasses. The master took his place in a squatting position, with a basin deployed to the west of him. The first candidate placed himself to the east of the basin, also squatting. With his hands, the guru sprinkled water on the student's back (tapping it several times), his arms, his stomach (tapping several times above the navel), his neck, and his face (tapping three times on the temples). Then the young man sprinkled water over his own face three times. Next, the master pronounced sentences that the candidate had to repeat, one at a time. The next student was subjected to the same procedures as in this sequence.

The basin was put aside, and the guru got up. He seized the *keris* (dagger) that he usually uses for the initiation rites. Facing west, he asked the candidate to face him at a distance of about a meter and a half. Then, with the *keris* handle in his right hand, he ran toward the young man and struck him in a zone between the navel and the chest (see fig. 2.1). Only 1.5 to 2 centimeters of the blade protruded beyond the fingers of his left hand, between his thumb and index finger holding the tip. The blade came in contact with the flesh without causing a wound. The sudden force of the blow knocked the student over, and two other experienced students caught him to prevent him from falling to the ground. The action was repeated three times. Then the guru turned the candidate around, repeating the procedure with a single blow to the back.

The guru next recited the final sentence of the prayer *windu kencana*, which the student had to repeat before striking the ground three times with his right heel. Then it was the turn of the other candidate to undergo the whole process, and this scenario was repeated with the four following students. The stipulation (*sarat*) that allows the candidates to retain the capacities enabled by the fast and the *windu kencana aji* ritual is that they should never again eat black slimy rice.

FIGURE 2.1 Mbah simulating the *windu kencana* initiation rite of the *keris*, Yogyakarta, 2005

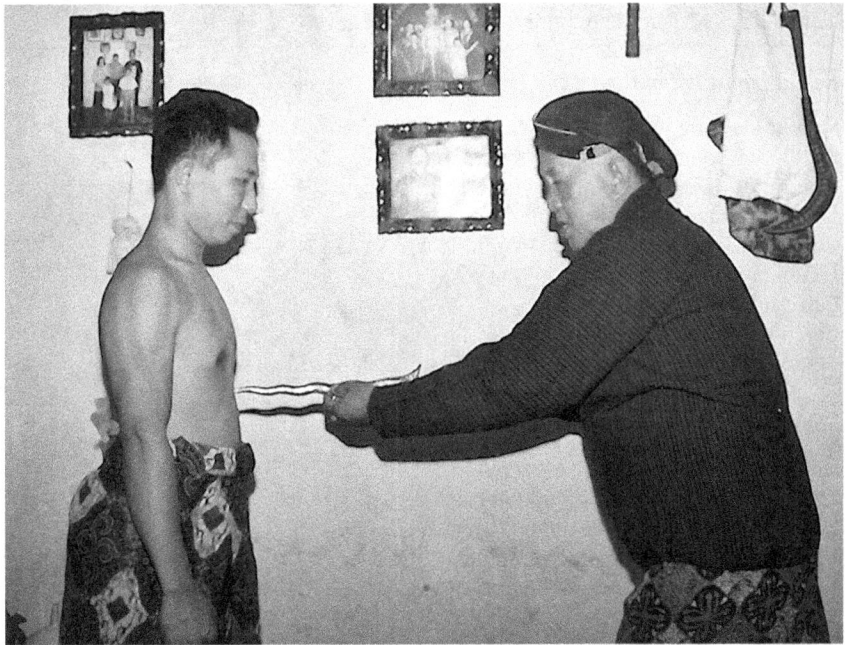

Photograph © Jean-Marc de Grave

At the end of this test, and after an accession rite specific to Mbah's two assistants, we returned to the courtyard where the final two candidates underwent a test linked to the *pangèlmunan*.

Before looking into this *aji*, I must make some additional remarks on the *windu kencana aji*. The first is that the teaching's introductory spell, *keblat papat kalima pancer* (see table 2.1), is actually the generic mantra to be recited before all *aji* invocations. I heard many similar mantras in Java that invoked the four sibling spirits. It thus appears that this cult is broadly followed in Java and that there is a mantra specific to each group of *kanuragan* or *kebatinan*.[10] In each case, the place of Man, or Ego, is set in a cosmological hierarchy. According to my analysis, the Javanese classification system—notably, for space and time—is immediately evident in this version (for an extensive review, see de Grave 2001: 49–60). It is first apparent with the 4-5 Javanese classification through 1 Ego and his 4 siblings; then with the 2-3 classification through the Cosmos, the Prince, and the Lord; and lastly with the central 1 binding the 4-5 together and also binding them to the Divine.

This classification system was first enumerated at the beginning of the last century by the Leiden School (see de Josselin de Jong [1916] 1977a; Pigeaud [1916] 1977; van Ossenbruggen [1916] 1977). Its proponents held that the 4-5 elements are oriented more toward worldly activities and the 2-3 elements toward spiritual activities, both being bound together by the ultimate 1 that dominates the hierarchical setting.[11] This mantra, then, represents a confirmation

---

TABLE 2.1 The generic mantra for all *aji* invocations

Keblat papat kalima pancer

Sadulurku bang wetan kang awujud putih
Sadulurku bang kidul kang awujud abang
Sadulurku bang kulon kang awujud kuning
Sadulurku bang lor kang awujud ireng
Sadulurku bang tengah kang awujud klawu ya aku
Kakang sukma rasa adhiku sukma sejati
Sira padha kumpula
Manunggala dadi siji
Jagad Agung Pengeran Agung dhuh Gusti Allah kawula nyuwun ...

Four Directions and the Fifth One in the Center

My sibling of the East in white color,
My sibling of the South in red color,
My sibling of the West in yellow color,
My sibling of the North in black color,
My sibling of the Center in gray color, myself,
My elder sibling the essence of feeling, my younger sibling the true essence,
    please muster up and unite to become just one.
Macrocosmos, Great Prince, please my Lord Allah your servant humbly begs ...

of the Leiden School's analysis. It also shows the magical value of these numbers and the way that they combine to call on the special forces of Nature to give Man a precise place in the Cosmos and to endow him with a special strength. This strength is tied to the local cults dedicated to the four sibling spirits and also to the Cosmos-Prince-Lord construction, which should be considered in relation to the Javanese Trimurti shrines that feature three main temples. Inherited from Hinduism, the Trimurti evolved locally in accordance with Sufi doctrines.

In addition to this categorization whereby cult elements are integrated into the Javanese social system, the notion of *windu kencana* is well-known in Java thanks to its evocation in classical literature, where it is also tied to cosmological references and especially to warfare. Significantly, we find it in a text whose author, Raden Ngabei Ranggawarsita, was reputedly the 'official writer and magus' (*pujangga*) of the royal palace of Surakarta. A poet who lived in the mid-nineteenth century, Ranggawarsita is very famous in Indonesia for his predictions. His manuscript is characterized by colorful language that implies several levels of comprehension understandable by those who are familiar with Javanese symbols. The text in question is titled *Sabda Tama* (The Essential Word).

According to Any (1990: 36), this manuscript is a prediction that concerns the end of an era called Kala Bendu (Period of Misfortune), which will be followed by a 'gilded period' or *windu kencana*. Ranggawarsita opens by depicting this terrible era as one characterized by the domination of attachments, selfishness, hypocrisy, and the desire for power. In the fourteenth verse of the text, the *pujangga* describes these attachments as flowing to the "yellow, red, and blue lights" that do not deal with "the teaching of the prophets" or "the true essence of God." The fifteenth verse continues: "One should remember. When the year of the yellow *windu* arrives, there will be white *wéwé* [a species of good spirits] armed with blue-black sugar cane sticks, and they will destroy the *wedhon* [a species of bad ghosts]." This paragraph may be interpreted as follows. The *wéwé* are youths whose hearts are pure (symbolized by the white color) and who represent Indonesia. The *wedhon* are the Dutch, who colonized Indonesia. The blue-black sugar cane sticks are the sharpened bamboo that the Indonesians frequently used (when they had nothing else at hand) to fight against the Dutch during the War of Independence. Ranggawarsita's text finishes by announcing the return to peace, joy, and harmony at the end of this hard period of fighting.

Several points connect warfare and *aji* as presented in the *Sabda Tama* to Mbah's *aji*. First of all, the predictions of Ranggawarsita are very well-known in Java, especially in the networks of Javanese mystics since Ranggawarsita was himself a mystic master. Thus, his prediction, as far as it concerns the independence of the country, could only attract the attention of the Indonesians. In connection with this, the *windu kencana aji* was transmitted by a master, Mbah Joyo Permono, to young men around 1948 who were fighting the Dutch—in the precise period and circumstances that correspond to the interpretation of Ranggawarsita's text cited above.

An additional element is that the weapons described in the text of the *pujangga* are pointed bamboo sticks that served in close-contact fights with opponents using pointed metal weapons—precisely the kind against which the *windu kencana aji* is supposed to render the initiate invulnerable, as discussed above. According to the old Javanese language specialist Kuntara Wiryamartana (pers. comm.), another point tied to martial activity (but also therapeutics, both being intrinsically related) is that, in such a context, the term *windu* could also be linked to its Sanskrit-originated root *bindu* (point) and, more precisely, to the 'vital points of the body' (*marma*, in ancient Javanese).[12] Thus, we may conclude that the *kanuragan* practice is evoked in classical divinatory poetry, which relates to its mythical dimension being rooted in social morphology. We will see other examples of this in the following analyses.

The Pangèlmunan

The next *aji* discussed here is called *pangèlmunan* or *klunthung waluh*. It aims to make the initiate invulnerable to the *gebragan*, a spear-like weapon armed with 40 metal points. The length of the fast is two days and two nights, during which nothing can be eaten or drunk. The *pangèlmunan* initiation ritual I attended was combined with the one previously described concerning the *windu kencana*. In the courtyard, the two candidates prepared to undergo the test. The procedure was similar to that for the *windu kencana* except that the weapon used here was a *gebragan*. As this initiation rite was the last of the night, the ritual meal was then served, after which most of the candidates returned home.

Differing from the other students, those who passed the *pangèlmunan* received a piece of white cloth (*lawon putih*), and the flower water in which the cloths had been soaked contained water of musky marrow (*waluh*). According to Mbah, the musky marrow (the one that was used measured about 45 centimeters and weighed around 4 kilograms) represents the strength of the *pangèlmunan*. The white cloth represents the purity (*kasucèn*) of the youths (*putra*) to whom the *pangèlmunan* is transmitted. Mbah explained that, to reach this level, the practitioner has to improve his behavior in order to truly purify himself. The 'key' by which the student would lose the *aji*, should it become necessary, is the *waluh* itself, which he would consume. The *pangèlmunan sejati* prayer is transmitted to him during the accession rite.

The term *pangèlmunan* requires some added commentary. First, the word is a deformation of the term *panglimunan*, which designates an *aji* (also called *aji siluman*) that makes a person invisible and which one can frequently find in popular or classical stories. Second, while the term *pangèlmunan* is described here with regard to the ceremony to render students invulnerable to the *gebragan*, in its older and more elaborate form it allows the initiate to become invisible. Parallel to these data, I must add that, tied to the question of invisibility (see more on this topic below), the musky marrow, or *waluh*, used as the 'key' to the *aji*, is related to the *ruwatan* purification ceremony (Sulaiman 1985). In the mythic story of Murwakala, the god Kala has obtained from Çiva, the king of the gods, the right to eat certain categories of human beings. At a particular moment, Kala is pursuing an adolescent called Jaka Jatusmati, the only son of a widow. After a while, as he is about to catch the youth, the god stumbles over a musky marrow in the middle of a backyard. He falls down and loses track of his prey, who makes the most of this mishap and disappears.

Thus, in this story we find two elements present in the *pangèlmunan*: the musky marrow and the disappearance. We even find the relation where the musky marrow is the 'key' to the disappearance, which echoes the *aji*. In the transmission of this *aji*, we also have the use of a white cloth, which represents purity, and the fact that the student must change his behavior in relation to this purity. The practitioner's state of purity is also present in the purity rediscovered by the victim of Kala following the ritual of *ruwatan*. It is necessary to add here that Mbah is also a ceremonial master of *ruwatan* rituals (see de Grave 1997: 546–549; on *ruwatan*, see Headley 2000). Therefore, he is familiar with the techniques used in the *ruwatan*. Mbah seems to have blended his knowledge of *ruwatan* and *kanuragan* together, although it is possible that his interpretation corresponds to an earlier tradition when the two rituals were not separate.

The Doa Gerak *Supplementary Form*

Unlike the preceding forms, *doa gerak* does not require an entire ceremony to be held. No 'key' or specific offering is attached to it. The object of this supplementary form is to get oneself invested with an animal spirit. The master rarely directs the practice, which often takes place on the sacred beach of Parangkusumo and, in 1995, was directed by Mbah's assistant, Mas Bambang. I should add that the mantra used for the *doa gerak* refers to the person of Abdulkadir Jaelani, the founder of the Qâdiriyah, a Sufi 'brotherhood' (*tarekat*) that reached Java in the seventeenth century and became established notably in Banten (West Java).[13] Denys Lombard (1990: 2:120) explains that the trance exercises practiced in this region under the term *debus* are linked to the knowledge of this brotherhood's initiated members. In a discussion on Jaelani and his brotherhood, Martin van Bruinessen (1995: 207–222) gives some indications about the practice of *debus* and its link to the teaching of the *tarekat*. The trance in question allows initiated members to become invulnerable to weapons and to fire.[14]

The Superior Level

Invulnerability knowledge is also taught at the superior level, but in this case it is in relation to wild animals and to fire (see also Neidel, this volume), no longer to man. Protective and auspicious teaching at this level is classified under the term *gineng*, which leads to higher-level practices aimed at preparing one's afterlife sojourn.

The term *gineng* refers to classical poetry and to the shadow play ritual (*wayang purwa*). One finds it in the works of *kakawin* studied by Kuntara Wiryamartana (1990: 99–101), particularly the *Arjunawiwaha* narrative. In it, *gineng* refers to a particularly powerful *aji* provided to the giant Niwatakawaca. It has made him completely invulnerable except in a certain part of his body situated in his mouth. The giant feels so strong that he wants to attack the gods, who ask Arjuna to become their champion. By chance, Arjuna has just reached the highest level of Çiva tantric meditation and is about to reach 'deliverance' (*moksa*), but he chooses instead to preserve the equilibrium of the world, following his 'holy duty' (*dharma*) as 'knight' (*ksatria*) of the kingdom. Nevertheless, this very high level of yoga enables him to obtain advanced warrior capabilities.

In the TG, *gineng* forms the basis on which the practices linked to 'authority' (*kawibawan*) and to mystical 'union' (*manunggaling kawula Gusti*) are developed.[15] I have not witnessed any ritual transmissions of *aji* tied to protection from wild animals. Nevertheless, I have seen high-level protective ceremonial transmissions classified as *gineng*. The first is called *gineng panyuwunan*—from the words *gineng* (whose signification in the TG is 'healing care') and *panyuwunan* ('prayer' in high-level speech)—which can be translated as 'care by prayer'. The elder members meet once a year after observing a week-long *mutih* fast. During the meeting, they drink consecrated water. They must also have previously recited the appropriate mantra every eve of Friday *Kliwon* and of Tuesday *Kliwon*. The practice linked to *gineng panyuwunan* reinforces previous teachings. Mbah comments that through *gineng panyuwunan* the feeling of serenity passes from the physical dimension to the spiritual. Here I describe the *gineng panyuwunan* ceremony that was held at the same time as the accession rites of the *windu kencana* and the *pangèlmunan* described above.

After announcing the program of the evening, Mbah sat in a corner of the prayer room. He placed flowers (red roses, jasmine, and champak) in a glass that contained consecrated water and prepared his benzoic resin burner. While the resin burned, he started to recite some prayers. Next, he lit three incense sticks and held them for a moment above his head and then above the flower water, while whispering formulas. He grasped the glass of flower water, placed it close to his mouth, and pronounced more formulas before circling it three times around the flame of the burner. He then returned the glass to its place at the left of the burner. Next, he asked the group of six elders to sit in a circle near the burner. A glass of water was placed in the center of the circle. The burner resin was revived by one of the assistants, Mas Bambang, and another assistant lit three sticks of incense that he placed in a small vase. A third assistant wrote on a paper the name of the woman to be healed and placed the paper in front of Mbah. The participants concentrated with their eyes closed. Their hands were pressed together in front of their chests with their fingers pointing upward. Mbah started to recite phrases in Javanese that were repeated one after another by the six men. Between the sentences, the name of the woman was spoken several times.

Then the glass of water was passed hand to hand by the men in a counterclockwise direction. Each one concentrated for a while with the glass in his hands while reciting the formulas silently. When the glass returned to the guru, he put it down in front of him. The closing prayer was recited and the *gineng panyuwunan* came to end. Then the consecrated water was poured into a small bottle. At this point, the tests linked to the accession rites for the *windu kencana* and the *pangèlmunan* as described above were held. After the ritual meal had been eaten and all of the younger participants had left, the elders placed themselves in a circle. Four bottles of water (three large and one small) were placed in the middle, and a glass of water circulated from hand to hand as before. The son of the guru also participated in the consecration of the water. This water was then poured into one of the bottles, after which closing invocations were pronounced. Everyone said goodbye to the guru and departed at 1:40 AM.

The second form of *gineng* is the *gineng pamungkas*, which serves to protect against bewitchments. The third one is called *gineng sangkan paran*—from *sangkan* (origin) and *paran* (destination)—and is tied to the Javanese ideas of 'the origin and the becoming of the being' (*sangkan paraning dumadi*). The fourth *gineng* teaching aims to provide protection against poisonous animals. The basic prayer for the *gineng* is the *keblat papat kalima pancer*, but the prayer *Gineng* of the *gineng panyuwunan* has itself become a generic prayer for the *kasepuhan* teachings.

High-level teachings are also directly oriented toward ritual authority. The *sri gamana sari*, for instance, consists of a prayer and hand gestures to be performed in a position of meditation related to the 'teaching of perfection' (*ngèlmu kasampurnan*). This meditation is reputed to bring *wahyu* (divine inspiration and strength) to the performer during the rite. If it works, a luminous yellow light appears on the top of the head. This special light is tied to the Sufi notion of *nur* ('light' in Arabic) and is explicitly related to *cahya* ('light' in Sanskrit) and to Çiva tantrism. It has given birth to the notion of *nur cahya* used in the TG school.

In Mbah's teaching, *nur cahya* designates the 'true essence of life'. *Nur* is linked to the 'soul' (*batin*). To enter in relation with *nur*, the powers of concentration must be 'ripe': one must be able to distinguish it with the eyes of the soul. The union of *nur* and *cahya* forms the *wahyu*. Kings and mythical heroes (both of which are considered to be great warriors), as well as saints and mystics generally receive the *wahyu*. This can take the form of a star coming from the sky. According to Mbah, this superior level of authority is best received when it is not imposed by force: it imposes itself, and everyone agrees to recognize it. In this respect, it differs from the 'junior' or basic level (*kaenoman*) of authority.

External Activities of the Master and the Javanese New Year's Eve

Mbah mastered other important rituals as well. During the second part of the 1990s and in the 2000s, he was often called to Jakarta, Surabaya, or other big towns to participate in *slametan* (generic Javanese auspicious ceremonies) or to conduct *syukuran* (thanksgiving rituals) aimed at protecting persons or places (shops, stores, houses, offices), particularly for Indonesians of Chinese descent (see de Grave 2001: 83–85). In addition to *ruwatan*, he also performed ceremonies linked to the life cycle (birth, circumcision, marriage, death).

The main ceremony that Mbah is responsible for is the Javanese New Year's Eve—the principal Javanese ceremony. The TG group prepares several months in advance, with around 70 persons involved in planning the event. Mbah directs the ritual ceremony, and high-ranking invited guests, including Javanese nobles, artisans, and traders and Indonesians of Chinese descent, also take part. The last part of the ceremony, before the ritual meal, consists in the *rebutan* ritual of dispute in which the people of the Gondosuman district physically argue among themselves about how to bring the holy water from different sacred places and place it in big jars (de Grave 2001: 85–89).

The Master's Masters, Pilgrimage, Ties to Warfare and Politics

Now I take a look at some people who have been direct masters of Mbah or masters of his masters. Their life and social background shed light on the TG's activities, all the more so since their graves are often visited by TG members. These pilgrimages are not formalized in the sense that they do not take place on a regular schedule and that their participants vary from one year to another. By attending pilgrimages, we can see who are the most important referent masters, founders, and ancestors in Mbah's lineage.

The main master of Mbah—and at the same time his 'elder uncle' (*pakdhé*)—was Joyo Permono. According to Mbah, Permono was the son of a secondary spouse of Sultan Hamengkubuwono VII. Mbah related that when his master lived in Yogyakarta, he had worked as a bus driver. After the first aborted clash against the Dutch in 1948, in which he participated, Permono fled to the village of Ngadirejo, situated at the top of a vast hill close to the city of Temanggung. From that moment on, he completely devoted himself to *kanuragan* and ceremonial activities. It is in the graveyard of this village that he was buried on 1 June 1977.

Members of the TG go to this gravesite, which is two hours away by car from Yogyakarta, at least once a year. This pilgrimage is generally made at the same time as another one to the grave of a *begawan* (an ascetic who attained the stature of saint), a 'commander in chief' (*panembahan*) of the kingdom of Majapahit, close to Temanggung. Another pilgrimage is also made frequently to the grave of Ki Tjindéamoh Tjindekémbar, from whom Permono's knowledge was supposed to have originated. A highly skilled officer of Sultan Agung, the main monarch of the Mataram dynasty, Tjindekémbar was buried in the royal cemetery of Imogiri in 1645. He has the reputation of having been provided with exceptional capacities of strength and invulnerability. The second master of Mbah was Gondo Sudiro. He was buried in 1975 in Yogyakarta's Pakuncen cemetery, where TG members often go.[16]

According to the chronological teachings and experience accumulated by Mbah, at the age of 20 he received the *wali sejati* (true saint) form in Banten while traveling around West Java. He received the *pangèlmunan* form later in

Ponorogo (East Java) from Mbah Ahmad Sayudi, who was still living in 1995 during my fieldwork. It was on the occasion of the 1948 clashes with the Dutch that he received *windu kencana aji* from Permono.

According to Mbah, at that time—with the Dutch wanting to return to Indonesia—Permono and other masters started to teach their knowledge more openly. They contributed by giving confidence to the young fighters and thus opened the way for a revival of *kanuragan*, especially starting in May 1948. Mbah relates that Permono participated in the 1948 rebellion by preparing the young combatants, among whom Mbah was to be counted, to fight against the Dutch. Mbah says that he had occasion to lead a group of soldiers and that they used the *pangèlmunan* form to become invisible: they removed their clothes and the Dutch could not see them, so that all the members of his group came back safely with none of them being captured.

After the war, Mbah maintained contact with these networks. In 1995, he invited me to participate in the annual pilgrimage organized by veterans in Yogyakarta to the tomb of Sultan Hamengkubuwono IX (in Imogiri), whom they considered to be their military leader during the war. However, Mbah's relationship to warfare was not restricted to the nationalist period. Since he taught *kanuragan*, Indonesian soldiers going to the front—inside Indonesia—frequently contacted him to transmit *aji* to them for purposes of invulnerability.

With reference to internal affairs, Mbah was also involved with the political opposition. He confided to me that he was contacted separately by representatives of the three principal political parties who asked him to train their respective members in invulnerability techniques during the period of the campaign that preceded the elections of June 1999. Three weeks before these elections, students of the TG and Mbah himself were threatened in the neighborhood of Tedjokusuman by Muslims of the Partai Persatuan Pembangunan (PPP, United Development Party), who judged the school's practices to be unorthodox from the standpoint of Islam.

Conclusion

To synthesize these descriptions of the TG school's activities, I first must emphasize what is unique to Javanese cults, for instance, the four sibling spirits cult, which is commonly used in Java for warlike purposes in *kanuragan*. We can then see how teachings such as *pangèlmunan* and *gineng* are tied to Javanese mythology and how *kanuragan* is explicitly embedded in the sociocultural context, climaxing in the large-scale organization of the school's Javanese New Year's Eve.

Another important point is the presence of Sufi elements. Through the mantra *keblat papat*, Javanese cosmology converges with the Sufi doctrine. This is also found in the teaching of *doa gerak*, which is explicitly related to the founder of the Qâdiriyah brotherhood, both of which are tied to monist conceptions of Sufism. According to Stephen Headley (2004), it is in this way that Islam must be considered as a proper Javanese element.

Tied to this cosmological background, the *windu kencana aji* teaching offers an actual example of how Javanese people are able to link cosmology and social events together, on this occasion through a nineteenth-century prediction concerning the anti-colonialist war in 1948. From this perspective, war and *kanuragan* are closely tied, as illustrated by the way in which Mbah's different masters played an active role in the independence war and how he himself used the *pangèlmunan* teaching in the fight against the Dutch. Thanks to this action, Mbah became a member of the war veterans organization and participated in the annual pilgrimage to the tomb of their military leader, Sultan Hamengkubuwono IX.

The fact that President Suharto exaggerated his own part in the War of Independence to the detriment of the sultan's role as a military leader[17] should be seen as a clue to understand better that the national perspective (of Suharto) has now overstepped the Javanese one (of the sultan). This shift has facilitated the introduction, in the Javanese social context, of more universal and standardized secular and Muslim ideologies. Nonetheless, the fact that contemporary Javanese soldiers and political representatives come to Mbah to ask for protection and that Muslim representatives threaten him because of his teachings signifies that *kanuragan* worship and rituals have persisted despite these other ideologies. This is evident in the way that Chinese secular traders come to Mbah from Jakarta to ask for protection and benediction for their possessions and activities.

As suggested at the outset of this chapter, the fact that diverse social groups are becoming interconnected through *kanuragan* activity allows us to develop an analysis in terms of different institutional networks and activities that either complete or compete with one another. On the one hand, we have the history of anti-colonial warfare using local techniques; older Javanese generations attached to the heritage of the *kanuragan* world, including its mythology and rituals; the presence of Sufi elements discredited by more orthodox trends of Islam; the relative absence of body practices such as martial arts, and even a rejection of them as subaltern techniques; and a relation between ancient practices of war (pilgrimages to warriors' graves of the Hindu-Buddhist period and of the Islamization period) and new ones (veterans of the independence war meeting on the sultan's grave, contemporary young soldiers and Chinese trade networks coming to Mbah for protection). In addition to these elements, one should also view Mbah's students (nobles, teachers, youths from the countryside) and elder members of the school (artisans, traders)—as well as his wife's central activities in the organization of rituals and the preparation of ceremonial meals—as direct links to traditional market activity.

On the other hand, facing this relative homogeneous value system and its embodied practices, we find oppositional forces that have recently grown stronger. Pressure is placed upon Mbah and his school, not only by orthodox Muslims, but also by a differentiated ideological perspective of modern martial arts schools that have adopted sport-like values and practices that are Javanese but also foreign, such as karate, kung-fu, and taekwondo. I should also highlight here a new trend that consists of organizing Javanese aestheticized rituals with no cultic dimension. However, these new trends are not basically opposed to *kanuragan*; instead, they represent an integral part of *kanuragan* (martial arts, aesthetic rituals), or they are at least connected to it (Islam through Sufism, modern nationalism). Members of the latter group may seem to be more organized and standardized and thus may appear to be growing faster than those of the first group. But Islam and modern nationalism, as we have seen, are completely integrated in Javanese society. From the inside point of view, this discussion has shown how *kanuragan* is present in the social basis of even the more standardized groups.

But what do present-day attitudes toward war magic and warrior religion teach us about sorcery, cognition, and embodiment? First, due to their inability to fit in with modern development and religious dogmas, it appears that sorcery and war magic are not valued from the government's point of view or from that of orthodox religion, be it Muslim or Christian. The social basis of magical practices, however, is so ingrained that even government and religious cadres, who are supposed to suppress these practices, still use them more or less secretly (see Bertrand 2002; Bonneff 2002). Based on the different networks involved in *kanuragan* activities presented in this chapter, we might conclude that Javanese war magic will remain socially active for a long time. Nonetheless, it must be acknowledged that growing trends—tied to modernist Islam, political democracy, sport, and other secular movements—tend to push sorcery and war magic to more reserved or specialized social categories.

Despite the ideological opposition of modernist Islam, war magic is effectively linked to religion, illustrated through the example of *kanuragan* and Sufism. In this perspective, the relation between *kanuragan* and religion must be understood according to wider trends within Islam. The development of radical Islam after the fall of Suharto in 1998, for instance, has given birth to another form of warrior religion. Whatever the menace that radical Islam poses in Indonesia, the question remains as to whether it is more threatening toward Javanese war magic than modernist Islam or secular trends.

Jean-Marc de Grave received his PhD in Social Anthropology and Ethnology from the Ecole des Hautes Etudes en Sciences Sociales (Paris), and his habilitation to supervise PhDs from the Université de Strasbourg. He is Associate Professor of Social and Cultural Anthropology, Director of the Anthropology Department at Aix-Marseille Université, and a researcher at the Institut de Recherches Asiatiques. In parallel to Javanese rituals and Malay martial arts, his research interests also include a comparative approach toward learning, apprenticeship systems, and wider issues of education and development in Asia. He is the author of *Initiation rituelle et arts martiaux: Trois écoles de kanuragan javanais* (2001), which was awarded the Jeanne Cuisinier prize.

Notes

1. The teachings of the school described in this chapter are addressed exclusively to men. Some similar teachings, but with no martial elements, occur in mystical or *kebatinan* groups that are widely open to women. Martial arts schools (the Javanese martial art is called *pencak*), which also are open to women, may use esoteric teachings of the same kind. In some cases, women become *kebatinan* or *pencak* masters.
2. To my knowledge, only Hooykaas (1974: 85–128) briefly mentions warfare as it relates to the cult of the four sibling spirits in Balinese manuscripts.
3. These researchers include Benedict Anderson (1972), Andrew Beatty (1999), Romain Bertrand (2005), Marcel Bonneff (2002), Clifford Geertz (1960), Stephen Headley (2000, 2004), Robert Hefner (1985), and James Siegel (2001).
4. With regard to present-day influences on Javanese society, see de Grave (2009) on the role of modern Javanese schools, martial arts from abroad, and Japanese and European body conceptions.
5. On this point, see also Neidel (this volume).
6. *Mutih* is more commonly called *nganyep*, a verbal form of the adjective *anyep* (tasteless, insipid).
7. On the Javanese calendar, see Damais (1967) and de Grave (2001: 343–344).
8. This ritual initiation was combined with three other rituals: the *pangèlmunan* described below, another rite of a higher level, and a ceremony linked to healing purposes called the *gineng panyuwunan*.
9. All of the TG's teachings and activities are conducted in Javanese, which is very different from the Indonesian national language, despite the fact that it comes from the same branch of the Austronesian family.
10. *Aliran kebatinan* (groups of mystics) were also very numerous in Java.
11. Mbah was preoccupied with these two complementary numerical classifications. For instance, in addition to the cosmological elements of the mantras based on five or three elements, he often spoke of the five Pandawa brothers of the Javanese epic, the *Mahabharata*, and of the five-note gamelan ensembles, and he was always using three-branched candleholders and three incense sticks during ceremonies and repeating one mantra three times, and so on.
12. For a discussion of the *marma* in the martial arts context, see Roşu (1981), Zarrilli (1998), and Zoetmulder (1995: 1:656).
13. Jaelani died and was buried in Baghdad in 1166. His eulogy appeared in Javanese (see Lombard 1990: 2:120).
14. For an exhaustive study on Banten ritual initiation, trance practices, and their social background and networks, see Facal (2012a). Compare with Facal (2010, 2012b) and Van Treche (2012).
15. The phrase *manunggaling kawula Gusti* means literally 'union of the servant and the Master', a hierarchical configuration in which God is the ultimate Master.
16. For a detailed description of the TG's pilgrimages, see de Grave (2001: 81–83).
17. After the fall of Suharto in 1998, the truth was re-established about the important military role played by Sultan Hamengkubuwono IX in the War of Independence.

References

Anderson, Benedict R. O'G. 1972. "The Idea of Power in Javanese Culture." Pp. 1-69 in *Culture and Politics in Indonesia*, ed. Claire Holt. Ithaca, NY: Cornell University Press.
Any, Anjar. 1990. *Raden Ngabehi Ronggowarsito: Apa yang terjadi?* [Raden Ngabehi Ronggowarsito: What Happened?] Semarang: Aneka Ilmu.
Beatty, Andrew. 1999. *Varieties of Javanese Religion: An Anthropological Account*. Cambridge: Cambridge University Press.
Berthe, Louis. 1968. "Parenté, pouvoir et mode de reproduction: Eléments pour une typologie des sociétés agricoles de l'Indonésie." Pp. 708-738 in *Echanges et communications: Mélanges offerts à Claude Lévi-Strauss*, ed. Jean Pouillon and Pierre Maranda. Paris: Mouton.
Bertrand, Romain. 2002. *Indonésie, la démocratie invisible: Violence, magie et politique à Java*. Paris: Karthala.
Bertrand, Romain. 2005. *Etat colonial, noblesse et nationalisme à Java: La tradition parfaite*. Paris: Karthala.
Bonneff, Marcel. 2002. "Semar révélé: La crise indonésienne et l'imaginaire politique javanais." *Archipel* 64: 33-37.
Damais, Louis-Charles. 1967. "Le calendrier de l'ancienne Java." *Journal asiatique* 255: 133-141.
de Grave, Jean-Marc. 1997. "Comparaison des activités et des valeurs ultimes de trois écoles javanaises de pratiques martiales (Yogyakarta - Java Centre)." PhD diss., EHESS.
de Grave, Jean-Marc. 2001. *Initiation rituelle et arts martiaux: Trois écoles de kanuragan javanais*. Paris: Archipel/L'Harmattan.
de Grave, Jean-Marc. 2008. "L'initiation martiale javanaise du point de vue des systèmes de transmission: Opposition entre javanisme et islam." *Techniques et culture* 48: 85-123.
de Grave, Jean-Marc. 2009. "Genèse du pencak silat moderne: La standardisation des arts martiaux indonésiens sous l'occupation japonaise et à l'époque de l'indépendance (1942-1965)." *Les actes de la recherche en sciences sociales* 179: 112-117.
de Grave, Jean-Marc. 2011. "The Training of Perception in Javanese Martial Arts." Pp. 123-143 in *Martial Arts as Embodied Knowledge: Asian Traditions in a Transnational World*, ed. D. S. Farrer and John Whalen-Bridge. New York: State University of New York Press.
de Josselin de Jong, P. E. [1916] 1977a. "Introduction: Structural Anthropology in the Netherlands: Creature of Circumstance." Pp. 1-29 in de Josselin de Jong [1916] 1977b.
de Josselin de Jong, P. E., ed. [1916] 1977b. *Structural Anthropology in the Netherlands: A Reader*. The Hague: Martinus Nijhoff.
Douglas, Mary. 1987. *How Institutions Think*. London: Routledge & Kegan Paul.
Elias, Norbert. 2008. *Quest for Excitement: Sport and Leisure in the Civilising Process*. 2nd ed. Ed. Eric Dunning. Dublin: University College Dublin Press.
Facal, Gabriel. 2010. "Banten (West Java)." Pp. 399-400 in *Martial Arts of the World: An Encyclopedia of History and Innovation*, ed. Thomas A. Green and Joseph R. Svinth. Santa Barbara, CA: ABC-CLIO.
Facal, Gabriel. 2012a. "Réseaux d'autorité, islam, institutions politiques: Les 'hommes forts' jawara de Banten (Indonésie)." PhD diss., Aix-Maseille Université.
Facal, Gabriel. 2012b. "Autorité et transmission à travers la relation aîné-cadet: Le cas de l'école de penca Cimande Pusaka Medal, Banten (Indonésie)." *Moussons* 20: 57-81.

Geertz, Clifford. 1960. *The Religion of Java*. Chicago: University of Chicago Press.
Headley, Stephen C. 2000. *From Cosmogony to Exorcism in a Javanese Genesis: The Spilt Seed*. Oxford: Oxford University Press.
Headley, Stephen C. 2004. *Durga's Mosque: Cosmology, Conversion and Community in Central Javanese Islam*. Singapore: Institute of Southeast Asian Studies.
Hefner, Robert W. 1985. *Hindu Javanese: Tengger Tradition and Islam*. Princeton, NJ: Princeton University Press
Hellman, Jörgen. 2009. "Creating Religious Bodies: Fasting Rituals in West Java."
   Pp. 59–74 in *The Body in Asia*, ed. Bryan S. Turner and Zheng Yangwen. Oxford: Berghahn Books.
Hooykaas, Christiaan. 1974. *Cosmogony and Creation in Balinese Tradition*. The Hague: Martinus Nijhoff.
Kuntara Wiryamartana. 1990. *Arjunawiwaha: Transformasi teks jawa kuno lewat tanggapan dan penciptaan di lingkungan sastra jawa* [Arjunawiwaha: Old Javanese Texts Transformation Considered through the Perception and Creativity of the Javanese Literary Circles]. Yogyakarta: Duta Wacana University Press.
Lombard, Denys. 1990. *Le carrefour javanais: Essai d'histoire globale*. 3 vols. Paris: Editions de l'EHESS.
Miyazaki, Koji. 1979. *Javanese Classification Systems: The Problem of "Maximal Correspondence."* ICA Publication Series No. 35. Leiden: Institute of Cultural and Social Studies Publication.
Miyazaki, Koji. 1988. "The King and the People: The Conceptual Structure of a Javanese Kingdom." PhD diss., Leiden University.
Pemberton, John. 1994. *On the Subject of "Java."* Ithaca, NY: Cornell University Press.
Pigeaud, Theodore. [1916] 1977. "Javanese Divination and Classification." Pp. 61–82 in de Josselin de Jong [1916] 1977b.
Roşu, Arion. 1981. "Les marman et les arts martiaux indiens." *Journal asiatique* 269, no. 3–4: 417–451.
Siegel, James. 2001. "Suharto Witches." *Indonesia* 71: 27–79.
Sulaiman. 1985. "Upacara tedhak sitèn di Jawa." [Earth Contact Ceremony in Java.]
   Pp. 101–107 in *Ritus peralihan di Indonesia*, ed. Koentjaraningrat. Jakarta: PN Balai Pustaka.
van Bruinessen, Martin. 1995. *Kitab Kuning: Pesantren dan Tarekat*. Bandung: Penerbit Mizan.
van Ossenbruggen, F. D. E. [1916] 1977. "Java's Manca-pat: Origins of a Primitive Classification System." Pp. 30–60 in de Josselin de Jong [1916] 1977b.
Van Treche, Mary. 2012. "Islam, politique et autorité en Indonésie: Le cas de l'organisation Pendekar Banten." Occasional Paper No. 19, IRASEC. http://www.irasec.com/component/irasec/?task=publication_detail&publicationid=332.
Zarrilli, Phillip B. 1998. *When the Body Becomes All Eyes: Paradigms, Discourses and Practices of Power in Kalarippayattu, a South Indian Martial Art*. New Delhi: Oxford University Press.
Zoetmulder, Piet. 1995. *Kamus jawa kuno-indonesia – jilid 1* [Old Javanese-Indonesian Dictionary – 2 vols. 1]. Jakarta: PT Gramedia.

Chapter 3

DISCOURSE OF DECLINE
Sumatran Perspectives on Black Magic

J. David Neidel

Magic, sorcery, and witchcraft constitute a suite of interrelated beliefs and practices that denote the projection of human agency through supernatural or mystical means.[1] Existing in nearly every region of the world, this phenomenon has long been of interest to scholars due to its seemingly problematic relationship with scientific rationality. Scholarly interpretations about the nature and function of magic, however, have varied over time. Three major interpretive frameworks for the study of magic can be identified, each of which differs in terms of its underlying assumptions about the empirical efficacy of magical practice and the persistence of related beliefs.

The first, an evolutionist framework, was widely used by colonial-era scholars and administrators in documenting the cultural beliefs and practices of subject populations. Influenced by the writings of Tylor (1871) and Frazer

Notes for this chapter begin on page 84.

(1890), these individuals often conceptualized magic as a pernicious and illogical element of traditional non-Western culture that had no direct material effect. Ignoring the long history and resiliency of magic in Europe, these analysts predicted that magical beliefs and practices would succumb to the forces of modernization.

The second, a structural-functionalist framework, emerged with the advent of professional anthropology in the early twentieth century. Influenced by the pioneering approaches of Malinowski (1922, 1935) and Evans-Pritchard (1937), these studies placed greater emphasis on examining the role that occult beliefs and practices played in explaining seemingly inexplicable events and in reinforcing or undermining certain social or political structures in those societies. This general type of analysis, which remains prevalent today, has shown that the earlier predictions of the demise of magic were incorrect. In fact, magic has proven to be incredibly resilient in the face of broader societal change. Still, like their evolutionist predecessors, these scholars tend to deny the empirical efficacy of magical practice. Rather than labeling the local people 'irrational', however, these scholars either redefine rationality relative to the cultural context or suggest that such beliefs and practices should be understood symbolically or metaphorically.

The third, a phenomenological framework, emerged following the development of the postmodern critique starting in the late 1970s. Challenging the Enlightenment projects of rationalism, empiricism, and universalism, scholars brought into question the degree to which objective accounts of magical beliefs and practices could be written. Individuals working within this framework typically became practitioners of the occult and examined its operations from inside the tradition (see, e.g., Favret-Saada 1980; Harner 1980; Stoller and Olkes 1987; Turner 1992). These scholars, like those of the structural-functionalist framework, assume the long-term persistence of magic, but give greater credence to the material efficacy, if not explicability, of indigenous magical practices.

While analysts working within each of these three frameworks have drawn upon 'raw data' from the field, scholarly assessments of magical beliefs and practices often marginalize local commentaries that provide indigenous perspectives on some of the questions that have energized scholarly interest in this field of inquiry. These questions include the following: What is the relationship between occult practices and rational explanation? How will magic beliefs and practices change over time? What societal factors contribute to the persistence or decline of magic? In order to explore how locals address some of these issues, this study focuses on the magical beliefs and practices of the people of highland Jambi in central Sumatra, Indonesia. An examination of this local discourse is interesting because it reveals a number of interpretations about these beliefs and practices that diverge from those of many Western scholars. In fact, local commentaries tend to be based on the assumption that local magical practices are materially efficacious but are nevertheless experiencing a decline. The nature of the decline and the reasons for it are discussed in this chapter.

Research Context

Highland Jambi constitutes the westernmost portion of Jambi province in central Sumatra (see map 3.1). Historically, this region was divided into three territories (*alam*)—Kerinci, Serampas, and Sungai Tenang—which stretch from the northwest to the southeast along the Bukit Barisan mountain range (Marsden [1811] 1966). Although the administrative status of these three territories has changed over time, with Kerinci currently a district and Serampas and Sungai Tenang forming a single sub-district (i.e., Jangkat) in the Merangin district, they are all still recognized as important territorial entities by the people in the region.

The early history of the region remains unclear, but the existence of an extensive series of megaliths and of ceramic remains points to a significant human settlement in the highlands by at least the thirteenth century AD (Bonatz et al. 2006; Tjoa-Bonatz 2009). The people of these settlements played an important role in the maritime trade with the coastal states that connected Southeast Asia with India and China by collecting gold and various forest products, which were funneled through a number of trade routes that ran between the highlands and lowland entrepôts (Coedès 1968; Miksic 2009; Wolters 1967). The people inhabited a number of independent villages, which were governed by councils of village elders, called *depati*, who played an important role in maintaining village customs (*adat*) and allegiances to federations that controlled the trade routes (Kathirithamby-Wells 1986; Marsden [1811] 1966; Watson 1992; Znoj 2001, 2009).

The difficult mountainous terrain and geographical distance allowed the people of highland Jambi largely to maintain their political autonomy from these lowland states, while benefiting from economic and cultural exchanges (Znoj 2001, 2009). The lowland sultans' repeated attempts to assert greater authority over the highland societies are well attested to by the existence of a large number of royal edicts (*piagam*). These edicts, along with a variety of other documents and personal possessions of the village ancestors, are maintained to this day by *depati* as community heirlooms (*pusaka*) (Gallop 2009; Kozok 2004; Marsden [1811] 1966; Neidel 2006; Voorhoeve 1941, 1970; Watson 1976, 2009).

After centuries of European involvement on the coasts, the Dutch finally occupied highland Jambi in 1903, at which time the traditional, relatively egalitarian form of government was transformed into a more hierarchical system. *Depati* gained greater authority under the colonial and post-colonial administration until 1976, when national-level administrative reforms replaced *depati* with officially appointed village heads (*kepala desa*) (Watson 1987; Znoj 2001). *Depati* have nevertheless remained very influential in village and regional government. During the colonial transition, the region also became more closely integrated into the colonial economy through the extension of cash crops, plantation agriculture, markets, and roads. The effect was most pronounced in Kerinci, where, due to its larger pre-colonial population and agricultural surplus, construction of a road connecting the highlands to the lowlands was completed by the early 1920s. As a result, Sungai Penuh, the capital of the Kerinci district, evolved into a significant highland market and administrative town.

MAP 3.1 Central Sumatra

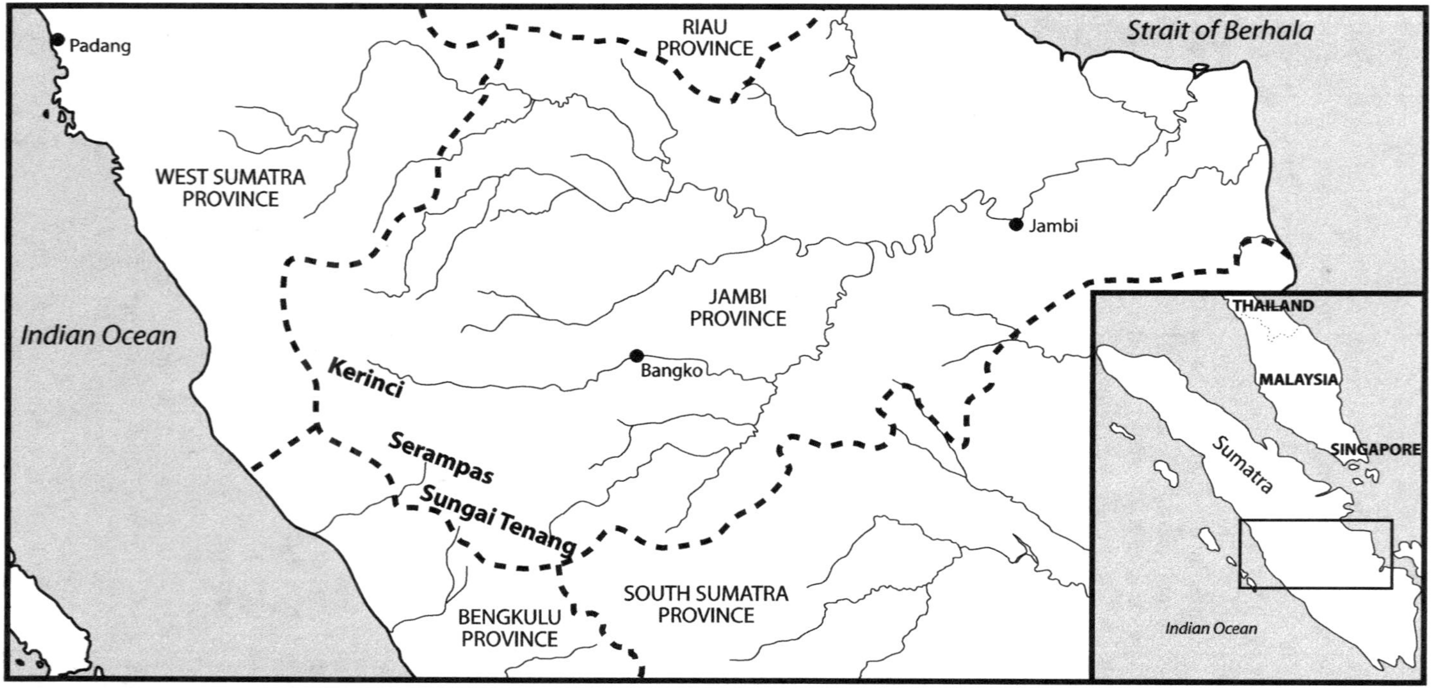

Source: Joy Natividad

The regions of Sungai Tenang and Serampas, in contrast, have for the most part remained more isolated.

The people of highland Jambi are primarily agriculturists, combining wet rice cultivation in the high rift valleys of the Bukit Barisan mountain range with several types of agroforestry systems on the surrounding hillsides (Aumeeruddy 1994). Coffee and cinnamon have been particularly important smallholder cash crops over the years, generating a significant amount of wealth for those with the land and labor needed to take advantage of the periodically high prices (Scholz 1982). Some people of Javanese descent, who were brought by the Dutch to work on the plantations, live in the northern portion of the Kerinci district. A limited number of people, including some of Minangkabau ethnic origins, are also employed as merchants, traders, and civil servants.

The population of highland Jambi is almost exclusively Muslim. Documentary sources suggest that Islam first entered the region in the late sixteenth and early seventeenth centuries (Watson 2009; Znoj 2001), but the initial adoption of Islam proved far from complete. As a result, the region has experienced a variety of reformist movements dating back to at least the mid-nineteenth century (Watson 1985; Znoj 2001). The degree to which more orthodox forms of Islam have supplanted pre-Islamic beliefs and practices—particularly those pertaining to ancestral worship—has been spatially heterogeneous, showing a wide range of intra- and inter-village variation.

Types of Magical Powers

Their lowland neighbors have long associated the people of highland Jambi with various magical or supernatural abilities (referred to locally as *kesaktian*, *ilmu*, or *ilmu kebatinan*). The people of Kerinci in particular are known for their reputed ability to transform themselves into tigers (Bakels 2000; Watson 1993: 203), whereas the people of Serampas are believed to practice 'black magic'.[2] For many of the highland people, there is an obvious sense of pride in their reputation as practitioners of magic, which undoubtedly has a history of being used for strategic advantage in their interactions with lowlanders. The supernatural has also become an important element of regional political identity. Kerinci, for example, is officially referred to as Sakti Alam Kerinci (the Magical Region of Kerinci), while its administrative capital, Sungai Penuh, is known as Kota Sakti (the Magical City).[3]

Given the prevalence of magical beliefs and practices in highland Jambi, I began to collect data on the subject through unstructured interviews and participant observation as an offshoot of a larger two-year project on natural resource conflicts that I undertook intermittently in southern Kerinci and Serampas between September 1999 and May 2003. Through this research, I collected a list of approximately 25 magical powers that are practiced in the region. These powers, some of which are known in other regions of Indonesia as well, include the following:

Angin punting beliung: the ability to send a destructive wind. This spell is used, for example, to destroy the house of an enemy.

Cunong: the ability to kill a person at a distance by sending a lethal disease. Unless the spell is countered, an affected person is predicted to die of a wasting-away type of illness.

Ilmu gayung: the ability to sever an opponent's 'heart strings' with the slash of a finger. If conducted correctly, the person is predicted to die within several days.

Ilmu kebal: invulnerability. Different types and degrees of invulnerability are said to exist, including invulnerability to fire, metal weapons, and bullets.

Ilmu kuat: superhuman strength. People with this power are said to be able to pick up cars, pull out trees by the roots, punch holes through cement walls, and so forth.

Ilmu macan: the ability to avoid being attacked by tigers while walking in the forest.

Pelakat bumi: the ability to completely immobilize a person. This spell is said to persist indefinitely unless the person is released through a counter-spell.

Most of the supernatural powers practiced in highland Jambi focus on killing or disabling an enemy or, conversely, on providing protection from attacks by humans, wild animals, or supernatural beings. While many practitioners focus exclusively on acquiring these 'offensive' and 'defensive' forms of magic, some also use their supernatural abilities for healing—a 'duality of shamans' (see Farrer and Jokic, this volume).

The Science of Invulnerability

Ilmu kebal, or the science of invulnerability, is probably the most common and sought-after form of magical power in highland Jambi—indeed, in much of Indonesia (see de Grave, this volume)—and is therefore worthy of an extended discussion. The prevalence of this supernatural ability in highland Jambi was suggested by the fact that a number of my informants claimed to have had this power themselves (assertions supported by others who saw them exercise that ability) before giving it up due to religious considerations (discussed below). In addition to those accounts, I also personally witnessed a number of students practicing *ilmu kebal* with their teacher. During that exercise, the students sat around a fire meditating while the teacher drew a machete blade across their chests and the back of their necks. The teacher then proceeded to hit the machete blade, which he had placed directly on their skin, with a heavy piece of wood (fig. 3.1). No injuries occurred, despite the fact that the machete was very sharp.

FIGURE 3.1 A student of *ilmu kebal* being tested with a machete

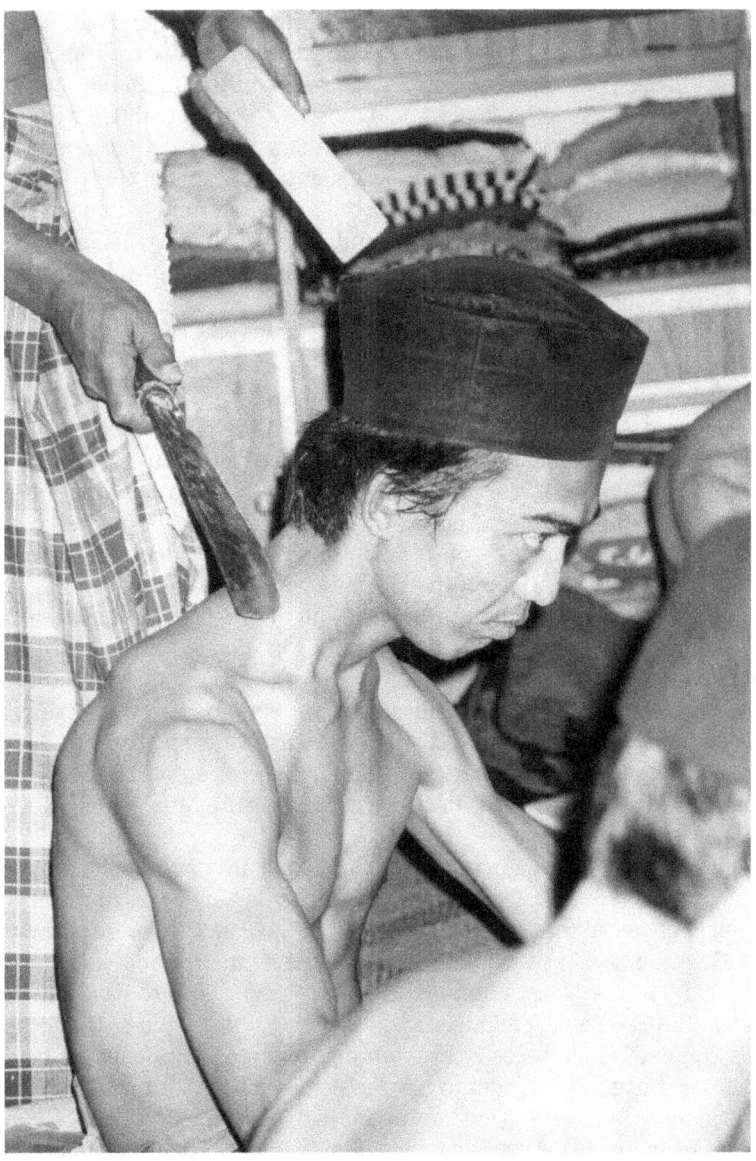

Photograph © Joy Natividad

Ilmu kebal is said to have played an important part in pre-colonial village life. Several *depati* explained that the possession of *ilmu kebal* was an unofficial prerequisite for holding *adat* titles. During the pre-colonial period, the heavy drinking of rice wine is reported to have been common during meetings of *adat* officials, sometimes leading to violent confrontations. Because those conflicts often included knife play, only those with invulnerability were willing to attend. The possession of *ilmu kebal* and other supernatural powers is also said to have played a key role in people's ability to protect the villages from wild animals and inter-village raids, as well as oneself from marauding bandits while traveling the trade routes that connected highland villages with lowland markets (Anon. 1972: 38). These types of dangers are well attested to in European documentary sources and by the prevalence of fortifications around former village sites (Neidel 2006, 2009).

The practice of *ilmu kebal* also plays a large role in local myths and legends. One particularly well-known story, for example, tells of Tiang Bungkuk, a man of the elite class from the lowlands who resettled in Kerinci upon being denied an appanage by the sultan of Jambi. Tiang Bungkuk is said to have shown such hatred for the sultan that he would kill any cock that crowed in the direction of Jambi City and any trader hoping to engage in trade with the royal court. In response to Tiang Bungkuk's obstruction of the main trade route between the highlands and lowland Jambi, the sultan sent some of his men to Kerinci to trick Tiang Bungkuk into submission. The sultan's men are said to have beaten Tiang Bungkuk, stabbed him unsuccessfully, and floated him down the river to Jambi City on the underside of a raft—but they could not kill him because of his *ilmu kebal*. The sultan finally succeeded in doing so only because Tiang Bungkuk's wife secretly tried to facilitate her husband's escape by sending him his magical *keris* (knife)—the only weapon in the entire world to which he was vulnerable—in a container of food that was opened by the sultan (Noerewan 2002; Yakin 1986).

In more recent times, a man known as Depati Parbo from the village of Lolo (located in the southeastern corner of Kerinci) is said to have displayed an extremely powerful form of *ilmu kebal* during the Dutch invasion of the region in 1903 (Anon. 1972; Watson 1978). Promoted by the regional government as a national hero (*pahlawan national*), Depati Parbo is said to have suffered no injuries during several prolonged battles with Dutch soldiers. Dutch bullets, locals contend, made holes in his clothing but could not penetrate his body. While Depati Parbo is thought to have gained some of his supernatural powers by practicing *pencak silat* (Indonesian martial arts) and studying with an area *dukun* (shaman), his exceptional power is believed to have been obtained by meditating on the site of a nearby volcano, Mount Kunyit (Anon. 1972).

Finally, *ilmu kebal* also plays a significant role in a number of traditional dances in the area. In the *tari asyik* dance, for example, female dancers are given various forms of challenges to overcome, including dancing on top of a board of nails (fig. 3.2), a sword blade, or broken ceramics, as well as amid burning flames. According to the dance leader, this invincibility is achieved through their possession by ancestral spirits (SCTV 2003).

FIGURE 3.2 Entranced dancer performing on a board of nails

Photograph © J. David Neidel

Modes of Transmission

Magical powers are said to have been passed down from generation to generation, starting with the earliest village ancestors. Origin stories often recount the arrival of village ancestors in the region and how relationships were forged—most typically through marriage—with various kinds of spirits and other types of ethereal beings, who were the original inhabitants of the area (Bakels 2000, 2009). It is believed that many of the village ancestors and spirits continue to inhabit the landscape, exerting influence over the daily lives of their descendants in the villages. *Dukun*, in particular, are believed to have direct personal relationships with these entities, from whom they themselves draw supernatural powers for the purposes of harming and healing. Because of their unique relation to the spiritual realm, *dukun* are the key to acquiring magical powers (*menutut ilmu*).

Two methods for obtaining these powers are commonly used. In the first, students learn them directly from a *dukun*. This typically requires the memorization of a mantra, which may be integrated with bathing and the enactment of a number of other rituals during auspicious times of the month. For students learning *ilmu kebal*, a period of testing often follows. According to two informants who undertook their training together, the whole process took three days. The first day revolved around memorizing the mantra. During the second day, the *dukun* tested each of the students to make sure that the magical power was taking effect by attempting to cut their hair and a lemon that was being held tightly in each student's hand. Finally, on the third day, the *dukun* hit the students on the back with a machete, drew the machete across their throats, and then had them bathe with burning oil. Injuries resulting from a student's lack of certainty about the efficacy of the power are said to be fairly common.

The second way to acquire magical powers is to request them directly from an ancestral spirit or another supernatural entity. To attempt this, a student is typically escorted to the grave of a particularly powerful ancestor by a *dukun*, who carries out a ritual involving the burning of *kemenyan* (incense made from the *Styrax benzoin* tree) before returning to the village. The supplicant, who is dressed only in the white cloth used to bury the dead, must spend the night alone, meditating (*bertapa* or *bertarak*) at the gravesite. According to numerous informants, the student is often, although not always, tested by the ancestral spirit, who appears in the form of a ghost, snake, tiger, or anything else that the person particularly is afraid of. If the supplicant passes these tests by not running away, the ancestral spirit reveals him- or herself to ask which magical ability is being sought. In most cases, the student will be given a mantra, stone, or some other object through which he (or occasionally she) can enact the requested power. In other cases, supplicants learn how to call upon the ethereal being to channel the power directly. In situations where the student asks for a power that the ancestor does not possess, the spirit may refer the individual to another grave where the power is available.

Invisible Inhabitants

The people of highland Jambi, and indeed many Indonesians, conceive of a close connection between the material world and an ethereal realm of existence (*alam gaib*). Within villagers' conceptualization of the latter, three main types of invisible beings exist: *jin* (genies), *orang gunung* (mountain people), and *poyang* (ancestral spirits), each of which will be discussed in turn.

Jin (genies) are invisible entities that, according to the Koran, were created by God out of fire. References to *jin* within the Koran show that these invisible entities can be 'good' or 'bad', depending on whether or not the *jin* adhere to the teachings of Islam. Most people in highland Jambi, however, seem to view them negatively, often using the terms *jin*, *setan* (Satan), and *iblis* (devil) interchangeably. *Jin* are said to reside in many locations throughout the landscape, although in Serampas they are most clearly associated with the numerous hot springs that are scattered throughout the area. A large hot spring located near the center of Serampas is considered a hub of *jin* activity. It is here that many people report having seen *jin*, which are said to appear as orbs of white light descending into the steam of the hot spring in the early morning hours. Because it is believed that *jin* can cause illness, villagers are very careful not to urinate in the vicinity of the hot spring or do anything else that could cause a *jin* to take offense.

Dukun are thought to be able to develop personal relationships with *jin* and to call upon them for assistance. One *dukun* in Serampas, for example, is said to have called upon *jin* to increase the activity of the hot spring during a visit by the district head (*bupati*). A promotional video of that visit filmed by the District Community Relations Department (see Anon. 2001) shows the *dukun* reciting a mantra, apparently causing the boiling hot water, which typically reaches a meter or so high, to shoot geyser-like to a much greater height. *Dukun* also call upon *jin* for magic that involves 'shooting from afar' (*tembak dari jarak jauh*) since the service of a *jin* is required to transport the spell's agent (whether it be wind, poison, or something else) to the intended target.

Orang gunung (mountain people), also known as *mambang*, are a race of invisible people who live in villages typically located on the tops of various prominent mountains throughout the region. Oral traditions and documentary sources describe how migrants to the region and village founders married with *orang gunung*, thus giving them political legitimacy (Bakels 2000, 2009; Watson 2009). Even today, villagers who have spent a significant amount of time in the forest claim that sounds from *orang gunung* villages, such as the crowing of a cock in the early morning hours, can sometimes be heard, but the villages themselves remain hidden. On a limited number of occasions, hunters and other individuals who are lost in the woods have been able to see and enter the villages. According to their stories, *orang gunung* are exceedingly beautiful, their food exceptionally delicious, and their villages immaculately clean.

In several stories, villagers who happen upon *orang gunung* villages decide to stay, not realizing that they have left the material world behind. Some men take *orang gunung* women as their wives and have children with them. Typically, these men are forbidden to look inside the cooking pot. If they do, they find no rice inside and realize that the entire realm is an illusion, at which point they are forced to return to the material world. In another story, some hunters decide to leave the village on their own accord. Before their departure, they are provided with food, which they discover, upon leaving the village, to be ant excrement.

While *orang gunung* are generally regarded as being well-mannered and tend to remain in their mountaintop villages, they are said to have the ability to transform themselves into various types of animals, including birds and pigs, which allows them to steal rice from the villagers' fields. They typically do not do so excessively, however, because the fields are actively protected by *poyang*. Villagers maintain good relations with *orang gunung* by inviting them to attend the *kenduri sko*, an annual village-wide ceremony held after the rice harvest. Attendance of *orang gunung* at a *kenduri sko* is made evident through possession trances that ensue during the ceremony.

As the original inhabitants of the area, *orang gunung* are considered to have great power, which they, like *poyang*, can bestow on people when requested. Depati Parbo, for example, is said to have gained his *ilmu kebal* and other supernatural abilities from Mendari Kuning, an *orang gunung* who married Sigindo Sakti, one of the founding ancestors of the neighboring village of Lempur. The vegetated crater of Mount Kunyit, where Depati Parbo is said to have meditated, is locally referred to as the Park of Mendari Kuning (Taman Mendari Kuning).

By far the most important entities with whom the villagers maintain a relationship are *poyang*. This term applies to all village ancestors, but it is most often used to discuss a small subset who, due to their possession of extraordinary supernatural powers, either abandoned their bodies at will or continued their earthly existence as ethereal entities following death. While most ancestral spirits remain invisible, *poyang* are said to have the power to transform themselves into various types of animals—often tigers—in order to roam the forests or descend to the village (Bakels 2000).

The relationship between ancestral spirits and villagers is one based on reciprocity. *Poyang* provide numerous types of services to the villagers, such as guarding their fields from *orang gunung* or helping to cure disease, and in return the villagers are expected to pay respect through various types of ceremonies. The most important single event in maintaining harmony with ancestral spirits is the *kenduri sko*. During this ceremony, the entire village and invited guests feast together, new *depati* are inaugurated, and village heirlooms (*pusaka*) are ritually opened for public viewing. *Poyang* make their presence known through spirit-possession trances (*keserupan* or *kemasukan*), in which ordinary villagers take on the identity of the village ancestors themselves. Individual families also hold smaller-scale *kenduri* (ceremonies) throughout the year in order to thank ancestors for interceding on their behalf. *Kenduri*, for example, can be held to celebrate a wedding or for the payment of *nazar* (a debt to be paid when a village ancestor grants a request).

Depati take the lead role in maintaining a positive relationship with village ancestors, with whom they have a genealogical link. *Depati* serve as the guardians of the village heirlooms and orchestrate and officiate over the various *kenduri*. They also mete out various punishments when villagers violate *adat*. If *depati*—and the village community more generally—did not fulfill these obligations, it is believed that the ancestors would become vindictive and seek retribution. Failure to perform the *kenduri sko*, for example, could result in the ancestors turning into tigers and raiding the village. Alternatively, they could take action to ensure a meager rice harvest. Village ancestors can also take punitive actions in the case of transgressions of *adat* law. Clandestine, adulterous affairs, for example, can bring tigers into the village and, on occasion, can even lead to the death of the individuals involved.

Discourse of Decline

Magic clearly remains a very important element of social life in highland Jambi. Young men still visit *dukun* in search of supernatural powers, villagers still channel ancestral spirits and *orang gunung* at *kenduri*, and some people still engage fearlessly in dangerous activities, such as casually picking up venomous snakes with their bare hands, making even local observers shake their heads in amazement. Nevertheless, there exists a local, generalized 'discourse of decline' in which modern-day magical practices are represented as being reduced relative to those from both the recent past, as preserved in oral history, and the ancient past of legend. What is so interesting about this discourse of decline, however, is the fact that, despite the common directionality (i.e., decline), the discourse is marked by several elements that are not necessarily shared by all commentators. These elements, which I summarize as declines in potency, practice, relevance, and believability, will be discussed in turn.

Decline in Potency

It would appear to be widely held in highland Jambi that the potency of magical powers has declined over time. Village ancestors, whose exploits are recorded in village histories and legends (*tambo*), are widely believed to have engaged in truly amazing feats of magical prowess, such as flying to the island of Java, raising the dead, or creating new stream channels overnight. These types of deeds are well beyond the abilities of modern-day practitioners. While this may simply be a reflection of people's tendency to construct a mythical golden age as a way to deal with the vagaries of the present (Steedly 1993), this decline in potency is also recognized as having occurred during the course of people's own lives, so that *dukun* who are now deceased are almost invariably regarded as having been more powerful than those who are still living. This general decline in magical potency is also implied in the common insult that certain villages are 'living off' the reputation of their ancestors.

Although the decline in potency is widely acknowledged, the reasons behind this change are rarely discussed. Indeed, the only explanation recorded in my field notes points to the inherent tensions in the relationship between teachers of potentially deadly powers and their students, who may use those powers to betray them. This is not surprising because betrayal of this nature is a common trope in Indonesian literature and legend. In Serampas, for example, one of the founding villager ancestors, Serampu Alam Sati, is said to have fled the region because his children repeatedly tried to kill him out of jealousy over his greater powers (Neidel 2006: 209). It is for this reason that *dukun* are often quite selective about whom they will and will not teach, often preferring people from outside the village with whom they will not have extended interactions, even if those people are petty criminals or thugs. Because of this problematic student-teacher dynamic, *dukun* are also said to adulterate their teachings (e.g., by changing certain words in the mantra) so that their version of the magic spell remains more powerful than that of their students. Continued from generation to generation, this process of adulteration is said to have led to a general decline in the potency of the magic practiced throughout the region.

Decline in Practice

Given the widespread belief in the supernatural and the almost universal acceptance of Islam in highland Jambi, discussions with locals frequently revolved around the question of which practices are permitted by Islam (i.e., 'white magic') and which are forbidden (i.e., black magic).[4] In those discussions, several general positions on the issue emerged. Some people argued that all magic was 'black' because it originated with Satan (sometimes disguised as an ancestor). Therefore, this group believed that it was inappropriate to use any kind of supernatural powers, including traditional healing methods that rely on the intervention of ancestral spirits. On the opposite extreme were those who argued that all magical powers originated with God, who had given them to chosen village ancestors, from whom the powers had been passed down, generation to generation. This group was tolerant of all supernatural powers, some going so far as to argue that magic used for immoral purposes would not be effective. Finally, an intermediate position was that the designation of magic as 'black' or 'white' depends on how the magic is used. If, as one informant explained, the magic was used to kill someone who was dangerous or evil, then it was white magic. If it had been used to kill someone who was innocent, it could safely be regarded as black magic.

Because of the moral uncertainty about these practices, a number of informants who claim to have had magical powers in the past had decided to give them up. Similarly, a couple of older men who had been respected *dukun* are said to have stopped their practice after having gone on the hajj, the Muslim pilgrimage to Mecca. This dynamic has been noted elsewhere in highland Sumatra as well (Bowen 1993). These personal disavowals of magic, however, were sometimes incomplete. For example, when one such informant came down with a chronic illness that could not be treated through Western medicine, he sought help from a village *dukun*, due to his growing suspicion that his former wife had used magic against him.

Decline in Relevance

In explaining the decline of occult practices in highland Jambi, several informants indicated that this change was occurring because various societal transformations had made the possession of magical abilities no longer as relevant as it once had been. Several examples will illustrate this point. First, in the past, people from other villages are said to have called upon *dukun*, asking them to serve as contract killers by using their magic to bring about the demise of individuals in a distant village or town. One colleague from Serampas explained, however, that nowadays people in the region have become *malas membunuh orang* (lazy to kill people). The informant attributed this decline to a general rise in village economic standards. It is no longer necessary for *dukun* to kill outsiders as a means of making money or for villagers to orchestrate the demise of family members in order to get a larger share of inheritance.

Second, although *dukun* in Kerinci and Serampas are still called upon by people from other areas to teach them supernatural powers, the importance of highland Jambi in this regard is said to have declined. This dynamic is explained by the fact that, over the years, students of magical abilities have themselves become teachers after having returned to their home regions, and people in lowland cities can often now find teachers closer to home. As a result, supernatural teachings have become more diffuse over time, causing highland Jambi to lose its monopoly. Those who still travel to highland Jambi are typically motivated by the desire to acquire what they hope will be more powerful magic by going to the original source.

Third and finally, the possession of supernatural powers is also seen to have become significantly less important in the selection of new *depati*. In one of the regions, for example, a young college graduate who was not well-versed in the traditional ways was chosen to be the head *depati* (*pamuncak*) of the entire region. While some of the elder *depati* grumbled about a change in criteria, the ability to interact with the bureaucracy of the regional government was now considered a more important job skill than being able to deal with the supernatural. Moreover, many of the *depati*'s tasks that once required magical powers, such as ensuring the safety of the village, are now the official duty of the police and military.

One countervailing trend to this decline in relevance, however, was the Kerinci district government's attempt to promote a type of 'spiritual tourism' (Arfenza and Wahjudi 2002; Natividad and Neidel 2003). In a national newspaper, the head of the tourism department was reported as saying, "Visitors can see *jin* and other strange things like supernatural creatures, if they indeed want to. We have prepared *pawang* [another name for *dukun*] who can guide tourists who want to see the other world that exists in Kerinci" (Mulyadi 2004). Two prototype events that were under discussion were performances by a group that channeled ancestral spirits and meetings with a *pawang* who would allow audience members to communicate directly with a *jin*. The promotion of these activities was clearly conceptualized as being a way to market the culture of Kerinci, while opposing the reformist influence of orthodox Islam.

Decline in Believability

One of my informants argued that magic is declining in the region because of the increase in people's skepticism, resulting from greater access to education. What was particularly interesting about this comment was the logical process that he used to justify his conclusion. This informant, citing stories about the ancestors' ability to fly, discounted such a possibility based on the fact that the Prophet Mohammad, who was an exceptional person and had a direct personal relationship with God, nevertheless had to walk with his followers from Mecca to Medina during the Hijrah in AD 622. If people could acquire the ability to fly, my informant concluded, surely Mohammad would have done so.

In Serampas and southern Kerinci, this element of the discourse of decline, which clearly reflects the influence of orthodox Islam as much as it does public education, was not as common as it is in other parts of the region, like certain villages in Sungai Tenang (see Znoj 2001). It is also important to note that informants who followed more orthodox Islamic beliefs did not necessarily discount the possibility of all magical practices. The limits to this discursive element seemed to reflect two factors. First, magical beliefs and practices are an integral and deeply engrained part of highland Jambi culture; their presence is hard to deny because it is experienced on a first-hand basis. Second, while followers of orthodox Islam have a long history of rooting out practices deemed *syirik* (polytheistic and taboo),[5] the Koran, which is regarded as the incontrovertible word of God, clearly establishes in its repeated discussions of *jin* and angels that there is more to this world than people can grasp with their five senses (Asyharie and Nuris 2001; Ulwan 1996).

Conclusion

I created the term 'discourse of decline' in order to combine several different types of local commentaries about the nature and direction of change in magical beliefs and practices in highland Jambi. This discourse is largely united by an assumption that magical practice does indeed have material effects. This assumption does not deny the existence of skepticism about certain practices; rather, it underlines the fact that highland society as a whole accepts that some people possess magical powers that are, according to a common refrain, 'strange but true' (*aneh tapi nyata*).

The assumption about the material efficacy of magic underlying the discourse of decline is in marked contrast to the dominant perspective within scholarly studies of magic, which, as with the evolutionist, either assume that the beliefs and practices are illogical or, as with the structural-functionalist, have tended to emphasize the metaphorical and symbolic qualities of local practice. The position of the structural-functionalists on magic, it should be pointed out, has largely replaced that of the evolutionists in professional scholarship today, possibly reflecting the laudable goal of protecting primitive peoples from accusations of 'irrationality'. In doing so, however, scholars run the risk of imposing their own ethnocentric views on the magical beliefs and practices of the people whom they study.

Regarding the future of magical beliefs and practices, the local commentaries are more in line with the assumptions held by the evolutionist scholars, who believed that magic was on an inevitable decline. These commentaries point to the erosive effect of political, economic, and social transformations on magical beliefs and practices. Of particular importance in this regard is the influence of modernist Islam. It is extremely important to note, however, that those people who have given up their supernatural abilities have done so on the grounds that magic is immoral or no longer needed, not that it is irrational or illogical, as many evolutionists assumed. Whether or not the local discourse of decline turns out to be any more accurate than the predictions made by analysts who adhere to the evolutionist framework remains to be seen. Scholars working within the structural-functionalist and phenomenological frameworks, with their proclivity to see people continually transforming magic to meet their current needs, may turn out to have had a perspective that is more accurate than that of local commentators. Regardless of what actually happens to the tradition of magic in highland Jambi in the long run, we should continue to examine local perspectives on the same questions that stimulate scholarly research.

Acknowledgments

This research project was made possible with institutional support from the Indonesian Institute of Sciences (LIPI) and Andalas University. Funding was generously provided by the Fulbright Hays Doctoral Dissertation Abroad Program and several institutions at Yale University, including the Center of Southeast Asia Studies, Center for International Area Studies, Agrarian Studies Program, Tropical Resources Institute, and School of Forestry and Environmental Studies. I would like to thank Michael Dove, Eric Worby, Carol Carpenter, and John Miksic, who provided guidance and feedback on this overall project, and Joy Natividad, whose assistance, including with the production of map 3.1 and permission to use figure 3.1, was fundamental to this project. Finally, I would like to express my deepest gratitude to informants and friends in Serampas and Kerinci for their myriad contributions to this research project.

J. David Neidel received his PhD in Forestry and Environmental Studies and Anthropology from Yale University in 2006. Based at Yale-NUS College in Singapore, he is the Asia Program Coordinator for the Environmental Leadership and Training Initiative, a capacity-building and training program of the Yale School of Forestry and Environmental Studies and the Smithsonian Tropical Research Institute. His current work focuses on facilitating forest restoration and degraded land rehabilitation in Indonesia, the Philippines, and Sri Lanka. He also continues to pursue his research interests in the historical and political ecology of biodiversity conservation and development.

Notes

1. There is little agreement on the usage of this terminology. Evans-Pritchard's (1937) distinction between witchcraft and sorcery, for example, has proven influential among Africanists but less so among scholars working in other parts of the world. Given the nature of the argument presented here, I have found it easier simply to clump these related beliefs and practices together and to use the terms 'magic', 'magical', and 'occult' as a form of shorthand.
2. In the Pasemah Highlands of South Sumatra, *tujuh serampu*, a term that refers to seven of the earliest inhabitants of Serampas, has come to mean "the sorcery of sending an evil curse" (Collins 1979: 50) and is considered one of the most dreaded and dangerous forms of black magic (Bart Barendregt, pers. comm., 8 August 2003).
3. The word 'Sakti' has taken on an additional meaning, standing as an acronym for the region's qualities that the government would like to promote: *sejuk* (cool), *aman* (safe), *kenangan* (memorable), *tertib* (orderly), and *indah* (beautiful).
4. This discussion was paralleled in a series of books, some translated into Indonesian from foreign languages, that I found in a bookstore at the regional capital, suggesting that such debates are prevalent in other parts of the Muslim world as well (see, e.g., al-Babithin 2002; Ar-Roisy 2000; Taimiyah 2001).
5. This history of suppressing non-orthodox beliefs includes actions taken against the Sufis (i.e., Islamic mystics), some of whom claimed to possess magical abilities (Arberry 1956: 119–121). It is probably not coincidental that Sufis played an important role in bringing Islam to Indonesia in the first place (Shihab 2002). The link between Sufism and supernatural powers is also highlighted by de Grave's work on *kanuragan*. See, for example, de Grave's chapter in this book.

References

al-Babithin, Abdul A. 2002. *Pengobatan Sihir dengan Sihir* [Treating Black Magic with Black Magic]. East Jakarta: Pustaka Al-Kaustar.

Anonymous. 1972. *Depati Parbo: Pahlawan Perang Kerinci* [Depati Parbo: Kerinci War Hero]. Sungai Penuh: Pemerintah Daerah Kerinci.

Anonymous. 2001. *Obyek Wisata: Si Cantik Dari Merangin* [Tourist Object: Beauty from Merangin]. Bangko: Hubungan Masyarakat, Sekretaris Daerah, Kabupaten Merangin.

Arberry, A. J. 1956. *Sufism: An Account of the Mystics of Islam*. London: George Allen & Unwin.

Arfenza, and Aji Wahjudi. 2002. "Turis Mancanegara Kagumi Keindahan: Bumi Sakti Alam Kerinci." [Foreign Tourist Amazed by Beauty: The Supernatural Region of Kerinci.] *Sakti*, August.

Ar-Roisy, Abu F. 2000. *Mengatasi Gangguan Jin Secara Islami* [Overcoming Disturbance from *Jin* Islamically]. Surabaya: Putra Pelajar.

Asyharie, M. A., and Anwar Nuris. 2001. *Bersahabat dengan Makhluk Halus: Malaikat dan Jin* [Befriending Ethereal Creatures: Angles and *Jin*]. Surabaya: Putra Pelajar.

Aumeeruddy, Yildiz. 1994. "Local Representations and Management of Agroforests on the Periphery of Kerinci Seblat National Park, Sumatra, Indonesia." People and Plants Working Paper. Paris: Division of Ecological Sciences, United Nations Educational, Scientific, and Cultural Organization.

Bakels, Jet. 2000. *Het Verbond met de Tijger: Visies op Mensenetende Dieren in Kerinci, Sumatra* [The Agreement with the Tiger: Perspectives on Man-Eating Animals in Kerinci, Sumatra]. Leiden: Research School of Asian, African, and Amerindian Studies, Leiden University.

Bakels, Jet. 2009. "Kerinci's Living Past: Stones, Tales, and Tigers." Pp. 367–382 in Bonatz et al. 2009.

Bonatz, Dominik, John Miksic, J. David Neidel, and Mai Lin Tjoa-Bonatz, eds. 2009. *From Distant Tales: Archaeology and Ethnohistory in the Highlands of Sumatra*. Newcastle upon Tyne: Cambridge Scholars Publishing.

Bonatz, Dominik, John David Neidel, and Mai Lin Tjoa-Bonatz. 2006. "The Megalithic Complex of Highland Jambi: An Archaeological Perspective." *Bijdragen tot de Taal- Land- en Volkenkund* 162, no. 4: 490–522.

Bowen, John R. 1993. "Return to Sender: A Muslim Discourse of Sorcery in a Relatively Egalitarian Society." Pp. 179–190 in Watson and Ellen 1993.

Coedès, George. 1968. *The Indianized States of Southeast Asia*. Ed. Walter F. Vella; trans. Sue B. Cowing. Honolulu: East-West Center.

Collins, William A. 1979. "Besemah Concepts: A Study of the Culture of a People of South Sumatra." PhD diss., University of California, Berkeley.

Evans-Pritchard, E. E. 1937. *Witchcraft, Oracles and Magic among the Azande*. Oxford: Clarendon Press.

Favret-Saada, Jeanne. 1980. *Deadly Words: Witchcraft in the Bocage*. Cambridge: Cambridge University Press.

Frazer, James G. 1890. *The Golden Bough: A Study in Magic and Religion*. London: Macmillan.

Gallop, Annabel T. 2009. "*Piagam Serampas*: Malay Documents from Highland Jambi." Pp. 272–322 in Bonatz et al. 2009.

Harner, Michael J. 1980. *Way of the Shaman: A Guide to Power and Healing*. San Francisco, CA: Harper & Row.

Kathirithamby-Wells, J. 1986. *Thomas Barne's Expedition to Kerinci in 1818*. Canterbury: Centre of South-East Asian Studies, University of Kent, Canterbury.

Kozok, Uli. 2004. *The Tanjung Tanah Code of Law: The Oldest Extant Malay Manuscript*. Cambridge: St Catharine's College and the Cambridge University Press.

Malinowski, Bronislaw. 1922. *Argonauts of the Western Pacific: An Account of Native Enterprise and Adventure in the Archipelagoes of Melanesian New Guinea*. New York: E. P. Dutton.

Malinowski, Bronislaw. 1935. *Coral Gardens and Their Magic*. London: Allen & Unwin.

Marsden, William. [1811] 1966. *The History of Sumatra: Containing an Account of the Government, Laws, Customs, and Manners of the Native Inhabitants, with a*

Description of the Natural Productions, and a Relation to the Ancient Political State of that Island. Kuala Lumpur: Oxford University Press.

Miksic, John. 2009. "Highland-Lowland Connections in Jambi, South Sumatra, and West Sumatra, 11th to 14th Centuries." Pp. 75–102 in Bonatz et al. 2009.

Mulyadi, Agus. 2004. "Wisata Alam hingga Dunia Gaib." [Eco-tourism to the Supernatural.] *Kompas*, 19 June.

Natividad, Joy, and J. David Neidel. 2003. *An Inside Look at the "Secret Valley": A Guide Book to Kerinci*. Sungai Penuh: Pemerintah Kabupaten Kerinci.

Neidel, J. David. 2006. "The Garden of Forking Paths: History, Its Erasure and Remembrance in Sumatra's Kerinci Seblat National Park." PhD diss., Yale University.

Neidel, J. David. 2009. "Settlement Histories of Serampas: Multiple Sources, Conflicting Data, and the Problem of Historical Reconstruction." Pp. 323–346 in Bonatz et al. 2009.

Noerewan, H. A. 2002. "Tiang Bungkuk Mendugo Rajo." *Kerinci Indepen*, November.

Scholz, Ulrich. 1982. *The Natural Regions of Sumatra and their Agricultural Production Pattern: A Regional Analysis*. Bogor: Central Research Institute for Food Crops.

SCTV (Surya Citra Televisi). 2003. "Gemulai Mistis dalam Tarian Mahligai." [Mystical Swaying in the Mahligai Dance.] 14 September 2003. http://www.liputan6.com/view/0,62435,1,0,1133340126.html (accessed 17 June 2007).

Shihab, Alwi. 2002. *Isam Sufistik: "Islam Pertama" dan Pengaruhnya hingga Kini di Indonesia* [Sufi Islam: "The First Islam" and Its Influences until Now in Indonesia]. Bandung: Penerbit Mizan.

Steedly, Mary M. 1993. *Hanging Without a Rope: Narrative Experience in Colonial and Postcolonial Karoland*. Princeton, NJ: Princeton University Press.

Stoller, Paul, and Cheryl Olkes. 1987. *In Sorcery's Shadow: A Memoir of Apprenticeship among the Songhay of Niger*. Chicago: University of Chicago Press.

Taimiyah, Ibnu. 2001. *Wali Allah Versus Wali Setan* [Representatives of God versus Representatives of Satan]. Jakarta: Pustaka Al-Kautsar.

Tjoa-Bonatz, Mai Lin. 2009. "The Megaliths and the Pottery: Studying the Early Material Culture of Highland Jambi." Pp. 196–228 in Bonatz et al. 2009.

Turner, Edith. 1992. *Experiencing Ritual: A New Interpretation of African Healing*. Philadelphia: University of Pennsylvania Press.

Tylor, Edward B. 1871. *Primitive Culture: Researches into the Development of Mythology, Philosophy, Religion, Language, Art, and Custom*. London: J. Murray.

Ulwan, Firya. 1996. *Misteri Alam: Jin* [Mystery of Nature: *Jin*]. Bandung: Pustaka Hidayah.

Voorhoeve, P. 1941. "Tambo Kerintji: Disalin dari Toelisan Djawa Koeno, Toelisan Rentjong dan Toelisan Melajoe jang Terdapat pada Tandoek Kerbau, Daoen Lontar, Boeloeh dan Kertas dan Koelit Kajoe, Poesaka Simpanan Orang Kerintji." [Kerintji History: Transcribed from Old Javanese, Rentjong Script, and Malay Writings Which Are Found on Water Buffalo Horn, Lontar Leaves, Bamboo, Paper and Bark Heirlooms Stored by the People of Kerinci.] Unpublished manuscript. Leiden: Koninklijk Instituut voor Taal, Land- en Volkenkunde.

Voorhoeve, P. 1970. "Kerintji Documents." *Bijdragen tot de Taal- Land- en Volkenkund* 126, no. 4: 369–399.

Watson, C. W. 1976. "Historical Documents from Sungai Tutung, Kerinci." *Masyrarkat Indonesia* 3: 35–49.

Watson, C. W. 1978. "Depati Parbo: A Case Study in Indigenous History." *Archipel* 15: 123–143.

Watson, C. W. 1985. "Islamization in Kerinci." Pp. 157–180 in *Change and Continuity in Minangkabau: Local, Regional, and Historical Perspectives*, ed. Lynn L. Thomas

and Franz von Benda-Beckmann. Athens: Ohio University Center for International Studies Center for Southeast Asian Studies.
Watson, C. W. 1987. *State and Society in Indonesia: Three Papers*. Canterbury: Centre of South-East Asian Studies, University of Kent at Canterbury.
Watson, C. W. 1992. *Kinship, Property and Inheritance in Kerinci, Central Sumatra*. Canterbury: Centre for Social Anthropology and Computing and the Centre for South-East Asian Studies, University of Kent at Canterbury.
Watson, C. W. 1993. "Perceptions from Within: Malign Magic in Indonesian Literature." Pp. 191–212 in Watson and Ellen 1993.
Watson, C. W. 2009. "*Tambo Kerinci.*" Pp. 253–271 in Bonatz et al. 2009.
Watson, C. W., and Roy Ellen, eds. 1993. *Understanding Witchcraft and Sorcery in Southeast Asia*. Honolulu: University of Hawai'i.
Wolters, O. W. 1967. *Early Indonesian Commerce: A Study of the Origins of Srivijaya*. Ithaca, NY: Cornell University Press.
Yakin, H. A. Rasyid. 1986. *Menggali Adat Lama Pusaka Usang di Sakti Alam Kerinci* [Exploring Old Customs and Worn-Out Heirlooms in the Supernatural Region of Kerinci]. Sungai Penuh, Kerinci.
Znoj, Heinzpeter. 2001. "Heterarchy and Domination in Highland Jambi: The Contest for Community in a Matrilinear Society." Postdoctoral thesis, University of Bern.
Znoj, Heinzpeter. 2009. "Social Structure and Mobility in Historical Perspective: Sungai Tenang in Highland Jambi." Pp. 347–366 in Bonatz et al. 2009.

Chapter 4

TAMIL TIGER RITUAL, WAR, AND MYSTICAL EMPOWERMENT

Michael Roberts

Faced with calamity, death, and prospective danger, people in the Indian world seek votive protection and aid from mystical forces of all sorts. In the Indian sub-continent and its offshoots, these anchors of succor and shields of protection are drawn from the transcendental religions long connected to the area and the localized belief systems associated with 'tribal' and allegedly 'primitive' peoples.

Four contemporary instances of protective practice introduce us to this phenomenon. First, Sanjay Srivastava (2007) observed urban healers, mostly Hindu but also Muslim, retailing amulets as protective charms on the pavements of Delhi. Amid the erotic sex manuals and 'footpath pornography' that

Notes for this chapter begin on page 101.

were vigorously peddled by vendors, he found advertisements for a "Tantric ring"; a "*māla* [chain] with 108 beads" that promised to "take away all your troubles, cast spells, pass exams"; and a booklet titled "Assam Bengal *ka jaadu*" that could "make humans disappear" (ibid.: 129, 130). Second, some Indian cricketers engage in sporting struggles with colored string bracelets around their wrists, in effect amulets that "have been blessed by some local godman."[1] Third, Jacob Copeman indicated that his relatives in Delhi who were afflicted by a blood disease kept their medicines beneath idols of Ganesh, Krishna, and Jesus Christ so that the cures would be blessed.[2] Fourth, Shyam Tekwani's camerawork in the late 1980s[3] captured a young Tamil Tiger fighter heading for combat duty with holy ash (*vipūti*) sharply and freshly emblazoned on his forehead in what is also called a *pottu* and is often a circle (see fig. 4.1).

All four examples indicate belief in supra-mundane forces, that is, powers beyond this world, powers that are intangible, mystical, and magical. They mark what Weber (1946; 1978: 174–205) would deem to be 'enchanted practice' at odds with secular rational thought (see also Roberts 2006: 77–79). These enchanted practices have usually involved the propitiation of forces associated with the transcendental religions we call Hinduism, Jainism, and Buddhism. But they could also embrace animist spirits and in more recent centuries have engaged Muslim saints (*pir*) and Christian figures.[4] The last examples highlight the considerable

FIGURE 4.1 Young Tiger fighter with holy ash on his forehead heads for the battlefield in the late 1980s

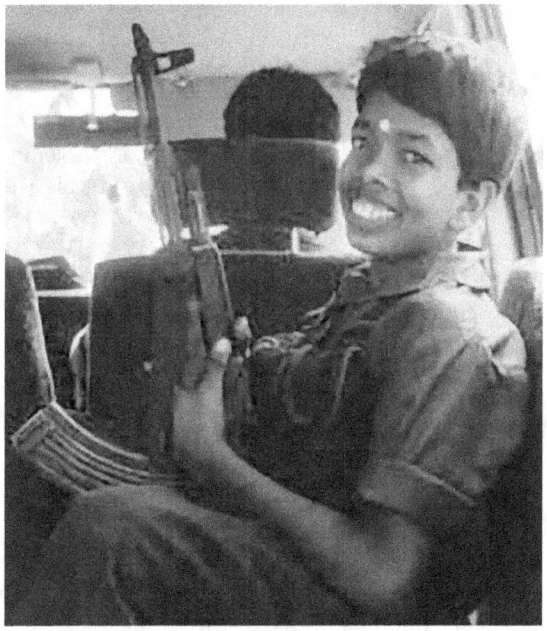

Photograph © Shyam Tekwani

cross-fertilization and pluralism of religious practice in South Asia. Thus, in Sri Lanka one finds Buddhists as well as Christians (and even a Muslim or two) at religious festivals associated with the deities of the Hindu world (Bastin 2002; Obeyesekere 1978, 1981; Roberts 2005c: 500–503). Hence, it is no surprise that a Tiger fighter of Christian persuasion should on occasion emblazon her forehead with 'sacred ash' in the manner of a Saivite person.[5]

These practices have extended to penances that involve considerable privation. Among those whom we have come to know as 'Hindus' (in all their variety), the powers of the deities are also stoked at regular intervals during festivals that involve teeming masses. When participants enter trance states of possession and ecstasy, they are understood to be agents of specific deities or a more general form of divine intervention.

The deities invoked are both male and female. The most popular are those who are amoral, that is, those known for the power of their wrath and for their affirmative responses to total devotion from a votive supplicant. These deities "may prove protective and beneficent at one time, then cruel at another" (Mines 2005: 126; see also Nabokov 2000). Several of these deities are female: Durga, Kāli, and Kannagi, for instance. Their iconic representations are in tune with such punitive force: "[T]he violence of their origins and their vengeful natures are often reflected in their murderous depictions as ... fanged terrifying women who look ready to bite" (Mines 2005: 133).

Given profound anxiety, it is hardly surprising that both protective shields and punishing forces carry commodity value. The pavement hawkers in Delhi referred to by Srivastava catered to popular prejudices by associating their amulets with Bengal and Assam, the two regions in the northeast of the subcontinent widely regarded as the primordial source of Tantric magic. The amulets on sale conveyed the ring of authenticity through such linkages. To those so oriented, they bespoke the power of encirclement.

We now face the unmarked question attached to three of our initial ethnographic examples: why does supra-mundane protection take an encompassing form, usually circular? For South Asia, the answer in surmise lies in Tantrism.

Religious Hybridity in Asia

Tantra as an umbrella concept refers to "a complex array of ritual, theoretical, and narrative strategies that are specific to their various ... contexts," but nevertheless have "a grouping of common denominators [permitting one to] classify these as so many varieties of a single tradition" (White 2000a: 5). Tantra emerged at some point "in the middle of the first millennium C.E." (ibid.: 20) and intertwined with the currents of thought and practice that we denote today as Vedism, Brahmanism, and Hinduism. Each of these terms should be comprehended as intertwined religious movements rather than doctrinal systems with clear boundaries; and we must heed White's insistence that "[n]o form of medieval Hinduism, Buddhism, or Jainism ... has been without a Tantric component" (ibid.: 7).

Religious practices in Asia are a challenge to those who have been nourished in the either/or epistemology of the modern West. Cross-fertilization of thought and practice has, I repeat, generated hybridity in form. We must therefore absorb White's (2000a: 12ff.) arguments about the imbrication of Tantric elements within the better-known transcendental religions. 'Imbrication' means the interlacing and fusion of threads of practice or belief in a mosaic form that is reproduced over time amid the changes that enter over the years. In meshing with Hinduism, Jainism, and Buddhism in their search for spiritual emancipation, Tantric practices encouraged the deployment of "ritual technologies" (ibid.: 12)—so that one sees Tantric *sādhakas* (practicers) pursuing various sorts of practical attainments, including astrology, medicine, and magic (White 2000a). Such attentiveness to supernatural forces was (and still is) nevertheless located alongside "a connecting thread ... between the magical and the spiritual" (Goudriaan 1979: 7).

One of the common denominators within the various threads of Tantrism was the use of the *mandala* (White 2000a: 13), that is, the "idealized circular model of the cosmos" (White 2000b: 629). Central to this visual aid to meditation was the Tantric representation of the energy levels of the universe as "a set of concentric circles (*cakras*) of hypostasized forms of the divine energy"; such divine energy could appear as "an array of divine, enlightened, perfected, demonic, human, or animal beings" (White 2000a: 10). These beings could also "manifest themselves on an acoustic level, as garlands or piled-up aggregates of phonemes (*mantras*)," or they could appear, "on a graphic level, as the written characters of the hieratic alphabets" (ibid.).

Two facets of Tantrism are pertinent to our focus on the principle of encompassment in relation to Tamil Tiger practice. First, Tantric practitioners believe in the possibility of a fusion with the sublime deity, a goal that is line with their tenet that "the 'microcosm' of the body is [homologous] with the 'macrocosm' of the ... world of the gods" (Goudriaan 1979: 8). So we have within Tantrism the reiteration of the Hindu idea of consubstantiation of self with a deity or deities (Fuller 1992: 73; Nabokov 2000: 8–9). Second, popular Tantra in many parts of India promoted the related notions of *vīra* (virile hero) and *siddha* (perfected being). The rites used by people to propitiate the various local deities included "the gratification of these beings through sacrificial offerings." The "supreme offering [was] none other than the bodily constituents of the practitioner himself." In the result, one found "an exchange of prestations in a heroic mode. Human practitioners [made] the supreme sacrifice of their own person, moving the Tantric deity to reciprocate with untold powers and supernatural enjoyments" (White 2003: 13–14). In short, one sees a dedication of self to the Greater Good, the Deity.[6]

The Tamil Tiger Kuppi

The gifting of oneself for the Greater Good of Thamilīlam (the insurgent state) was one of the fundamental principles enjoined on all those who were recruited to the Liberation Tigers of Tamil Eelam (LTTE), being embodied in the concept of *uyirayutham*. *Uyirayutham* refers to the gifting of one's life as a weapon and thus describes a person whose suicidal action is a *that-kodai* or 'self-gift' (Chandrakanthan 2000: 164; Roberts 2005a: 13; 2005b; 2006). Its material form was embodied in a *kuppi*, a vial containing cyanide that all Tiger fighters carried on the promise that they would bite the vial if they were in imminent danger of capture. The *kuppi* was a pragmatic instrument devised by the LTTE as a defensive tool that would save their personnel from the rigors of torture. But it was also sculpted into their mythology in ways that consolidated their *esprit de corps*.

The *kuppi* was also a talisman of selfless zeal: it told the world that the LTTE fighters possessed a remarkable intensity of commitment. None of the other Sri Lankan Tamil groups that had taken to arms in a quest for independence in the period from 1983 onward had adopted this tool and its symbolism. There is little doubt that the LTTE garnered widespread admiration among the Sri Lankan Tamil populace for their quality of *arppaNippu* (dedication, offering, gift, sacrifice).[7] Thus, the *kuppi* also functioned as a propaganda device in the competition for support among the various armed groups during the initial stages of the LTTE's war effort.

Velupillai Pirapāharan (1954–2009), who founded the LTTE in May 1976, was captivated by the action of another budding revolutionary, Ponnudurai Sivakumāran, who swallowed cyanide when the police cornered him in 1974.[8] Pirapāharan told a BBC team that he himself began to carry cyanide quite early in his career as the LTTE leader. Thus, the *kuppi* was eventually rendered into a badge of initiation for all Tiger fighters after their training—as graphically depicted in a BBC documentary (see Lambert 1991) filmed in the LTTE territories.[9]

This emblem, the *kuppi*, was usually worn as part of a necklace (*māla*). That, clearly, was the most pragmatic manner in which to carry a tool that one has to use quickly. But whatever the practical advantage of such a device, it can hardly be lost on Tamils that the *kuppi* was (is) in appearance similar to the *thāli* (also written as *tāli*).

In its original form, the *thāli* was a turmeric-stained string that was placed around a woman's neck by her spouse at the rite finalizing their marriage.[10] Among Tamils, this simple token could be embellished by gold emblems or pellets of various kinds threaded onto the string. Or the necklace itself could be a gold or silver ornament that bore more than just protective value. It is the meaning attached to the *thāli*, however, that is central: the *thāli* signifies a permanent bond—should the wife cut the *thāli*, the relationship would be severed (Mines 2005: 39).

My early juxtaposition of *kuppi* and *thāli* was originally a surmise. This interpretative leap has since been confirmed by Trawick's (2007: 81) ethnographic finding: "[T]he pendant around the neck [of Tiger fighters] signifying submission to a particular discipline (*kaddupādu*) is a variform of the marriage pendant signifying, for women, the renunciation of personal freedom in the service of husband and family." Significantly, the concept *kaddupādu* is often linked in modern Tamil expressions as part of a trinity with *kadamai* (duty, obligation) and *kaNNiyam* (decency).[11] This triumvirate of cultural values has a puritanical thrust associated with sectarian and group discipline.

Like the *thāli*, therefore, the *kuppi* embodied a binding relationship—in this case, between each fighter and the LTTE (and its cause of Eelam). It was also a form of defensive empowerment. Both the *kuppi* and *thāli* immediately bring to mind one of our opening gambits, the image of a Tantric amulet. It is the encompassing form in which these 'tools' were worn that leads one to reflect upon a whole array of practices in the Hindu world that involve circular acts of protection or commitment.

Encompassment in Hindu Practices

The Tantric amulet is but one example of a species of shamanic practice deployed by many forest-dwelling and agricultural peoples of archaic time who faced the vicissitudes of environment and disease without the benefits of advanced technology. It is a form of enchanted practice that invests the principle of encompassment with magical force. We can speak of such encompassing acts as encirclement, but this should not be taken literally because a box or rectangle can also encompass. Indeed, the architectural composition of a Hindu temple usually involves a series of concentric box-edifices encompassing the central core with its inner sanctum, a sanctum that is also understood to be a 'root seat' and 'seed chamber', which is at once the primordial source of life and, metaphorically, a Mount Meru looming over the universe (Bastin 2002; Shulman 1980).

The placement of art designs in white rice powder, known as *kolams*, on the threshold of dwellings by their occupants is intended to "protect the household, and specifically [to] protect its female inhabitants" from evil spirits (Bastin 2002: 136), while also signifying "a state of auspiciousness" (Nagarajan 2007: 87). The power of protection resides in the intricate design and the various astrologically determined patterns—namely, forms of *cakra* (the wheel of *dharma*)—that they select (see fig. 7.1 in Bastin 2002: 135). Referencing Diana Eck's work on *darshan*, Nagarajan (2007: 97) states: "The designs of *kolams* ... [also] reflect symbolic *tirthas* (crossings)—that is, spaces to be crossed with a consciousness of the sacred."[12] *Kolam* art designs are also drawn in front of deities in shrine rooms. Thus, these *kolam* designs are forms of *mantra*, *tantra*, and *yantra*. In effect, what we have is protection sought through what one can call 'astrological alignment', a form of parallelism or 'analogue magic'.

In a further testament to encompassment, it is a conventional practice for young boys to be ritually invested with a string or cord around the waist, an encircling device that is threaded through a brass capsule with a letter or symbol contained within it. This is the *nūl kaddu*, a protective charm. Used at the vulnerable childhood stage, its principal purpose is to provide protection, and one commonly observes little boys running around naked—except for a cord and amulet around their waists.

Just as significant are the collective rites of encompassing protection. One of the most fundamental rituals of protection and life renewal in agrarian and fishing villages in India and Sri Lanka involves elaborate ceremonial processes that culminate in a circumambulation of the village, known as the *pradakshina*. This act of boundary marking separates the vulnerable, civilized, and superior from the surrounding *katu*, the wasteland that is ghost-ridden, wild, and dangerous (Mines 2005: 40). The *pradakshina* is a mode of protective encompassment that is also regenerative: it is designed to secure divine boons for the fertility of people and ample harvests in the village.

These are just a few of the many illustrations of encircling spiritual acts in the world of Hindu worship (in all the varieties marked by the term 'Hindu'). Central to much Hindu worship are actions and substances that further an identity of being between the worshipper and the superior divine power, understood as a Good and/or Force. The devotee seeks to disembody him- or herself in the process of embodying the divine figure that he or she is propitiating. This identity of being is revealed/effected not only "by the sequential logic of [a] ritual as it unfolds" (Fuller 1992: 72), but also by a multi-media 'assault' on all the senses that seeks to enfold and subsume the participants in one 'globe'.

It is because of its englobing and pervasive capacities that a camphor flame is a favorite 'tool' in a Hindu *pūjā* (prayer ritual) in front of a deity's image, an act that is often scheduled for its climax. We are speaking here of *ārati* (also *ārathi*, *aarthi*), a rite of worship involving the encompassing ambience of light and fume. At this moment,

> the divine and human participants are most fully identified in their common vision of the flame and hence in their mutual vision of each other—the perfect *darshana*. God has become man and a person, transformed, has become god; they have been merged and their identity is then reinforced when the worshiper cups the hands over the camphor flame, before touching the fingertips to the eyes ... Light, most especially the camphor flame, is thus an extraordinarily potent condensed symbol of the quintessentially Hindu idea, implied by its polytheism, that divinity and humanity can mutually become one another, despite the relative separation between them that normally prevails in this world where men and women live and must die. (Fuller 1992: 73)

The *bhakti* movement, commencing from about the sixth century CE, encouraged individuals to seek the realm of divinity through personalized devotion to a deity without resort to intermediaries. *Bhakti* has been "a theology of embodiment" where one's devotion is "embedded in the details of human life" (Prentiss 1999: 6). By linking a focused mind to a loving heart, the devotee is believed to secure unity with the deity through participatory love-linked-to-awe (Cutler 1987: 1, 8, 10–11; Fuller 1992: 156–158, 164–169, 210–217; Prentiss 1999: 6–7, 15–18).

One expression of this theme was inscribed within a Saivite devotional poem in Tamil called the *Periya Purānam*, produced in the twelfth century by Cēkkilār. This is a hagiography about 63 Tamil Saiva *tontars* (servitors) or *nāyanmārs* who extend unqualified commitment to Lord Siva. The *nāyanmārs*' absolute devotion inspires them to pursue fierce acts in sacrificial mode against their own loved ones and against themselves. In brief, their "emotional intensity of *anpu*" (or love) drives them "far beyond normal moral boundaries" to an "excess of blood and death"—an excess that pleases Siva because it embodies total devotion.[13] Here, then, was an outstanding story of sacrifice of self for a Greater Good. The *Periya Purāṇam*, I note, was not an archaic text. It was transmitted as poetry, chant, and performative act in the Tamil vernacular. In short, it entered literary fare as well as folklore throughout much of the Tamil world in the modern era.[14]

Thus, we witness here the ultimate offering to divine form: the gift of oneself. For the vast majority of Hindu devotees, this esteemed act is not practicable. Arduous journeys of pilgrimage on religious occasions or surrogate acts of sacrifice serve as alternative paths. At many religious festivals, the culminating act that involves the sacrifice of goats or lambs—a rite called *velvi*[15] by Tamil speakers—is one such moment. It is a ritual of renewal as well as an act of defensive girding through divine power. At the Bhadrakāli festival in Udappu along the western coast of Sri Lanka, the amassed worshippers yell "Arōharā" as a goat's neck is cut off. Since the animal is garlanded and the ceremony occurs within a *pandal*, or temporary structure, the ethnographer Tanaka (1991: 119) suggests that the rite has affinities with a marriage ceremony. So we come full circle to the *velvi*'s analogy to the *thāli* of marriage rites and the binding promise of the *kuppi*, which is adopted by every warrior inducted into the fighting force of the LTTE.

To sum up in point form, these terms have the following meanings:

- *thāli* = binding discipline of self in marriage;
- *velvi* = sacrificial gift and a promise to a deity, one that carries the bondage of a vow;
- *kuppi* = binding self to one's peers and to the Greater Good via a promise of defensive sacrifice for one's comrades.

It is no surprise that Tamil teenagers in the Eastern Province in the late 1990s firmly believed that joining the LTTE was a path to death (Trawick 2007: 81–86, 110, 129–130, 171, 176). This was a road that significant numbers were prepared to take.

Dead Body Politics

Such propaganda by deed was quickly elaborated by the propaganda around the dead, confirming Verdery's (1999: 27) notion of "the political lives of dead bodies" (see also Roberts 2008). The LTTE initiated practices of homage to their dead in ways that created a sacred topography and mobilized Tamil sentiment in favor of the leadership of the Tamil liberation struggle. On 27 November 1989, "around six hundred LTTE cadres assembled at a secret venue in the Mullaitheevu district jungles of Nithikaikulam" to commemorate what they call Māvīrar Nāl or Great Heroes Day (Jeyaraj 2006).

This was a revolutionary measure that involved shelving Hindu practices of cremation (Roberts 2005b; 2005c: 499–500). Between 1989 and 2004, the commemorative process was incrementally expanded on an epic scale, occurring simultaneously at numerous sites, especially the 21 impeccably maintained *tuyilam illam* (resting places), where the countless Tiger fallen have been 'planted' or commemorated by plaque.[16] Here, then, was a striking reversal: the *tuyilam illam*, like cemeteries elsewhere in the world, became sacred terrain and were explicitly deemed to be 'holy places' and 'temples' (see Harman 2011; Natali 2008; Trawick 2007: 245). This moment engendered a community of suffering across the length and breadth of the Tamil country and along Tamil networks across the world. The lamentation, however, was gilded by pride and a celebration of worth (Roberts 2005b: 81–82). Indeed, as Schalk (2003: 404) tells us, Heroes' Week was celebrated as an *elucci nāl*, that is, a "Day of Edification" or "Day of Rising."[17]

Māvīrar Nāl *and Cosmic Encirclement*

The Heroes Week over the seven days culminating at 6:05 PM on 27 November was a state ritual, a ritual *of* Thamilīlam *for* Thamilīlam.[18] Māvīrar Nāl was grand theater, but theater displayed locally and suffused with evocative cultural motifs and artifacts, while being imbricated with religious principles and enchanted hues. Within a context involving widespread cross-fertilization between religions and where Christian practices are a thin veneer upon a Hindu foundation (Bastin 2002; Bayly 1989: 454ff.; Obeyesekere 1978; Stirrat 1992), the religious hues within cultural forms were invariably Saivite, the dominant form of Hinduism among Tamils in both India and Sri Lanka.[19]

The LTTE honored their dead *māvīrar* (great heroes) during Māvīrar Nāl by displaying their pictures in their home locality. The garlanded photographs were placed in a series along the walls of a shed, the *māvīrar mandapam*, built especially for the purpose. The color scheme of the pillars separating sections of the shed replicated that of temple pillars, while the whole ambience was strikingly Saivite-cum-Hindu.[20] The walls displayed meaningful scenes from the Tamil heritage that reached back into India (Roberts 2005b: 78–82). One illustration must suffice. Amid the colorful paintings of palatial houses, several calling to mind chalets and chateaux in Switzerland or other regions in northern Europe (see fig. 3 in ibid.: 79), was one scene where the image of an attractive and corpulent woman with a pot held at her waist appeared to smile down benignly at photographs of dead women that had been placed in front of the backdrop (see fig. 4.2). This puzzled me until the scholar Karthigesu Sivathamby explained that the backdrops were intended to convey the idea of pleasant surroundings and abundance.

This imagery of plenitude gains emphasis by reference to the religio-cultural values associated with the pot in Tamil culture, its regular use in rituals of regeneration such as Tai Pongal (or Ponkal), and its widespread deployment in LTTE mobilization work in Sri Lanka as well as abroad. Diane Mines's (2005) village study in South India provides specifics that carry generalized validity for much of the Tamil-speaking country, if not much of India. The *ponkal* or boiled rice dish[21] has to be interpreted in the context of temple festivals known as *kotai* held throughout the summer months in southern India.[22] By cooking rice in pots and by offering personalized vows (*nērtikkatan*) before a deity, the people of a village see themselves as producing general fruits (*palan*) or benefits

FIGURE 4.2 Photographs of Female *Māvīrar* Surrounded by Tropes of Abundance at a *Māvīrar* Shed in Velvittathurai, November 2004

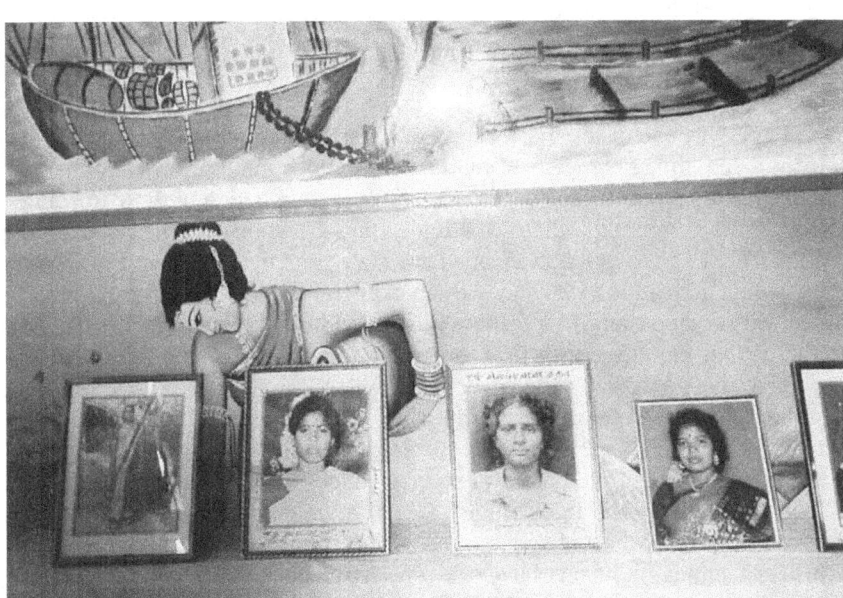

Photograph © Michael Roberts

(*nanmai*, lit., 'goodness') as well as specific outcomes, such as getting a loan to build a house (ibid.: 42, 149, 151).[23] In the village festival studied by David Mosse (1994: 316), the heated goddess from outside was understood to be "the virginal or ascetic form identified with Durga or Kali" and was "carried from the water source [a well] to the village temple in the form of a ritually prepared pot containing milk which [was] said to 'boil over' with the goddess's power."

In sum, therefore, the scenes surrounding the revered Tiger *māvīrar* were pleasant. They evoked thoughts of goodness and conveyed notions of abundance, plenitude, fructification, and renewal, suggesting the birth of a new 'era'. And that is not all. Arrays of *māvīrar* photographs were displayed on one occasion at Pirapāharan's old school, Maheswara College in the Eastern Province, in a blaze of lights set within a red background (see fig. 24 in Roberts 2007a). One could not have asked for a better replication of the encompassing principle of *ārati*. In addition, at the entrance to the *tuyilam illam* in the frontline town of Vavuniya, a profuse cluster of white flowers, almost certainly the fragrant, wild jasmine *nitya kalyāni*, encircled the LTTE flag.[24]

This was not an isolated instance. In my observations in 2004, every official LTTE building at Kilinochchi had a flagpole—bearing the LTTE's totemic flag—encircled by white jasmine. Likewise, the official epitaph to the LTTE fighters who had died in capturing Kilinochchi, intended as an inspiration for renewed vigor, was encircled in orange stone by replicas of the *karthigapoo* or glory lily, the flower selected by the LTTE in 2003 as their official emblem (see figs. 7, 9 in Roberts 2006). These were all officially ordained state actions. They embodied (embody) the principle of 'cosmic encirclement'.

Liminality and LTTE Inventiveness

The LTTE was one of the most innovative insurgencies in the history of insurrection. Here the reference is to military technology and improvisations in the face of adversity that enabled its leaders, over a long period of time, to counter forces (Sri Lankan and Indian) that had superior resources. This capacity also enabled the LTTE to function as a de facto state from mid-1990 until early 2009. Engaged in a liberation struggle with an explicit ideology of sacrifice, the LTTE as an organization and its personnel as individuals confronted an existential threat. What has been shown at the empirical ethnographic level, as well as interpretative surmise, is the manner in which—as Kapferer (2002: 21) puts it—the LTTE personnel worked "intuitively ... by extending and adapting" the "available cosmologies" in support of this project.

Anthropology has laid great store by the concept of 'liminality', and Kapferer (2002: 22) stresses the vitality of this concept when he argues that magical activity in the modern world often arises in "spaces apart from everyday life" (ibid.: 22). Such liminal moments have the capacity to be "major sites of invention" (ibid.: 21). In the story of the LTTE as a state actor, the *māvīrar* rituals were a major invention within Sri Lankan Tamil culture. In replacing cremation with burial, the LTTE converted what would normally have been considered polluted mortuary sites into holy temples (Natali 2008; Roberts 2005b: 75; 2005c: 499–500). The *tuyillam illam* became places where the kinsfolk and friends of the deceased went to interact with those who had sacrificed themselves for the cause. And it was not only to lament: "They talked with them, scolded them, praised them, cajoled them, and they asked for help to bear the horrors of [their] terrifying war" (Harman 2001: 3). In this view, it is argued that the LTTE reproduced the "very substance of a religious impulse that embodied a form of traditional Tamil religiosity" (ibid.: 5). Deploying Kapferer, one can modify Harman's emphasis on tradition. One can argue that the whole corpus of practices involving *māvīrar* veneration was a modernizing innovation and a practice of re-enchantment that re-energized the 'magic' of a specific religious worldview. In these terms, the result is a new hybrid composition (cf. Kapferer 2002: 20).

Concluding Remarks

Both cosmic and astrological alignments are threaded within the multifaceted range of LTTE practices, both commemorative and military, without necessarily being the predominant elements in their calculations. Furthermore, on some occasions Tiger functionaries indulged in votive thanksgiving acts or flower offerings that were suffused with religious principles, thus securing connections with their 'lineage' dead (Roberts 2006: 76–80). Critical military operations were also girded by propitiatory acts involving key functionaries. The Tiger assassination team intent on killing Rajiv Gandhi went to a Pillaiyar *kōvil* in Chennai lorded over by Ganapati[25] before heading for Sriperumbedur because one of the assassins, Dhanu, "wished 'to say her final prayers'" (Roberts 2010: 38). After their successful strike at Sriperumbedur, on 25 May 1991 the operational commander Sivarāsan took the remainder of the team to Tirupati, South India's most famous pilgrimage center, on "a thanksgiving trip" (Kaarthikeyan and Raju 2004: 50). This thanksgiving vow to cosmic forces was in keeping with a similar act by Velupillai Pirapāharan about seven years earlier. When a shipment of arms secured by the LTTE from Lebanon was landed secretly in Tamilnadu in 1984, thereby reducing their dependence on India and giving the LTTE an edge over the other militant Eelamist groups,[26] Pirapāharan "tonsured his head as a mark of thanksgiving to the Hindu gods [and] quietly traveled to [the] pilgrim town of Palani to pray at the hill temple of Murugan, his favorite deity" (Narayan Swamy 2003: 110).

Those readers who are wedded to positivism and its either/or rationality may conceivably deem the circumstantial character of some evidence marshaled here as inadequate. However, I underline my arguments by taking my cue from D. S. Farrer's (2008) essay on Malay healing arts and the inspiration it has drawn from Alfred Gell's (1999) work on art objects and the 'technology of enchantment'. The issue raised by this act of prompting can be phrased thus: what do the practices that I have outlined, whether flower offerings, garlands, tonsured heads, or amulets around the neck, achieve? Clearly, without ethnographic backing, the answers are speculative, although built on *a priori* grounds.

Take the *kuppi* worn around the neck by most LTTE soldiers. It was adopted, as I revealed earlier, at a powerful rite of induction that served to bind the soldiers to their peers and to the LTTE cause. Such rites, which are typical of military training in all parts of the world, are intended to implant loyalty to one's peers and the unit of operation. Here, one's unit becomes a single element in a larger force that is set up as the ultimate goal in life. Sporting teams also work in this way. Such practices are facets of the generalized technology of 'beguilement', a modern form of enchantment that works within and through the psychology of instrumental rationality.

Thus, arguably, the *kuppi* sustained self-confidence among Tiger fighters by reminding them that they were a special breed of persons, rather like the heroic figures of the archaic Tamil past and recent (Tiger) past—those deified humans of enshrined *natukal* power.[27] In this sense, the *kuppi* extended its carrier's agency in a manner similar to Gell's (1998: 6, 31) interpretation of art objects, such as the Asmat shield or the painted prows of Trobriand war canoes, which are understood by their creators to generate awe in the enemies whom they face (see Farrer 2008). One can therefore suggest that the Tiger fighters were inspired to believe that they transcended quotidian life. In this way, the *kuppi* was also good instrumental psychology, although its effects were not necessarily successful at all times.[28]

While this psychological boost was partly meant for defense against torture, all Tiger warriors were aware of the first LTTE suicide attack. Carried out by

Vallipuram Vasanthan, known as Captain Miller, in an explosive-laden truck, it pulverized an army camp at the Nelliyadi school on 5 July 1987. Miller's was the first suicide attack by the Black Tigers, a wing of the LTTE that was trained to mount suicide missions. His action, one can assume, was also etched in the minds of Sri Lankan fighting forces. Nelliyadi came to symbolize the penetrative power of suicide attacks on land or sea, carrying the potential to instill fear in the enemy. Certainly, some LTTE personnel believed that the enemy was frightened by the Tigers in general, whether Black Tigers or ordinary soldiers (Trawick 2007: 118, 162). So the mystique of the *kuppi* and the serial record of its military successes captivated the LTTE's own fighting personnel and promoted self-confidence.

In review, therefore, the cyanide vial, the *kuppi*, can be interpreted as a form of distilled power and "congealed agency" that enhanced the "ongoing agentive capacity" of Tiger personnel (Copeman 2004: 135; see also Farrer 2008; Gell 1999; Roberts 2007b). It was thus part of the technology of enchantment. In this argument, the play of instrumental rationality intertwines with a stress on the belief in cosmic powers.

Note, moreover, that the LTTE dead were commonly described through a "formulaic phrase" that runs thus: *vīramāna maranam adainta*—"[having] attained a heroic death" (Trawick 2007: 84; see also ibid.: 102). This terminology and their status as *māvīrar* linked the dead, in my interpretation, with a significant strand of belief in Tamil culture, namely, the belief in *pey* (ghosts) and "lesser 'demonic' beings including the army of invisible supernatural warriors (*vīrans*: a term denoting power and heroic valour) who attend figures like Aiyanar and Munisveran" (Bayly 1989: 32–33; see also White 2003: 3–4, 8).

Consider therefore a further dimension within the cultural backdrop: "Tamil culture draws no distinct boundary between gods and adored persons, creatures, or things: the dead are deities of a kind, and so are children and movies stars" (Trawick 2007: 107). Rather than reinforcing Trawick's own leanings, these strands of information provide circumstantial support for the speculation that the *māvīrar* may have been invested with divine power and the punishing cosmic capacities of those 'attendants' serving Kāli, Murugan, and other deities of just cause.[29]

The latter proposal is explicitly tentative in character. In contrast, several pieces of evidence, some circumstantial and others empirically sustained, have been assembled within this chapter to establish the fact that Tiger personnel, including some of the highest rank, resorted to ritual practices of protection or invocation in connection with momentous operations. The tonsuring of one's head by males is a form of 'embodied practice' among Saivites and Tamils that encapsulates a religious orientation toward divine power. It is thus a form of enchantment in the Weberian sense (opposed to secular, rational modes of being). In the context of military operations, Pirapāharan's tonsuring of the head and expressions of thanks to powerful deities at Palani in 1984 can be deemed, metaphorically, if not literally, as 'war magic'.

Acknowledgments

This chapter would not have been possible without the assistance of several friends who responded to many of my questions. Extra-special thanks are conveyed to S. V. Kasynathan, Maya Ranganathan, K. Sivathamby, David Gordon White, and Sanjay Srivastava. Among others who helped me on specifics are Darshan Ambalavanar, David Mosse, S. Nataraja, Anoma Pieris, Fr. Aloysius Pieris, Shyam Tekwani, Rajesh Venugopal, S. Visahan, Richard Weiss, Mark Whitaker, and the late D. Sivaram.

Michael Roberts is an Adjunct Associate Professor of Anthropology at the University of Adelaide and the author of numerous works on the Tamil Tigers. Educated in the discipline of history at the University of Peradeniya and Rhodes Scholar for Ceylon in 1962, he taught at Peradeniya from 1966 to 1976 before moving sideways into anthropology at the University of Adelaide in 1977. His many publications encompass social mobility, social history, agrarian issues, peasant protest, popular culture, urban history, caste in South Asia, practices of cultural domination, and nationalism. His main focus has been Sri Lanka, and his present concern is a comparative study of martyrdom. He is one of the central figures behind the new site http://sacrificialdevotionnetwork.wordpress.com and also manages http://thuppahi.wordpress.com, http://www.flickr.com/photos/thuppahi, and http://cricketique.wordpress.com.

Notes

1. Deepak Mehta, e-mail note, 6 March 2008.
2. Jacob Copeman, personal communication, 2010. See also Copeman (2004).
3. Eventually becoming embedded within the LTTE, Tekwani began entering the north from late 1983 onward, embarking from Rameswaram and working with different Tamil militant bodies until the LTTE became the main arm. From late 1987, some of his missions were via Colombo, but through LTTE contacts. See Pratap (2001: chap. 1) for one account of the latter. These secret visits included the period when the Indian Peace Keeping Force was in occupation, from 1987 to early 1990.
4. For illustrations of the forces propitiated by these practices, see Bayly (1989: 27–33, 141), Fuller (1992: 48–49), Mosse (1994), and van der Veer (1994: 33–53, 58–61, 200–201).
5. This woman was Sita (code name), who was then a mother and an ex-fighter still linked to the LTTE (Trawick 2007: 88–89). Note Sita's response when faced with Trawick's challenging reaction: "In our movement all religions are one" (ibid.: 87).
6. Apart from the readings cited, this review was aided by Flood (2006).
7. On *arppaNippu*, see Schalk (1997: 66, 69, 76) and Hellmann-Rajanayagam (2005: 123). One also has the form *ArppaNam*. Both mean "the performance of dedication as well as that which is dedicated" (S. V. Kasynathan, e-mail note, 30 March 2007).

Also see Pratap (2001: 102–104), Roberts (2005c: 496; 2007a), and Trawick (2007: 184, 185, 207).

8. Pirapāharan himself did not swallow a cyanide capsule when cornered on the battlefield on 18–19 May 2009; he died in a firefight (Roberts 2012). Details about Sivakumāran are from Narayan Swamy (1994: 29), Roberts (1996: 252–254), and T. Sabaratnam in chapter 7 ("The Cyanide Suicide") of a serialized book that is available on the web (http://www.sangam.org/Sabaratnam/PirapaharanChap7.htm).

9. See the BBC documentary film *Suicide Killers* (Lambert 1991) for the oath and other details. For evidence of Pirapāharan's god-like status in Tamil circles, see Pratap (2001: 70–72, 102–104), O'Duffy (2007: 265), and Trawick (2007: 85, 125, 182–183).

10. S. V. Kasynathan, personal communication; Mines (2005: 38–39).

11. S. V. Kasynathan, telephone conversation, 6 January 2008; Darshan Ambalavanar, e-mail communication, 7 January 2008.

12. "Stepping on the *kolam* is like stepping into the Ganges River," one Tamil woman told Nagarajan (2007: 97).

13. This paragraph is based on comments kindly sent by Darshan Ambalavanar of Toronto that corrected questionable facets of my previous reading of Hudson (1990). On *vannanpu* or 'violent love', also see Vamadeva (1995).

14. On 1 January 2007, Darshan Ambalavanar sent me this note about the *Periya Purāṇam*: "It was continuously taught in Saiva and probably broader Tamil literary circles ... At the same time, the stories of the *nāyanmārs* constitute the stuff of Saiva devotion." He added that it was "carried by Vellalar and castes close to them," so the issue as to whether it was diffused to the non-orthodox castes and *dalit*s (lower class, or untouchables) should be treated as an open one.

15. Etymologically, the multivalent term *velvi* can refer to (1) spiritual discipline, (2) the site of a rite, or (3) service or worship and thus can designate a desire or offering in search of a goal. In pointing this out with the aid of his dictionary, the scholar Karthigesu Sivathamby (1932–2011) added that it is related to the mythological image of *kalavelvi*, where the *pey* (evil spirits) dance on the battleground and make *ponkal* (gruel) from the gore of the fallen (information conveyed in November 2004). Also see Pfaffenberger (1979: 260), Roberts (2006: 74–75), and Tanaka (1991: 72, 114, 118–119).

16. The LTTE does not bury the remains of a person. It conceives its mortuary operations to be a 'planting' and speaks of the bodies as *vitai* (seeds) and *viththudal* (bodies that have become seeds) that will soak into the soil and fructify as ash (Hellmann-Rajanayagam 2005: 123–124, 138, 141; Schalk 1997: 79). See also http://www.TamilNet.com, 6 July 1999. *Viththudal* is the combination of two words: *viththu* (seed, semen), where the *th* represent the *t* with a dot underneath it when the diacritic is available, and *udal* (body). I was assisted here by S. V. Kasynathan in correcting a misprint in Hellmann-Rajanayagam's article.

17. For an elaboration of the concept *elucci*, assisted by e-mail exchanges with Rick Weiss in New Zealand, see Roberts (2010).

18. This review is aided by my observations of one such week in the Jaffna Peninsula and environs of Kilinochchi in 2004 and by Roberts (2005b: 76–92; 2005c; 2006).

19. I am influenced here by the terminology adopted by Bastin (2002) and Trawick (2007).

20. This was the firm opinion of Vineeta Sinha of the National University of Singapore after I showed her pictures of the inside of two sheds taken during my visit to Jaffna in November 2004. Sinha has done extensive research on Hindu gods in southern India.

21. This boiled rice dish has to be prepared "in a special way on open fires, often cooked on thresholds" (Mines 2005: 222). The Tai Ponkal holiday "is associated

with agricultural productivity, kinship connections, and celebration of the Tamil New Year" (ibid.).
22. *Kotai* literally means 'gift'. Thus, regeneration is through offering, dedication.
23. For illustrative details on the use of pots in Sri Lanka, see Bastin (2002: 137, 168–169, 186, 195) and Tanaka (1991: 66, 78–98, 102–122).
24. See also the garlands around *tuyilam illam* epitaphs in figure 23 in Roberts (2007a).
25. The god Pillaiyar, also known as Vināyakar (Remover of Obstacles), Ganesh, and Ganapati, among other names, "is the most beloved and revered of all the Hindu gods, and is always invoked first in any Hindu ceremony or festival. He is the son of Parvati (the wife of Shiva, the Destroyer, the most powerful of the Hindu trinity of principal gods." See http://www.lankalibrary.com/myths/ganesh.htm.
26. Between August 1983 and July 1987, the Indian government and the state authorities of Tamilnadu actively supported and sponsored the several Eelamist fighting forces and established military training camps for most of them. The LTTE had at least 11 batches of soldiers trained at such camps, some of which were run by the LTTE. It is widely believed that TELO was the group most favored by the Indian authorities. However, TELO and other factions such as PLOTE were totally dependent on India for its arms and ammunition. Pirapāharan had the foresight and the connections to secure his own lines of armament.
27. *Natukal* (also written as *nadugal*) are more or less equivalent to 'hero stones' (*vāragal*) and 'memorial stones' in southern India. They are burial epitaphs for *sannyāsin*, *sati*, and other such heroes who have been vested with divine power and have become sites of supplication.
28. Some Tiger soldiers did not bite into their cyanide capsules when capture was imminent (Shyam Tekwani, pers. comm.).
29. The previous quotation from Trawick is from part of a section where she refers to an ethnographic situation at the house of a friend, an ex-female fighter who had placed a garland around each photograph of a dead friend adorning the rooms. The picture of Pirapāharan, however, had no garland. Trawick deploys this fact to contend that treating the leader as a god in this manner would be contrary to the LTTE's proclaimed position that it is "a secular movement" (Trawick 2007: 107). But there are two counterpoints to this argument. First, in Indian convention, garlanded photographs are a conventional way of indicating that people are dead, whereas Pirapāharan was not yet deceased at the time and thus was not quite a *māvīrar*. Second, despite this, there is some evidence that Pirapāharan was expressly likened to a god by senior LTTE personnel (O'Duffy 2007: 265). Female fighters such as Sita and Nalini also beatified him—that is, he was depicted as 'beautiful' and a "man of goodness" (Trawick 2007: 85; see also ibid.: 81, 183).

References

Bastin, Rohan. 2002. *The Domain of Constant Excess: Plural Worship at the Munnesvaram Temples in Sri Lanka*. New York: Berghahn Books.

Bayly, Susan. 1989. *Saints, Goddesses and Kings: Muslims and Christians in South Indian Society, 1700–1900*. Cambridge: Cambridge University Press.

Chandrakanthan, A. J. V. 2000. "Eelam Tamil Nationalism: An Inside View." Pp. 157–175 in *Sri Lankan Tamil Nationalism: Its Origins and Development in the 19th and 20th Centuries*, ed. A. Jeyaratnam Wilson. London: Hurst.

Copeman, Jacob. 2004. "'Blood Will Have Blood': A Study in Indian Political Ritual." *Social Analysis* 48, no. 3: 126–148.
Cutler, Norman. 1987. *Songs of Experience: The Poetics of Devotion*. Bloomington: Indiana University Press.
Farrer, D. S. 2008. "The Healing Arts of the Malay Mystic." *Visual Anthropology Review* 24, no. 1: 29–46.
Flood, Gavin. 2006. *The Tantric Body*. London: I.B. Tauris.
Fuller, C. J. 1992. *The Camphor Flame: Popular Hinduism and Society in India*. Princeton, NJ: Princeton University Press.
Gell, Alfred. 1998. *Art and Agency: An Anthropological Theory*. Oxford: Oxford University Press.
Gell, Alfred. 1999. "Vogel's Net: Traps as Artworks and Artworks as Traps." Pp. 187–214 in Alfred Gell, *The Art of Anthropology: Essays and Diagrams*, ed. Eric Hirsch. London: Athlone Press. Originally published in 1996 in *Journal of Material Culture* 1, no. 1: 15–38.
Goudriaan, Teun. 1979. "Introduction: History and Philosophy." Pp. 3–67 in Sanjukta Gupta, Dirk J. Hoens, and Teun Goudriaan, *Hindu Tantrism*. Leiden: Brill.
Harman, William. 2011. "Embracing the Martyred Dead: *The Tuyilam Illam* as Sacred Shrines for the Sri Lankan Tamil Tigers." Paper presented at the conference of the American Academy of Religion at San Francisco, November.
Hellmann-Rajanayagam, Dagmar. 2005. "And Heroes Die: Poetry of the Tamil Liberation Movement in Northern Sri Lanka." *South Asia* 28, no. 1: 112–153.
Hudson, D. Dennis. 1990. "Violent and Fanatical Devotion among the Nāyanārs: A Study in the *Periya Purāṇam* of Cēkkilār." Pp. 373–404 in *Criminal Gods and Demon Devotees*, ed. Alf Hiltebeitel. Delhi: Manohar.
Jeyaraj, D. B. S. 2006. "No Public Speech Ceremony for LTTE Chief This Year?" Transcurrents, 26 November. http://transcurrents.com/tamiliana/archives/234.
Kaarthikeyan, D. R., and Radhavinod Raju. 2004. *The Rajiv Gandhi Assassination: The Investigation*. Slough: New Dawn Press.
Kapferer, Bruce. 2002. "Introduction: Outside All Reason—Magic, Sorcery and Epistemology in Anthropology." *Social Analysis* 46, no. 3: 1–30.
Lambert, Stephen, prod. 1991. *Suicide Killers*. Documentary film, 49 min. BBC Inside Story series.
Mines, Diane P. 2005. *Fierce Gods: Inequality, Ritual, and the Politics of Dignity in a South Indian Village*. Bloomington: Indiana University Press.
Mosse, David. 1994. "Catholic Saints and the Hindu Village Pantheon in Rural Tamil Nadu, India." *Man* (n.s.) 29, no. 2: 301–332.
Nabokov, Isabelle. 2000. *Religion against the Self: An Ethnography of Tamil Rituals*. Oxford: Oxford University Press.
Nagarajan, Vijaya R. 2007. "Threshold Designs, Forehead Dots, and Menstruation Rituals: Exploring Time and Space in Tamil *Kolams*." Pp. 85–105 in *Women's Lives, Women's Rituals in the Hindu Tradition*, ed. Tracy Pintchman. Oxford: Oxford University Press.
Narayan Swamy, M. R. 1994. *Tigers of Sri Lanka*. Delhi: Konark Publishers.
Narayan Swamy, M. R. 2003. *Inside an Elusive Mind*. Colombo: Vijitha Yapa Publications.
Natali, Cristiana. 2008. "Building Cemeteries, Constructing Identities: Funerary Practices and Nationalist Discourse among the Tamil Tigers of Sri Lanka." *Contemporary South Asia* 16, no. 3: 287–301.
Obeyesekere, Gananath. 1978. "The Fire-Walkers of Kataragama: The Rise of *Bhakti* Religiosity in Buddhist Sri Lanka." *Journal of Asian Studies* 37, no. 3: 457–476.

Obeyesekere, Gananath. 1981. *Medusa's Hair: An Essay in Personal Symbols and Religious Experience.* Chicago: University of Chicago Press.

O'Duffy, Brendan. 2007. "LTTE: Majoritarianism, Self-Determination, and Military-to-Political Transition in Sri Lanka." Pp. 257–287 in *Terror, Insurgency, and the State: Ending Protracted Conflicts,* ed. Marianne Heiberg, Brendan O'Leary, and John Tirman. Philadelphia: University of Pennsylvania Press.

Pfaffenberger, Bryan. 1979. "The Kataragama Pilgrimage: Hindu-Buddhist Interaction and Its Significance in Sri Lanka's Polyethnic Social System." *Journal of Asian Studies* 38, no. 2: 253–270.

Pratap, Anita. 2001. *Island of Blood: Frontline Reports from Sri Lanka, Afghanistan and Other South Asian Flashpoints.* New Delhi: Viking.

Prentiss, Karen P. 1999. *The Embodiment of Bhakti.* Oxford: Oxford University Press.

Roberts, Michael. 1996. "Filial Devotion and the Tiger Cult of Suicide." *Contributions to Indian Sociology* 30, no. 2: 245–272.

Roberts, Michael. 2005a. *Narrating Tamil Nationalism: Subjectivities and Issues.* Colombo: Vijitha Yapa Publications.

Roberts, Michael. 2005b. "Saivite Symbols, Sacrifice, and Tamil Tiger Rites." *Social Analysis* 49, no. 1: 67–93.

Roberts, Michael. 2005c. "Tamil Tiger 'Martyrs': Regenerating Divine Potency?" *Studies in Conflict & Terrorism* 28: 493–514.

Roberts, Michael. 2006. "Pragmatic Action and Enchanted Worlds: A Black Tiger Rite of Commemoration." *Social Analysis* 50, no. 1: 73–102.

Roberts, Michael. 2007a. "Blunders in Tigerland: Pape's Muddles on 'Suicide Bombers' in Sri Lanka." Heidelberg Papers in South Asian and Comparative Politics. Working Paper No. 32, November 2007. South Asia Institute, Department of Political Science, University of Heidelberg.

Roberts, Michael. 2007b. "Suicide Missions as Witnessing: Expansions, Contrasts." *Studies in Conflict & Terrorism* 30, no. 10: 857–887.

Roberts, Michael. 2008. "Tamil Tigers: Sacrificial Symbolism and 'Dead Body Politics.'" *Anthropology Today* 24, no. 3: 22–23.

Roberts, Michael. 2010. "Killing Rajiv Gandhi: Dhanu's Sacrificial Metamorphosis in Death?" *South Asian History and Culture* 1, no. 1: 25–41.

Roberts, Michael. 2012. "Velupillai Pirapāharan: VEERA MARANAM." Thuppahi's Blog, 26 November. http://thuppahi.wordpress.com/2012/11/26/velupillai-pirapaharan-veera-maranam.

Schalk, Peter. 1997. "Resistance and Martyrdom in the Process of State Formation of Tamililam." Pp. 61–84 in *Martyrdom and Political Resistance: Essays from Asia and Europe,* ed. Joyce Pettigrew. Amsterdam: VU University Press.

Schalk, Peter. 2003. "Beyond Hindu Festivals: The Celebration of Great Heroes' Day by the Liberation Tigers of Tamil Eelam (LTTE) in Europe." Pp. 391–411 in *Tempel und Tamilien in zweiter Heimat,* ed. Martin Baumann, Brigitte Luchesi, and Annette Wilke. Wurzburg: Ergon Verlag.

Shulman, David D. 1980. *Tamil Temple Myths: Sacrifice and Divine Marriage in the South Indian Saiva Tradition.* Princeton, NJ: Princeton University Press.

Srivastava, Sanjay. 2007. *Passionate Modernity, Sexuality, Class, and Consumption in India.* Delhi: Routledge.

Stirrat, R. L. 1992. *Power and Religiosity in a Post-colonial Setting: Sinhala Catholics in Contemporary Sri Lanka.* Cambridge: Cambridge University Press.

Tanaka, Masakazu. 1991. *Patrons, Devotees and Goddesses: Ritual and Power among the Tamil Fishermen of Sri Lanka.* Kyoto: Institute Research in Humanities, Kyoto University.

Trawick, Margaret. 2007. *Enemy Lines: Warfare, Childhood, and Play in Batticaloa*. Berkeley: University of California Press.
Vamadeva, Chandraleka. 1995. *The Concept of Vannanpu "Violent Love" in Tamil Saivism, with Special Reference to the Periyapuranam*. Uppsala: Uppsala University Religious Studies.
van der Veer, Peter. 1994. *Religious Nationalism: Hindus and Muslims in India*. Berkeley: University of California Press.
Verdery, Katherine. 1999. *The Political Lives of Dead Bodies*. New York: Colombia University Press.
Weber, Max. 1946. "Religious Rejections of the World and Their Directions." Pp. 323–359 in *From Max Weber: Essays in Sociology*, ed. H. H. Gerth and C. Wright Mills. London: Routledge & Kegan Paul.
Weber, Max. 1978. *Max Weber: Selections in Translation*. Ed. W. G. Runciman. Cambridge: Cambridge University Press.
White, David G. 2000a. "Introduction: Tantra in Practice: Mapping a Tradition." Pp. 3–38 in White 2000b.
White, David G., ed. 2000b. *Tantra in Practice*. Princeton, NJ: Princeton University Press.
White, David G. 2003. *Kiss of the Yoginī: "Tantric Sex" in Its South Asian Contexts*. Chicago: University of Chicago Press.

Chapter 5

SHAMANIC BATTLEGROUND IN VENEZUELA

Željko Jokić

In South America, and more specifically Amazonia, the dark side of shamanism has been largely neglected by researchers due to Western prejudices against violence and a discriminatory emphasis on the more positive, healing aspects of shamanism (Whitehead and Wright 2004a). As a result, the pervasive malignant elements of Amazonian shamanism have been either misrepresented or completely excluded in ethnographic accounts, and the overall picture has been distorted. A few fairly recent studies have attempted to redress this imbalance by focusing on malevolent magical practices, various forms of assault sorcery and witchcraft, and offensive, destructive aspects of shamanistic practices (Whitehead 2002; Whitehead and Wright 2004a; see also Brown 1988). These works have demonstrated that the dark side of shamanism is not only an omnipresent part of the ethnographic realities of various Amazonian groups but also

Notes for this chapter begin on page 124.

an indispensable component of their cosmo-shamanistic systems. The central argument in this chapter is that such an omission and the resulting (mis-)representation of other life-worlds constitute a reproduction of colonial ways of knowing due to "both the denial of radical cultural difference and the refusal to think through its consequences" (Whitehead and Wright 2004b: 1). Farrer (this volume; 2009: 24–25) likewise argues that a blind spot or gap in understanding the shamanic other can result in problems of misplacing the subject.

In the case of the Yanomami, however, radical cultural differences were reinforced and highlighted from the beginning. In fact, even before the first permanent contacts were established with missionaries in 1951, the Yanomami had acquired the reputation, mainly from the neighboring Ye'cuana, of being warlike and primitive. For the missionaries (especially the evangelical New Tribes Mission), the Yanomami became the 'poor souls' who needed to be saved, while their shamans became the 'agents of Satan'. The Yanomami's negative image was further reinforced by some scholars—notably, by the anthropologist Napoleon Chagnon (1968, 1992), who characterized them as an inherently fierce, violent, and drug-ridden people living in a chronic state of warfare. Even today Yanomami are considered the prime example of ignoble savages, Stone Age remnants who are a window into our own past. Sponsel (1998) argues that the exaggeration of Yanomami aggression and violence has been used against them by the state. Tierney (2000) claims that Chagnon's overt focus on violence helped to justify the invasion of Yanomami territory in search of gold. Albert (1988) similarly maintains that portrayals of Yanomami as violent barbarians can be used to rationalize the violation of their human rights (see also Borofsky 2005).

With regard to the issue of destructive magical activities, ever since the pioneering work of Evans-Pritchard ([1937] 1977) among the Azande in Africa, the classificatory distinction has been made in anthropology between witchcraft and sorcery, on the one hand, and, by extension, shamanism, on the other. However, this distinction as defined by the Africanist model (ibid.) does not match other ethnographic realities—in this instance, that of Amazonian cultures (Farrer, this volume). In the literature on Amazonia, witchcraft and sorcery have largely been assimilated under the category of shamanism (Whitehead and Wright 2004). The reason for this is the inherent duality of the shamans' powers, which is reflected in their ability both to heal and to kill—the common shared characteristic of many shamanic complexes throughout Amazonia. In fact, one of the fundamental aspects of Amerindian shamanism is its ambivalence toward shamanistic power (Brown 1988; Crocker 1985; Hugh-Jones 1996). The same practitioner who can cure and protect his or her kin with the help of assistant spirits can also use those spirits for the purpose of inflicting harm and death to others.

This chapter, which is based on my fieldwork among the Yanomami of the Venezuelan Upper Orinoco River Region in 1999–2000, aims to address this dual aspect of *shapori (hekura) mou* (the Yanomami shamanistic complex)—namely, the dialectic between offensive and defensive shamanism, with particular emphasis on its malignant side. My intention here is not to reinforce negative views on Yanomami culture, such as those discussed above, but to address this aspect of Yanomami shamanism and lived reality from the point of view of positive and negative reciprocity as a governing principle of Yanomami society (see Lizot 1994).

Among the Yanomami, assault shamanism, various forms of sorcery, and other magical manipulations for the purpose of inflicting suffering, illness, and death are always present in everyday life. During my fieldwork in two Yanomami communities, Mahekoto-theri and Sheroana-theri, I observed almost on a daily basis numerous healing sessions performed by the *shapori* (shamans) in both communities, but also various acts of magical assault directed at distant enemies. There is a general agreement in the existing Yanomami literature that the *shapori* use their *hekura* spirit-helpers for the dual purpose of curing their own people and attacking and killing their enemies. The primary motive for magical assaults is vengeance and retribution for past deaths. Some research papers dealing with this topic provide more or less balanced accounts of shamanism, with frequent emphasis on its positive aspects (see, e.g., de Barandiarán 1965; Wilbert 1963). Two studies that stand out due to their focus on shamanism's malevolent aspects are Lizot's (1985) book *Tales of the Yanomami*, in which a chapter titled "Eaters of Souls" describes the action of a soul-eating shaman, and Chagnon and Asch's (1973) controversial film *Magical Death*, which shows a group of Shamathari shamans involved in a collective ritual of paedophagy (i.e., consumption of children). These examples as well as my own case studies reveal part of a wider Yanomami socio-cosmic system based on the governing principle of exchange and reciprocity, in this instance a negative type of reciprocity. Positive reciprocity, which involves mutual obligations with regard to the exchange of trade goods and the sharing of food, occurs within a single community or between neighboring communities at a short distance from each other. Negative reciprocity involves a cosmic circuitry exchange of magic attacks and shamanic assaults between distant communities, and it is primarily motivated by revenge (Alès 2000; Lizot 1994).

A Yanomami *shapori*, akin to his colleagues from other Amazonian ethnic groups, is first and foremost the 'master of spirits'. The relationship between the *shapori* and his assisting *hekura* spirits is generally described as one of mutual cooperation, whereby the actions of the *hekura* abide by the will and intentionality of the shaman (de Barandiarán 1965; Goetz 1969; Wilbert 1963).[1] While this is certainly true to some extent, in this chapter I argue that, due to the malevolent nature of the Yanomami cosmos and its extracorporeal spirit-denizens, the *shapori* engaged in the act of killing sometimes must do this for the purpose of appeasing those spirits who demand human souls. In order to maintain the cosmic balance, the shaman at times has to take the life of others in order to save the life of his own kin. These harmful activities form an integral part of the Yanomami shamanistic complex. Their cosmo-geographical patterns and flow of cosmic vital force enhance our understanding of wider social relations and provide insight into the historical transformation of the practice and meaning of shamanism and sorcery within the context of modernity and culture change.

Ethnographic Context

The Yanomami are the southernmost and largest of four linguistic Yanoama sub-groups, numbering somewhere between 7,500 and 8,000. The majority of their territory is situated within the Parima-Tapirapecó National Park in the far southeastern corner of Venezuela's southernmost state, Amazonas, a large section of which was declared part of the Upper Orinoco-Casiquiare Biosphere Reserve in 1991. The Yanomami's territory is covered by dense tropical forests and forested mountain ranges, stretching from the Parima Mountains in the east down to the Brazilian border and incorporating the adjacent areas of northern Brazil. On the northern side, it borders that of the Sanema. The southernmost part of the Yanomami's territory in Venezuela, which was the main area of my field research, incorporates the headwaters of three major regional rivers: the Orinoco, Mavaca, and Siapa.

Altogether, I spent just over a year living in two Yanomami communities: Mahekoto-theri and Sheroana-theri. The first community is situated in Platanal, one of the three Salesian missions established in the early 1950s. Lured by the missionaries, the Mahekoto-theri people abandoned their semi-nomadic existence and settled on the left bank of the Orinoco River, where they remain up to the present day. Platanal is nowadays a meeting place for many Yanomami, who go there to exchange trade items and visit their relatives. The mission consists of a church-sponsored bilingual school for children, a rural health clinic with a doctor in charge, and an adjacent hospital building. The second community, Sheroana-theri, is linked through kinship ties with some Yanomami of Mahekoto-theri. This small inland community is situated approximately three hours upriver by boat from Platanal where the forest trail begins and then eight hours on foot from the Orinoco River.

In the area of my research (see map 5.1), there is a general pattern that involves the negative exchange of shamanistic assaults, malignant magical activities, and mutual witchcraft accusations among numerous communities situated along, or in proximity to, the Orinoco River. These include the Sheroana-theri, Mahekoto-theri, and distant Shamathari communities located toward the south in the Siapa River basin.[2] For the Sheroana-theri, other potential enemies performing magical assaults come from communities clustered around the Mavaca mission. It is important to mention that both present-day Sheroana-theri and the community of Pishaansi-theri that originally settled in Mavaca were part of the same 'mother community' by the name of Namowei-theri before they split up due to a dispute around the mid-1940s (Chagnon 1968; Jokić 2003). The ongoing animosity between these groups stems from this historical fission. Magical assaults resulting in illness or death can sometimes be attributed to non-Yanomami shamans and their assisting spirits, usually from the neighboring Ye'cuana people. This region represents a large-scale geographical theater of intercommunal dialectics between offensive and defensive types of *shapori mou* practice that generate an endless cycle of tit-for-tat revenge and *hekura* assaults. It is a macro-universe of the principally repetitive activities engaged in by *shapori* from different communities.

MAP 5.1 Research area in the Upper Orinoco River region

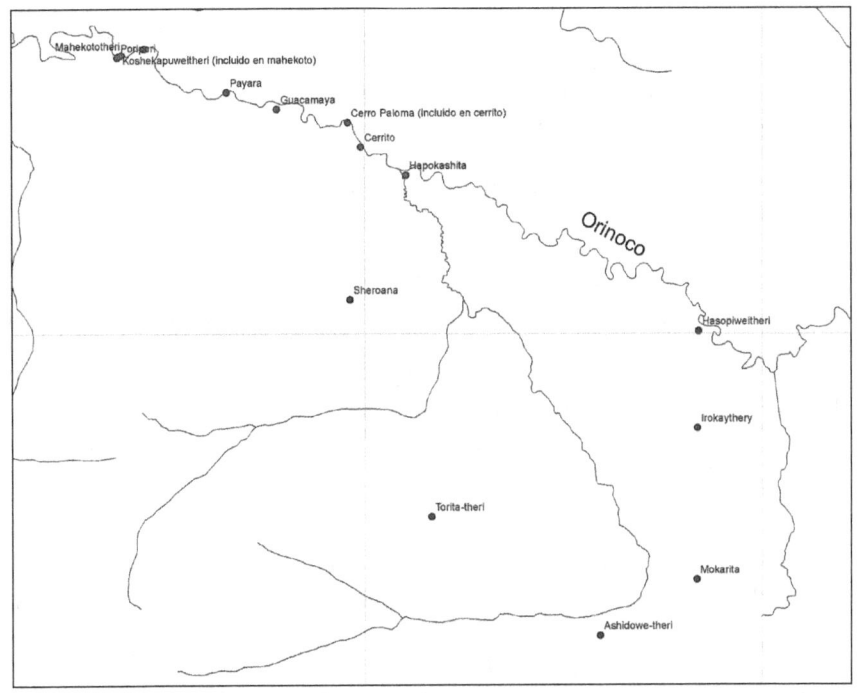

Source: PNEO-FS, Ecoepidemiology Unit, SACAICET

Cosmos, *Hekura*, and Initiation

Yanomami conceive of the whole universe as consisting of five separate but interconnected celestial and terrestrial layers or 'cosmic discs', each having its own proper name. Together, they form one bounded cosmic totality, which is contained within the abdomen of a giant cosmic boa (*hetu mïsi*). In the Yanomami language, *hetu* means boa constrictor, and the suffix *mïsi*, attached to the name of each separate cosmic disc, signifies 'abdomen' (Lizot 1999). Structurally, all of these cosmic discs are positioned on top of each other along the vertical cosmic axis. Each separate layer is at the same time a world in itself, with its own horizontal dimensionality limited by the top and bottom surfaces of each layer. Although all cosmic discs exist in their own right, the bottom surface of each disc becomes the top surface of the one below.

These distinct cosmic layers represent different structural parts or changing conditions of the cosmic whole as a set of different stages, from new to old and from male to female. In other words, each cosmic disc represents a state of the cosmos or condition of the cosmic boa's abdomen as a fragmented totality, which is reflected in the names of each respective disc. As Wagner (1991: 167) puts it: "When a whole is subdivided in this way it is split into holographs of itself." The uppermost layer is the young cosmos in its genesis, that is, the 'new abdomen' (*oshe mïsi*), while the layer farthest down is described as an 'old woman' (*hetu mïsi suwë pata*). Both celestial and terrestrial realms mirror each other, and together they constitute the primal totality, which I will call the 'cosmic body'—an alternative term for the classical idea of the macrocosmos. It is through the earth level that the male and female cosmic principles converge at the moment of regeneration, transformation, and the death and rebirth of the universe. The earth disc, where the Yanomami (human beings) live, is encapsulated by the celestial vault, the central cosmic component where the whole cosmic order is manifested.

The Yanomami cosmos is not a friendly place. It is inhabited by various cannibalistic, anthropomorphic ancestral beings, with each stratum having its own denizens (*hekura*). The sky is home to a number of celestial beings, including Mothokariwë (Sun), Periporiwë (Moon), Yaru (Thunder), Watawatariwë (Thunder's son), and Yamirayoma (Lightning), among others. The terrestrial disc, the 'world of the living', is covered with vast tropical rainforests and is home to a number of malevolent beings, chief of whom is Irariwë, the 'ancestral jaguar' (see fig. 5.1). Finally, the subterranean layer is populated with Amahiri—Yanomami ancestors who once lived on earth but sank underground due to the collapse of the sky. A constant menace to the Yanomami, the Amahiri's shamans frequently engage in maleficent acts. Various *hekura* pose an ongoing threat

FIGURE 5.1 A *shapori* transformed into the ancestral jaguar Irariwë

Photograph © Željko Jokić

to the Yanomami, inflicting illness and death by stealing and eating their vital essences. It is only through the process of shamanistic initiation that these extra-corporeal spirit-beings can become domesticated and put into the service of the *shapori*. However, the same shamans can—and customarily do—use these embodied spirits for harmful purposes.

Explicit knowledge of representations of the cosmos is generated implicitly in the lived experience of the shamanistic initiation and the 'construction' of the cosmic body or shaman's corporeal microcosm, which is itself a replica of the Yanomami cosmos. While I have discussed this process at length elsewhere (Jokić 2006, 2015; see also Lizot 1985: 87–105), here it is important to mention briefly that the initiation essentially entails the metamorphosis of a human being into a *hekura* being, which is reflected in the Yanomami term for initiation—*hekuraprai*. The neophyte calls the ancestral spirits to come from the various corners of the universe, inviting them to invade the interiority of his body.

This process eventually culminates in the experience of death and rebirth, after which the same *hekura* spirits become embodied and continue living inside the new *shapori*. The shaman himself becomes a *hekura* after receiving various bodily components and attributes of other *hekura*, such as the crown of light (*watoshe*) (see fig. 5.2), which enables him to see at a distance and inside others' bodies, and toucan wings (*hoko*), which enable him to fly. Together with these, the new *shapori* receives the spirit-path (*pei yo*),

FIGURE 5.2 A candidate receives the crown of light (*watoshe*) during a shamanic initiation

Photograph © Željko Jokić

spirit-house (*shapono*), *hekura* hammocks (*yii*), and a cosmic mountain (*pei maki*). All of these bodily components, together with the embodied *hekura*, form one complete, self-enclosed system. The shaman's cosmic body is not only a symbolic blueprint of the cosmos but also its source and an instrument of its manifestation.

Each individual *shapori* has a distinct set of personal *hekura* that operate together as a unit. The shaman's body represents their headquarters, with each constituting a separate microcosm, a self-contained whole that co-exists with other shamans and their respective embodied systems of personal *hekura*. Various *shapori* operate simultaneously within a transpersonal field of macrocosmic *hekura* powers. In other words, there is a 'point of touch' in the distance that separates the various *shapori*. They affect each other directly in a sphere of shared or overlapping modes of consciousness, generated by their embodied *hekura* helpers and, of course, by the copious hallucinogens used during shamanistic activities. Each individual *shapori* participates in the sphere of conscious intersubjective relations with other *shapori*, mediated by their *hekura* and the psychotropic snuff *epena*.

Apart from being engaged in a kind of intra-shamanic warfare against each other, *shapori* readily summon their personal *hekura* spirits for the purpose of affecting other people, whether by inflicting misery and death on them or by helping them to recover from the same effect. Through song and dance they are able to reach a trance state of consciousness, which is in essence their re-experience of death. Trance, or the realm of death, at the same time becomes a specific dimensionality of consciousness during which the *shapori* are able to undergo multiple metamorphoses into any of their embodied *hekura* spirits. In this state whereby the *shapori*'s self is fused with that of the *hekura*, the powers and abilities of the *hekura* are used to heal or to inflict misfortune.

Ambiguous Shamanic Powers

Through the experience of initiatory death and rebirth, the neophyte reaches a specific mode of being as he assumes the new identity of a living spirit 'in the flesh'. This new dual mode of existence—as an immortal *hekura* occupying the perishable physical body—confers on the *shapori* a new social status, coupled with a set of duties and responsibilities toward his residential group. Within his own community, the *shapori* is always engaged in healing protective acts (see fig. 5.3). Yet the same practitioner can use his powers to send illness and to inflict harm or death on members of other distant communities; in this latter sense, he becomes an enemy. Therefore, a *shapori*'s social status is relative to the situation and to the possibly conflicting points of view of the two or more sets of villages involved.

While a *shapori* can save life, he can also take life. He is responsible for order but can also create disorder. He becomes both protector and defender of the community, shielding his people from the intrusions of the outside *hekura* and enemy shamans. But at the same time he becomes an aggressor, a predator,

FIGURE 5.3 A *shapori* engaged in protective, integrative activities in his own community

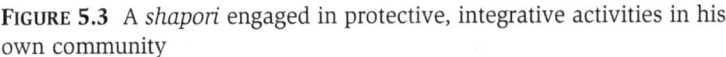

Photograph © Željko Jokić

preying upon the young and weak in distant communities (see Cocco 1972: 423). This dual aspect of Yanomami shamanism and the ambiguity of the shamans' powers is a common characteristic of Amazonian ethnographic realities. However, this is by no means the case everywhere. In some instances, the role of shamans is more delineated. For example, among the Warao, who inhabit the area of the Orinoco River delta, the distinction between dark and light shamanism is more obvious (Wilbert 1972, 2004).

While an individual *shapori* can heal or harm, each case of affliction implies both defensive and offensive types of shamanistic activities employed by different practitioners. For analytical purposes, I distinguish between these two types of shamanistic actions similarly to how Farrer (this volume) defines war magic as both defensive and offensive. But, in reality, each case simultaneously involves elements of either sickness infliction or *hekura* attack by one or more *shapori*, on the one hand, and the follow-up treatment or rescue countermeasures employed by another *shapori*, on the other. This, of course, only applies to cases in which a health disturbance is caused by a deliberate act involving human agency, whether it be an enemy shaman or an *ōka* sorcerer. Such an act always requires the counteractive action of another shaman.

Each *shapono* community is a micro-universe, subject to principally protective and curative activities by resident *shapori*, but the *shapono* dwelling is also an arena of *shapori*'s assaults on members of other *shaponos* (see fig. 5.4). Structurally, it is a replica of the Yanomami universe and, at the same time, a manifestation of the cosmic order—the place where social and cosmic orders converge (Lizot 1976, 1985). The open central area is the celestial arch, which curves down and touches the earth at the point of the horizon, where the higher part of the roof terminates. This communal space in the building is intended for festivities and other collective events, such as shamanistic sessions and body cremation ceremonies. Yanomami tend to perform these activities near the roof's

FIGURE 5.4 Transformed into a moon *hekura*, the *shapori* searches for a victim outside a *shapono*

Photograph © Željko Jokić

edge or the lower part of the sky, while the very center of the house is rarely used. The earthen floor of the *shapono* corresponds to the earth itself—the central disk of the universe. The area of domestic family life, offering shelter and safety, begins at the rim of the roof, while the lower roof's edge demarcates the circumference of the earth's disk.

Body, Illness, and Death

Yanomami knowledge of the human self-constitution, as revealed through shamanism, is of central importance to any understanding of the processes of illness, cure, and death. There are three main components of the Yanomami multiple soul: *pei puhi*, *pei mɨ āmo*, and *noreshi*. On the one hand, *pei puhi* is associated with will power, thought, emotion, and belief (Alès 2000; Chagnon 1992; Lizot 1999). On the other hand, Chiappino (1995) identifies *puhi* as a vital principle or cosmic force that saturates all of existence, including human bodies. The main difference consists in either viewing *pei puhi* as a mental capacity or assigning it an existential status. The *shapori* Ruweweriwë from Sheroana-theri described *pei puhi* as a 'breath' that resembles *horoi* (white down used in shamanistic rituals). He stressed the anthropomorphic quality of *puhi* that is part of a person. *Pei mɨ āmo* is another vital principle, with each body part having its own *mɨ āmo*. It can be lost or stolen and is susceptible to *hekura* attacks. After the person's death, the *pei mɨ āmo* transforms into *no porepi* and migrates to the sky. Finally, *noreshi* is a unique constitutive part of a person with dual manifestation: it is simultaneously a part of the human embodied soul and a specific animal located in the forest. Both parts are inseparable and symbiotic, mirroring each other's actions. Damage to or the loss of one affects the other. Each of these soul components plays a part in the nosology of sickness.

For the Yanomami, events surrounding sickness, various types of accidents, snakebites, and eventual death are not merely coincidences or random occurrences or the outcome of bad luck. These disturbances are considered to be the result of an offensive act committed by *hekura*. In this context, illness is seen as a general disruption of the micro-bodily and, by extension, macro-social equilibrium, and it is believed to be provoked by an intentional act of assault shamanism. On a micro-bodily level, a sick person may experience a range of symptoms depending on the nature of the malady, thus undergoing changes from being in a state of good health (*temi*) to being sick (*hariri*). In other words, sickness implies a total change of the state of the individual—from corporeal equilibrium to disequilibrium. Each case of sickness is unique despite certain commonalities that are manifested as clearly discernible symptoms, such as pain, shortness of breath, fever, or general malaise. At the same time, on the macro level, each case of individual sickness affects the social harmony of the whole group, whose security is suspended until the *shapori* eventually re-establishes the balance. Illness, in this sense, implies that something is wrong with the whole being and not just a particular part. It is not only a malfunction of a single person but also a disruption of the unified process of living for everyone.

In the Yanomami life-world, bodily and socio-cosmic disequilibrium erupts when something external invades the corporeal interiority and causes fever, pain, or death. In this instance, the *shapori*'s duty is to expel the intruder from the body—and the community—and, in doing so, to re-establish corporeal and social balance. Alternatively, illness or death results when soul-snatching *hekura*, such as Periporiwë (Moon) or Mothokariwë (Sun), seize and consume someone's *pei mɨ āmo*, with or without the *shapori*'s help. The cure consists of the *shapori* finding the lost *mɨ āmo* and inserting it back into the body (Cocco 1972: 403; Lizot 1999: 27). In order for the balance of life and harmony to be re-established, that which is foreign and disruptive must be removed or that which is missing must be brought back and restored to its proper place. The treatment of an individual person by the *shapori* is thus extended to an entire community as well as the whole cosmos.

An abrupt change of well-being can also be brought about through the manipulation of certain magical objects such as arrows or thorns, which are sent by enemy *shapori* for the purpose of damaging a person's *pei puhi*. This magical activity produces sharp pain and sometimes death. Ruweweriwë from Sheroana-theri explained to me that the pain produced by the tearing of the *pei puhi* commonly occurs in specific places in the body: the solar plexus (*shitikari*), the area just above the kidneys, the forehead, and sometimes the leg or foot. Through suction and vomiting, the *shapori* extracts the magic thorn sent by an enemy *shapori*. He then dispatches the object back to where it came from, customarily a distant Shamathari community or Mavaca or Sejal. Once the magic needle or arrow is expelled from the body, the *shapori*, with the help of his *hekura*, proceeds to 'repair' a person's damaged *pei puhi*.

Finally, sickness and death can also be inflicted through 'war sorcery', which is generally understood to involve certain ritual practices for the purpose of inflicting "misfortune, disease, destruction, or death" on an opponent (Farrer, this volume). The Yanomami generally recognize two lethal types of magical practices: *mayo hëri* and *ōka*. In order to effect harm, the malefactor in the first instance carefully collects earth bearing someone's footprint (*mayo*). This earth is then mixed with some herbs (*hëri*) and heated over hot flames while chanting is performed. *Shapori* say that this will cause a person to develop a fever and die.

Ōka sorcery is a technique of covert war magic that can sometimes trigger a real war. It involves the invocation of specific spells coupled with the use of a powder made from the poisonous *aroari* plant (*cyperus articulatis* or *cyperus corymbosus*) that is found primarily in the Siapa River region. The Shamathari are renowned as experts in this lethal magical practice. The *ōka* sorcerer travels on foot to a targeted community and blows *aroari* powder in the direction of a passer-by on the forest path, either from a distance or nearby through a blowpipe or from the palm of his hand. The victim of *ōka* experiences an inner heat that can be extinguished only by the superior fire of the shaman's *hekura* (Lizot 1985). The Yanomami claim that *ōka* sorcery almost certainly results in an agonizing death after a short period of time and that often not even the *shapori* can save the victim.

Case Studies

During my fieldwork I witnessed various successful and unsuccessful instances of malignant shamanistic activities, considered from the standpoint of both victims and perpetrators. These hostile acts involved soul theft, the use of various magical projectiles, and killing from a distance by strangling. For the purposes of this chapter, I will focus primarily on the last act by providing two complementary examples from the community of Sheroana-theri. In the first instance, the victim was a little boy from the same community who died as a result of a *hekura* attack executed by the Shamathari *shapori* from the distant community of Narimipiwei-theri. The second instance was a retaliatory magical assault on a boy from Narimipiwei-theri, carried out by Ruweweriwë, the chief *shapori* from Sheroana-theri. These two cases are complementary as they represent two distinct but interlinked examples of assault shamanism: the first from the victim's standpoint, the second from the perspective of the predator *shapori*.

One day, a young boy from Sheroana-theri suddenly became ill. His condition progressively deteriorated, and he died two days later. The *shapori's* diagnosis was that the Shamathari *shapori* from the community of Narimipiwei-theri had introduced *shawara* sickness during the boy's sleep and had finished him off days later. I first found out from the boy's mother that he was not well. She said that for the past two days her son had been complaining of pain in his abdomen and blood in his feces. The day before he died, I saw that the amount of blood in his feces had increased significantly. On the day of his death, as his mother held him in her arms, a red, jelly-like substance oozed from his anus. He did not suffer from diarrhea. Lying next to them on the ground were solid, dark-red feces and vomit. Moments before he died, the boy turned very pale. He screamed a few times and started looking around, his eyes full of fear. One of the *shapono* dwellers mentioned *hekura*. People started crying. To them he was already lost, for the situation had become extremely grave. As fate would have it, Ruweweriwë was away, taking part in a week-long fishing expedition on the Shanishani River. Moments before passing away, the boy opened his mouth, gasping for air in panic as his little body started twisting. Suddenly, his frightened look changed, and with eyes full of anger and in a deep adult voice he said: "Ya amishi" (I am thirsty). A second later, the fear and desperation were present again in his eyes. He called to his mother and father one last time before his chest stopped all movement.

A week after the above incident, Ruweweriwë performed an act of revenge by taking the life of a boy purportedly from the same community of Narimipiwei-theri. This example is hence from the perspective of the predator *shapori*, with the focus not on the victim but on the act of ritual killing itself. For this occasion, Ruweweriwë summoned the Moon *hekura* Periporiwë. After inhaling large doses of *epena*, he crouched and leaned forward, almost touching the ground with his forehead. His body suddenly started shaking and wobbling; it lost all its firmness and natural stability, resembling one big jelly-like mass. He then stood up, crossed his arms on his chest, and started rolling his eyeballs. This was the sign that Periporiwë had arrived, rising up from the ashes and being born again into this world through the *shapori*'s body. Periporiwë started slowly encircling the *shapono,* preying on his victim. After making the full circle, the *shapori* spoke in a child's voice, "Nape, nape ya amishi" (Mother, I am thirsty), while leaning against the house post. He then sat on the ground repeating the same phrase a few more times. The boy was obviously scared and confused, his breathing fast and shallow. He was looking around, touching his body in discomfort and calling his mother. The *shapori* then made a movement as if ripping his skin open with his hands. Then he placed what appeared (to us onlookers) to be an invisible rope around his own neck a few times before strangling himself with one energetic movement upward. His body dropped lifeless to the ground. He then got up, and a female voice started weeping: "Pushika, pushika" (My child). The boy had died, strangled by Periporiwë as his mother was crying for him.

Body Intrusion and the Dynamics of the Cosmic Flow

The above examples of combative shamanism demonstrate that magical practices and the accompanying social experience of violence, sickness, and death are first and foremost embodied practices (Farrer, this volume; Kapferer 1991, 2003), with the body being a locus of magical action involving the victim and several shamans. The primary power of Yanomami *shapori* is their ability to access the interiority of others' bodies with the help of their assisting *hekura,* whether for the purpose of healing or killing. When the *shapori*'s cosmic body is set in motion during a trance, the interiority of others' bodies 'opens up' and becomes externalized as it fuses with the intentionality of the *shapori*'s consciousness. In other words, during a healing or killing session, and with the help of his personal *hekura,* the *shapori* is capable of accessing human bodies: he enters bodies directly, as in the aforementioned cases of *hekura* attacks, or he detects and extracts from bodies an object of witchcraft or other invading *hekura*. In this way, the practicing *shapori* discovers in the victim a 'body fault' or an intruding *hekura,* or he himself becomes the intruder of another body. In the case of predatory shamanism, *shapori* prefer babies and small children as their potential victims rather than adults. Infants are easy targets as their souls are unstable and not yet fully formed; thus, the chances of a successful outcome are much higher.

In the same manner that defensive shamanistic activities involve two complementary phases of diagnosis and subsequent cure, undertaken with the assisting *hekura,* assault shamanism generally consists of two steps: surveillance of the terrain for the purpose of detecting the potential victim and the follow-up attack. In our second example, the *shapori* Ruweweriwë first undertook an ecstatic journey to the intended destination in order to locate the chosen victim (see fig. 5.4). Upon returning to the Sheroana-theri locale, he assumed the identity of the mighty *hekura* Periporiwë, whose specialty is eating children's delicate souls, and attacked a little boy. When I asked him to describe his journey, he replied that it is like looking at a photograph or a television screen (*noreshi*) in front of his eyes.

During the killing act, the somatic space of other people's bodies becomes accessible to the predator *shapori* in the same way that the interiority of the human body opens up to the *shapori* involved in the healing act. If the intruder into another's body is a *hekura/shapori*, when he is detected, the *shapori* who undertakes a countermeasure assumes the full identity of the intruding *shapori* by merging his *hekura* with the intruding one—in effect, becoming that *shapori*. In this instance, what follows is a direct clash between the two *shapori*, and their degree of experience and power often determines if the victim will live or die.

It is misleading to assume that the *shapori* always sends his *hekura* to kill, as this implies that they (the *hekura*) do the job for him, as appears to be the case with Sumatran *dukun* and their assisting *jin* (see Neidel, this volume). Instead, when the *shapori* sends his *hekura*, he *is* in fact that *hekura*. The ritual action thus takes place simultaneously at two different locations.[3] In my second example, although Ruweweriwë was physically present in Sheroana-theri, he invaded the victim's body while in a trance state as the cannibalistic Periporiwë, and his own body became possessed simultaneously by the victim. Not only was the frightened boy's death materialized in front of us, but also the victim's mother was crying through the *shapori* after the boy had allegedly died. At the moment of the boy's death, the *shapori*, who was strangling himself in front of us, also died or experienced the victim's death directly, as his lifeless body collapsed to the ground.

What motivates a shaman to commit an offensive act? The primary reasons are vengeance for a previous attack and competition among various shamans. It is evident that assault shamanism involves negative exchange and reciprocity. The *shapori* from the Upper Orinoco River region are engaged against their distant enemies in a perpetual cycle of retaliatory revenge and magical assaults that affects not only the competition among them but also the victims of their aggression. Thus, this 'supernatural warfare' involves not only individual fates but broader community relations as well. While offensive acts of assault shamanism are clearly part of hostile human intentionality motivated primarily by vengeance and rivalry, I argue that malignant shamanistic activities are also non-human acts. They are cosmic activities driven by the key attribute of the spirits that shamans embody—their compulsion to eat human flesh. In other words, although the Yanomami *shapori* intentionally engage in predatory acts for the purpose of inflicting harm and death, when they metamorphose into a jaguar or moon spirit during a trance, they are fully endowed with the characteristics of these cannibalistic spirit-beings.

When the *shapori* perform offensive acts due to the cannibalistic nature of meat-hungry (*naiki*) *hekura* spirits, this is then reflected in shamans' songs. For example, on one occasion during my fieldwork, Ruweweriwë was singing and thus calling the spirit of a vulture, Watupariwë, describing him in the song as dangerous and meat-hungry. During a ritual that same night, Ruweweriwë allegedly devoured a soul component of a girl from a distant community. On another occasion in Platanal, the chief *shapori* from Mahekoto-theri, Enano, was telling his spirit-helpers to get up from their bodily hammocks, announcing through song that the meat-hungry *hekura* Periporiwë had arrived and was angry, craving human flesh and refusing to leave. In order to appease him and to prevent him from snatching a soul of someone from his own community, Enano had to seize a soul from a distant village while in the guise of the same moon *hekura*. In order to maintain a cosmic balance, the *shapori* must satisfy the spirits' cravings; otherwise, they become a threat to his own community. In this way, the Yanomami *shapori* help to balance the predatory forces of the cosmos. In a similar manner, Whitehead (2002: 221) writes that *kanaimà* ritual killers of the Guyana highlands carry out sacrifices in order to provide "human nourishment" to appease the Lord Jaguar and satisfy his cravings. Behind this interchange of rivalry, power, and disempowerment is the universe, which is driven by the cyclic flow of vital force that swings between the processes of life and death, health and illness, equilibrium and disequilibrium.

Concluding Remarks: Shamanism and Culture Change

The destructive aspects of Yanomami shamanism are an indispensable part of their shamanistic complex. Various forms of hostile shamanistic activities and *hekura* attacks employed by the *shapori* are complementary to the socially integrative countermeasures used by the same *shapori* to heal sufferers or to save the lives of affected victims. The 'moral ambiguity' of Yanomami shamans—especially as it concerns hostile acts of magical assaults motivated by vengeance, jealousy, and competition for power and prestige—is the reason why the general categories of shaman and sorcerer overlap. In this sense, shamanism and assault sorcery, at least in the Yanomami case, represent an overlapping and interweaving process rather than strictly separated activities that reflect universal categories. The exception to this is the distinction between shamanism and *ōka* sorcery. While the Yanomami *shapori* can sometimes be a *ōka* sorcerer, the latter is not necessarily a shaman. *Ōka* does not require initiation and can be employed by anyone. The *ōka* sorcerer utilizes substances and spells, works in secret, and directly attacks members of enemy villages. After their killing raids, *ōka* are subjected to a specific purifying rite called *unokai*. Unlike *ōka* sorcerers, shamans use *hekura* powers overtly in their malicious magic attacks against distant communities, they have little or no direct contact with each other, and they do not need any purification after their malevolent activities (Lizot 1985). What both malicious shamanism and *ōka* sorcery have in common is their tendency to promote the continual need to retaliate, since each suspected death by either technique requires the settling of scores by the same means.

After the first permanent contacts with missionaries were established during the 1950s, the spread of previously unknown epidemics and health threats brought misery and multiple deaths to the Yanomami, and this, in turn, resulted in the general increase of sorcery accusations. Ferguson (1992, 1995) goes to the extreme, arguing that Yanomami warfare and, by extension, an increase in harmful magical activities came about due to the presence of and competition for metal tools and other manufactured goods. The population decline was primarily attributed to epidemics of diseases introduced by Westerners, which Yanomami identify as *shawara*. The magnitude of deaths from various epidemics led to an overall increase in sorcery accusations and intercommunal warfare, which, in turn, contributed further to population loss. During my fieldwork, Yanomami repeatedly attributed today's relatively small-sized contemporary communities, as compared with the larger communities of the past, to *ōka* sorcery, *hekura* attacks, and *shawara* sickness sent by hostile *shapori*. Conflicts between the various groups have had a particularly devastating effect since firearms were introduced to the Yanomami (see Ferguson 1992).

Destructive aspects of Yanomami shamanism and sorcery still persist in a contemporary post-contact situation of culture change. However, the general crisis has propelled some *shapori* to call for a cessation of traditional hostilities and for unification against a common outside threat. This is more prevalent in Brazil where the impact of the national society on the Yanomami population has been much more severe than in Venezuela, due to differences in government policies (Albert 1988). In the wake of tragic events that brought multiple deaths and misery to Brazilian Yanomami, Davi Kopenawa, a shaman and an activist from the Toototobi region in Brazil, emerged as a new prophetic leader, warning about the threat of a malicious *shawara* smoke that will cause the sky to collapse and bring about the end of the world (Kopenawa and Albert 2013). Aspiring to unite all Yanomami against a common peril, Kopenawa sought to create a sense of pan-Yanomami identity. A combination of his shamanistic knowledge of the cosmos and familiarity with the Christian doctrine prompted him to act on behalf of all Yanomami by creating a powerful synthetic cosmo-shamanic discourse composed of Western concepts blended with Yanomami mythology vis-à-vis the impending danger.

Continuing to speak out, Kopenawa particularly urges all remaining *shapori* to stop their bellicose activities and unite the powers of their *hekura* in order to prevent the sky from collapsing, for the shamans are the only ones who are capable of preventing this cosmic catastrophe. As long as there are living shamans, the sky will remain on high, and the symbolic distance between the two cosmic levels will be maintained. The destruction of the world parallels the decline in shamanism and any further possibility of the manifestation of the cosmos. Without shamans, the symbolic order collapses as the sky crashes to earth and the experience of a differentiated cosmos comes to an end. Consequently, "[t]he basis for life in this world as it is known ... no longer holds" (Sullivan 1988: 45). Within the overall cosmological matrix, shamans, in this sense, are responsible for preserving life and maintaining the existential balance as much as they are involved in taking life.

In the context of post-culture contact, the meaning and content of sorcery, witchcraft, and assault shamanism show historical change. Assault sorcery and hostile shamanistic activities are embedded in a process that reveals how community relations have changed over time. The transformation of society is reflected in the transformation of sorcery. This change is concurrent with the emergence of pan-Yanomami identity and more and more frequent calls to put an end to belligerent activities against each other and to unite against threatening forms of new magic, in which the global peril overshadows local conflicts.

Željko Jokić is Visiting Fellow at the School of Archaeology and Anthropology, Australian National University. Formerly, he worked as Research Assistant at the Australian Institute of Aboriginal and Torres Strait Islander Studies and as Anthropologist Investigator at the Amazonian Centre for Research and Control of Tropical Diseases in Venezuela, where he also worked as a Consultant for the Onchocerciasis Elimination Program for the Americas. His main research interests include indigenous health and medical anthropology and the philosophical foundations of social theory and phenomenology.

Notes

1. Hereafter I will use masculine pronouns when referring to Yanomami shamans because they are predominantly male.
2. Shamathari is a collective name for a group of interrelated Yanomami communities that have little or no physical contact with the Yanomami from the Orinoco River area.
3. The phenomenon of bilocation is common to shamanism. Rasmussen (1979), for example, writes that during the shamanistic séance, the Inuit shaman and a female Sea Spirit were simultaneously in the house and at the bottom of the sea.

References

Albert, Bruce. 1988. "La fumée du métal: Histoire et représentations du contact chez les Yanomami (Brésil)." *L'Homme* 28, no. 106–107: 87–119.
Alès, Catherine. 2000. "Anger as a Marker of Love: The Ethic of Conviviality among the Yanomami." Pp. 133–151 in *The Anthropology of Love and Anger*, ed. Joanna Overing and Alan Passes. London: Routledge.
Borofsky, Robert. 2005. *Yanomami: The Fierce Controversy and What We Can Learn from It*. Berkeley: University of California Press.
Brown, Michael F. 1988. "Shamanism and Its Discontents." *Medical Anthropology Quarterly* 2, no. 2: 102–120.
Chagnon, Napoleon A. 1968. *Yanomamö: the Fierce People*. New York: Holt, Rinehart and Winston.
Chagnon, Napoleon A. 1992. *Yanomamö: The Last Days of Eden*. New York: Harcourt Brace Jovanovich.
Chagnon, Napoleon A., and Tim Asch, dirs. 1973. *Magical Death*. Documentary film, 29 min. Distributed by Documentary Educational Resources.
Chiappino, Jean. 1995. "El Coloso Yanomami Frente al 'Nuevo' El Dorado. Representaciones del Ser Humano y del Medio Ambiente: Un Envite de la Participación Comunitaria al Desarrollo Regional." Pp. 175–204 in *Amazonas Modernidad en Tradicion*. Caracas: GTZ/CAIAH-SADA AMAZONAS.
Cocco, Luis. 1972. *Iyewei Theri: Quince Años Entre los Yanomamos*. Caracas: Edicion Escuela Tecnica Popular 'Don Bosco'.

Crocker, Christopher. 1985. *Vital Souls: Bororo Cosmology, Natural Symbolism, and Shamanism*. Tucson: University of Arizona Press.
de Barandiarán, Daniel. 1965. "Mundo Espiritual y Shamanismo Sanema." *Antropologica* 15 (December): 1–28.
Evans-Pritchard, E. E. [1937] 1977. *Witchcraft, Oracles, and Magic Among the Azande*. Oxford: Clarendon Press.
Farrer, D. S. 2009. *Shadows of the Prophet: Martial Arts and Sufi Mysticism*. Dordrecht: Springer.
Ferguson, R. Brian. 1992. "A Savage Encounter: Western Contact and the Yanomami War Complex." Pp. 199–227 in *War in the Tribal Zone: Expanding States and Indigenous Warfare*, ed. R. Brian Ferguson and Neil L. Whitehead. Santa Fe, NM: School of American Research Press.
Ferguson, R. Brian. 1995. *Yanomami Warfare: A Political History*. Santa Fe, NM: School of American Research Press.
Goetz, Inga S. de. 1969. *Uriji Jami! Life and Belief of the Forest Waika in the Upper Orinoco*. Caracas: Cultural Association Humboldt.
Hugh-Jones, Stephen. 1996. "Shamans, Prophets, Priests, and Pastors." Pp. 32–75 in *Shamanism, History, and the State*, ed. Nicholas Thomas and Caroline Humphrey. Ann Arbor: University of Michigan Press.
Jokić, Željko. 2003. "Hekura Mou: A Phenomenological Analysis of Yanomami Shamanism." PhD diss., University of Sydney.
Jokić, Željko. 2006. "Cosmo-genesis or Transformation of the Human Body into a Cosmic Body in Yanomami Shamanistic Initiation." *Shaman: Journal of the International Society for Shamanistic Research* 14, no. 1–2: 19–39.
Jokić, Željko. 2015. *The Living Ancestors: Shamanism, Cosmos and Cultural Change among the Yanomami of the Upper Orinoco*. New York: Berghahn Books.
Kapferer, Bruce. 1991. *A Celebration of Demons: Exorcism and the Aesthetics of Healing in Sri Lanka*. 2nd ed. Bloomington: Indiana University Press.
Kapferer, Bruce, ed. 2003. *Beyond Rationalism: Rethinking Magic, Witchcraft and Sorcery*. New York: Berghahn Books.
Kopenawa, Davi, and Bruce Albert. 2013. The Falling Sky: Words of a Yanomami Shaman. Trans. Nicholas Elliott and Alison Dundy. Cambridge, MA: Belknap Press of Harvard University Press.
Lizot, Jacques. 1976. *The Yanomami in the Face of Ethnocide*. Copenhagen: International Secretariat of IWGIA.
Lizot, Jacques. 1985. *Tales of the Yanomami*. Cambridge: Cambridge University Press.
Lizot, Jacques. 1994. "Words in the Night: The Ceremonial Dialogue—One Expression of Peaceful Relationships among the Yanomami." Pp. 213–240 in *The Anthropology of Peace and Nonviolence*, ed. Leslie E. Sponsel and Thomas A. Gregor. London: Lynne Rienner.
Lizot, Jacques. 1999. *Cosmovisión, Enfermedad y Muerte entre los Yanomami*. Unpublished report for the Centro Amazónico de Investigación y Enfermedades Tropicales, Puerto Ayacucho.
Rasmussen, Knud. 1979. "A Shaman's Journey to the Sea Spirit." Pp. 308–311 in *Reader in Comparative Religion: An Anthropological Approach*, ed. William A. Lessa and Evon Z. Vogt. New York: Harper & Row.
Sponsel, Leslie E. 1998. "Yanomami: An Arena of Conflict and Aggression in the Amazon." *Aggressive Behavior* 24, no. 2: 97–122.
Sullivan, Lawrence E. 1988. *Icanchu's Drum: An Orientation to Meaning in South American Religions*. New York: Macmillan.

Tierney, Patrick. 2000. *Darkness in El Dorado: How Scientists and Journalists Devastated the Amazon*. New York: W. W. Norton.
Wagner, Roy. 1991. "The Fractal Person." Pp. 159–173 in *Big Men and Great Men: Personifications of Power in Melanesia*, ed. Maurice Godelier and Marilyn Strathern. Cambridge: Cambridge University Press.
Whitehead, Neil L. 2002. *Dark Shamans: Kanaimà and the Poetics of Violent Death*. Durham, NC: Duke University Press.
Whitehead, Neil L., and Robin Wright, eds. 2004a. *In Darkness and Secrecy: The Anthropology of Assault Sorcery and Witchcraft in Amazonia*. Durham, NC: Duke University Press.
Whitehead, Neil L., and Robin Wright. 2004b. "Introduction: Dark Shamanism." Pp. 1–20 in Whitehead and Wright 2004a.
Wilbert, Johannes. 1963. *Indios de la Región Orinoco-Ventuari*. Caracas: Fundación La Salle.
Wilbert, Johannes. 1972. "Tobacco and Shamanistic Ecstasy among the Warao Indians of Venezuela." Pp. 55–83 in *Flesh of the Gods: The Ritual Use of Hallucinogens*, ed. Peter T. Furst. New York: Praeger.
Wilbert, Johannes. 2004. "The Order of Dark Shamans among the Warao." Pp. 21–51 in Whitehead and Wright 2004a.

Chapter 6

CHANTS OF RE-ENCHANTMENT
Chamorro Spiritual Resistance to Colonial Domination

D. S. Farrer and James D. Sellmann

> That night I shot down an American B-52 bomber over Guam. I don't know what possessed me.
> — Leonard Iriarte, from fieldnotes

When religion, magic, and sorcery enter, or prepare to enter, the battlefield or site of operations, they take on an embodied presence beyond the casting of spells and prayers. This chapter weaves together the disparate and arcane threads of war magic and warrior religion that persist from ancient times into the ethnographic present to show that war magic and warrior religion are ongoing embodied cultural positions that reflect and respond to economic, military, and colonial conditions. A site of strategic US Navy and Air Force military bases, Guam now prepares for impending military build-up. War magic and warrior religion serve as lenses that enable the study of colonial domination where the battle lines fault across military, economic, and political frames toward cultural fronts. Combining historical and philosophical investigations with ethnographic observations of a Chamorro chant group, I Fanlalai'an, this chapter locates war

Notes for this chapter begin on page 143.

magic and warrior religion as strategies of resistance and of colonial oppression. In the process, a Weberian analysis of re-enchantment explains the forms cultural resistance takes to oppression and offers an alternative narrative device to discourses of cultural survival and reinvention (Benjamin 1996, 2014; Scott 1990).

In his informative discussion of Micronesian religion and magic, Glenn Petersen (2009) offers the following definitions for the terms 'magic' and 'sorcery'. Magic, he writes, refers to "practices and techniques (usually in the form of spells) employed by individuals to achieve one sort or another of relatively benign control over either the supernatural realm, nature (especially to enhance the growth of local crops or manage local weather), or other people (particularly in the form of 'love magic' meant to cause one person to become enamored of another) ... By 'sorcery', on the other hand, I mean the use of basically similar techniques in the service of negative or malevolent ends, either to inflict damage on the possessions, crops, or health of others or, in some cases, to kill them" (ibid.: 197).

War magic and warrior religion challenge such standard individualized meanings. They need to be regarded as cognitive, embodied, and practice-based forms of resistance to domination (Scott 1990). At the same time, they are methods through which power and authority may be imposed, in this case colonial authority via Catholicism. War magic and warrior religion do feature malevolent and benevolent spells and prayers, but the practices can only be understood when considered within the context of the social, historical, and cultural frameworks of an overarching 'battle for hearts and minds'—in other words, when situated within the context of ongoing enchantment, disenchantment and re-enchantment (Benjamin 1996; Elkins and Morgan 2009; Farrer 2009; Graham 2007; Ritzer 2005; Weber 1946).[1]

In *Shadows of the Prophet*, Farrer (2009: 39) has argued that magic should be regarded in three frames: (1) cognitive, informed by myth, perception, and belief; (2) performative (liminal ritual being especially apposite for the release of mystical forces); and (3) embodied. Gell's (1999) notion of the 'technology of enchantment' and the 'enchantment of technology' employed in the anthropology of art is augmented here with perspectives drawn from the anthropology of performance, to offer the notions of the 'performance of enchantment' and the 'enchantment of performance'. The performance of enchantment refers to *techniques du corps* (body techniques) honed to such a degree through practice, rehearsal, and performance that their execution takes on a magical appearance and creates an uncanny effect upon the audience (Mauss 1979). Correspondingly, the methods and procedures used to draw power from the unseen or sacred realm are referred to as the enchantment of performance (see also Farrer 2008: 32; 2012). This chapter puts the framework of war magic and warrior religion within a theoretical rubric of performance, enchantment, and re-enchantment and sets up a discussion of spiritual resistance against the colonial territorialization of Guam. From the perspective of Chamorro chant, or the art-with-agency-that-wants-to-survive, the Chamorro recovery and reinvention of magical practices signify an advance rather than a cultural regression.

Guam and Chamorro Culture

Guam, now often referred to by the indigenous people as Guåhan, is the largest island in Micronesia.[2] Located at 13.5 degrees north latitude and 144.7 degrees east longitude, it is the southernmost isle of 15 in the chain of Mariana Islands on the edge of the western Pacific near the eastern side of the Philippine Sea. The indigenous people of the Marianas link themselves to an ancient Chamorro culture that extended throughout the archipelago, reaching from Guam to Uracas Island at 20.5 degrees north latitude. Although not all of the islands were inhabited, they were all used to acquire resources.

On 6 March 1521, the Portuguese explorer Ferdinand Magellan landed on Guam and promptly took the archipelago for Spain, naming it Islas de las Velas Latinas (Islands of the Lateen Sails). After the loss of a skiff, Magellan then renamed it, somewhat ironically, Islas de los Ladrones (Islands of the Thieves) and proceeded with a party of forty men to burn down 40 or 50 houses and kill seven men in the recovery of the skiff (Lessa 1975: 16). If the Spanish had had an archaeologist on board, however, they might have chosen Isla de los Muertos Antiguos (Island of the Ancient Dead) as the name for Guam, since its beaches can be likened to pincushions dotted with human remains, some up to 2,500 years old (Carson 2011; DeFant 2008).

Issues of the reliability, validity, and accuracy of historical and anthropological materials about Guam are controversial subjects (Carter et al. 2005; Cunningham 1992; Fritz [1904] 2001; Hattori 2004; Lessa 1975; Rogers 1995; Russell 1998; Thompson 1969; Underwood 1985).[3] Archaeologist Mike Carson's (2010: 1627) report, using "new radiocarbon chronology for the Ritidian archaeological site in Guam, verifies that the earliest human presence on Guam was around 1460–1300 cal. BC."[4] Previously, Laura Thompson (1969: 54–55), basing her analysis on an examination of Hans G. Hornbostel's 1920s research and artifact collection, speculated that the taller and more technologically sophisticated people, who used *latte* stones in their constructions, invaded the original inhabitants around 1,200 years ago and established themselves as the ruling class (*matua*).[5] Precise details remain to be uncovered, yet no doubt the later settlement was also Austronesian (Vilar et al. 2013). As Horridge (1995: 154) says in *The Austronesians*, "the seaways were open, once explored," and there was nothing to stop people from sailing all over the place.

An iconic feature of the Mariana Islands is the *latte* stone, the probable foundation for houses (*guma'*), including men's houses and outbuildings for canoes (Morgan 1988; Waterson 1997: 7). Employed for Chamorro construction and habitation from approximately 900 to 1700 CE (Carson 2012b), the *latte* stone is a toadstool-like structure comprised of two pieces of limestone—a semi-circular capstone (*tåsa*) that rests upon an upstanding pillar (*haligi*). The largest array of *latte* stones was used to construct the Taga House—a building that stood 15 feet high—on the island of Tinian to the north of Guam. The population of the Mariana Islands during the *latte* period, as with all topics on ancient Guam, is a subject of ongoing debate. Below we quote Carson at length to demonstrate the tentativeness of any attempt to make pronouncements on ancient Guam civilizations:

> [T]he archaeological evidence shows a large-scale change in material culture starting with the *latte* period. The reason for this major change could be a new population of people, but it also could be internal development. I would argue that it was due to a mixture of new people, materials, and ideas. It is marked by the appearance of *latte* stones as house structures, along with large coarse pottery, stone mortar-pestle complex, introduction of rice, and intrusion of rats ... The *latte* period also was when the smaller northern islands in the Marianas first were settled. The larger islands in the south were settled for a few thousand years previously. This evidence would suggest a larger number of people in the region after AD 900–1000 ... Anyway, I would hesitate to say anything definite about a population replacement per se. Rather, I would emphasize inter-island contacts and communications, wherein the Mariana Islands (and other island groups) saw a mix and flow of people, materials, and ideas over time. One critical time certainly was at the beginning of the *latte* period AD 900–1000.[6]

Leonard Z. Iriarte, a Guam chant leader, whose contributions we shall begin to address shortly, responded to Thompson's point above as follows: "We are fed up with hearing that only the ancient Chamorros can tell us anything about the present." This comment expresses local irritation over the historical cliché that Chamorro culture was wiped out by the Spanish conquest and mass Filipino migration to the islands. Despite the efforts of Spanish colonialism to destroy the Chamorro culture and the early American colonial ban against speaking the language, Chamorro continued to be passed down through centuries of matrilineal practices (although fluent speakers are now primarily found among the elders). Traditional Chamorro dances have disappeared, but they are in the process of being reinvented, often with recourse to Hawaiian and other Polynesian dances—perhaps becoming products of 'creating the past', as Keesing (2000) suggests (but see also Trask 2000). Further, it is accepted that most Chamorro clans today bear the surnames of Spanish, European, Chinese, Japanese, and a plethora of other ancestors, as evidenced by names such as Cruz, Calvo, Hattori, Okada, Sgambelluri, and Underwood. Nevertheless, the Chamorro persist as an ethnic, cultural, and linguistic entity (Diaz 2010; Judy Flores 2004). Ongoing studies among the contemporary Chamorros draw from and reflect upon archaeological and historical research concerning the so-called ancient Chamorros, and these combined understandings fuel the process of Chamorro re-enchantment. Local re-enchantment exhibits qualities that range from carefully researched indigenous materials to outright cultural plagiarism, in addition to the occasional New Age influence (Farrer 2009: 37–38; Prince and Riches 2001).

Iriarte leads a Chamorro chant group, I Fanlalai'an, whose mission is to define Chamorro culture.[7] According to Iriarte, the chant (*lålai*) is the most respected form of Chamorro artistic expression; chants preserve information and facilitate the remembrance of past events. Significantly, both the words in chants and the chanting of words are magical. The cultural revitalization of the Chamorro people is considered essential to ensure their cultural continuity in the face of American colonialism. In 2010, the then governor of Guam proposed that the indigenous name Guåhan should replace the Americanized name Guam. For Iriarte, who has been compiling a lexicon of indigenous non-Spanish Chamorro words for over 12 years, Guåhan does not simply mean "a place that has (something of value)." Guåhan might also mean "we have a (perceived) threat." This was said in regard to an impending US military build-up. According to a report in the *Pacific Daily News*, "[a]bout 8,600 Marines and their 9,000 dependents will be relocating from Okinawa in Japan to Guam in coming years" (Matthews 2010). Due to a range of factors including local protests, however, the build-up has been considerably reduced and delayed. When asked about the possibility of independence for Guam, Iriarte said that it would be a good thing, provided that "Guam is [recognized as] the capital of Micronesia ... the worst thing that could possibly happen to us [is] what happened to Hawaii as that would just further disenfranchise the island."

The term 'magic' is loaded with pejorative connotations and requires qualification. In the Chamorro language, *åtte* means 'magic', 'trick', or 'stratagem'. Iriarte considers *åtte* as the root word of *latte* and regards the *latte* sites as sacred burial places of great magical power. In this context, magic does not denote a stage show, sleight of hand, or other form of deception, illusion, or trick. Rather, it is used to refer to beliefs and practices that are understood to be an effective and warranted means to obtain desired results (Swain and Trompf 1995: 147). Magic, then, is looked on as a hybrid form of proto-science, medicine (*åmot*), and religion. Such beliefs and practices (*hinengge*) are used to cure or solve problems and conflicts brought on by people or the environment. These include illness (*malångu*), famine, and natural disasters, such as floods, typhoons, storms (*goyof*), earthquakes, and tsunamis, as well as internal and external social conflicts or disputes (*inaguaguat*). When social conflict escalates to a serious degree of violence (*takmomyon*),[8] such violence is referred to as war (*mumu*).

Ancient Chamorro Cosmology

The term 'ancient Chamorro' is used here to refer to the indigenous inhabitants of the Mariana Islands, known as *taotao håya* and *gihaya*. In Sellmann's terms, the Micronesian and Chamorro cosmologies are not monisms. Monism proposes that the world is composed of one material substance or spiritual force. According to this theory, plurality—the many—is either an illusion or reducible to 'the One'. The Micronesian and Chamorro worldviews are not dualisms: the opposing forces are not separate. In the Micronesian non-dual worldview, which may have originated in Southeast Asia, opposites interact, interconnect, and interpenetrate into and through each other. Life and death are intimately interconnected, and this is particularly true in Chamorro culture.

All people discover that life leads to and terminates in death, but Americans (Amerikånu or, in the Hawaiian terminology, *haole*) may find it difficult to recognize that death (*finatai*) or the dead (*måtai*) support life here in this world. In dualistic fashion, many Westerners expect either an afterlife that is very different from this one or no afterlife at all, depending on their degree of disenchantment. In part, the non-dual worldview explains why for ancient or pre-modern Micronesians, and for the ancient Chamorros, the deceased ancestors were considered to be part of the present world and members of the living community. For the ancient cultures, the spirits of the deceased (*taotao mo'na* or *mananiti*)[9] did not leave this world for another, transcendent world beyond. This is particularly the case for the ancient Chamorros, who kept the skulls of their ancestors in their homes and made offerings to them on certain occasions. The ancient peoples of Micronesia attempted to live in harmony with and maintain a balance between the interactions of opposing forces—the high/up/right/east/south/male and the low/down/left/west/north/female (Alkire 1972).[10] The male and female generative forces (*manaman*, in Chuukese) constitute a hylozoistic (living) world (Oliver 1989: 136). These forces procreate the next generation; likewise, the cosmic male and female forces commingle and generate the sky world above and the island-sea world below. These are not two separate, distinct worlds—on the contrary, like male and female, they intermingle. In pre-modern Micronesian and Chamorro religion, the spirits or gods are either forces of nature or apotheosized ancestors. Their spirit-powers are localized and limited (Hezel 1995).

The Micronesian identity is rooted in a person's lineage, and hence intrinsic family and clan relationships are factors related to land possession and occupation on Guam (Petersen 2009: 22, 76–77). It is through their ancestors that living people connect to the environment. The lineage establishes people's totemic relation to the fish in the ocean, the land, the creatures on the island, and the stars in the sky. The world is alive, and in it humans are understood to share kinship relations with natural objects or animals while taking part in regulated behavioral practices associated with totems (Fischer 1957). Instead of rigid, structured belief systems, the Micronesian world is based on a rigid, structured family-social system. Relationships of interdependency and exchange define who and what a person is—identity does not hinge on a person's abstract beliefs about the world, the state, or God. The sky world is a continuation of this world with correlations between the gods and the forces of nature. There is an exchange system between the gods or ancestor spirits and humans, and in many ways the afterlife is a continuation of this life.

The non-dual perspective of the Chamorro people is further seen in the journal of Fray Juan Pobre de Zamora, who visited the nearby island of Rota in 1602. He relates an exchange that took place between his friend Sancho and some Chamorro elders. Sancho asked who had made the heavens, the earth, and the ocean (see Driver 1993: 23). From a European (also enchanted, although dualistic) perspective, Sancho expected the elders to say that God, the First Cause and Prime Mover, had created the world. The Chamorros, however, thought the question was foolish. They replied that they themselves make the heavens by looking at them, the earth by tilling the fields, and the ocean by fishing and sailing on it. Expecting a causal answer, Sancho considered their response to be foolish. But the Chamorros had a different worldview: they understood that things have value and meaning when humans engage and work them. The object perceived depends on the perceiving subject to be the kind of thing it is, and the subject, in turn, is construed, at least in part, by standing in relationship with the object. The subject and the object are intertwined in a non-dual relationship that gives rise to a form of 'enchanted rationality'.

The concept of the 'center' plays an important role in the Micronesian non-dual worldview. Micronesian cosmology is organized around the focal point of a center: the interaction and interpenetration of the bipolar opposites are harmonized by maintaining balance at the center. This is especially true of Micronesian navigation techniques. The navigator (*fa'ulos*) must continually negotiate his course from the center of the star compass as his position changes (Alkire 1972: 489). The ancient Chamorros believed that Guåhan was the center of the world, and Fouha Rock (also known as Creation Point) was their *axis mundi* (García [1683] 2004: 173). Possibly, like most Pacific Islanders, they viewed the world as a flat disk covered by the sky world, like an upside-down bowl (Goodenough 1986). A paradisiacal afterlife was to be lived either in the sky world or in an underworld. Within this cosmology there were 'currents' or passageways that connected the underworld, this world, and the sky world.

After gaining some understanding of Micronesian cosmology, a contemporary reader can begin to acknowledge that the use of magic in the ancient Pacific is not just a misguided appeal to serve a fallacious cause, as it is usually presented to be. In the non-dual worldview, objects and people take on extraordinary powers based on either their direct contact with certain people, places, and things or their indirect, correlated connection with certain people, places, and things. In the non-dual cosmology the pairs of opposites correlate with each other based on the perceived energy field generated by each thing. Day attracts evening; life attracts death. By understanding and manipulating the energy fields of things and people, the ancient arts of making (magic) were constructed to assist humans in achieving specific goals, contributing to the value of their lives.

Chamorro Warfare and War Magic

In the early accounts of European contact, the ancient Chamorro people are depicted as naked (see Lessa 1975: 120–123). The men and women wore their hair long, and the women may have blackened their teeth and bleached their hair blonde (ibid.: 125). Iconic pre-contact rock art, in the form of pictographs and petroglyphs, survives to this day. One of the most famous depictions is that of a former chief called Gådao, a man renowned for his tremendous physical strength (Heathcote 2006). Gigantism is a common feature in the Chamorro myths. Legend has it, for example, that the ancestral spirit (*taotao mo'na*) Gåtos traveled with his soldiers to a river that was impossible to ford, so he extended his penis and they walked across on that.

The Chamorro arsenal consisted of short spears (*tokcha'*), thrown spears (*tokcha' dåggao*), clubs (*dåmang*), the sling (*atupat*), sling stones (*acho' atupat*), and fireballs. Spear points were often made from human tibia. When metal was introduced, the machete became the preferred weapon. The Chamorros dug trenches and built walls for both offensive and defensive maneuvers. According to historical sources, a Chinese Buddhist trader named Choco Sangley, who was shipwrecked in a storm in 1688, was living among the Chamorros when the Jesuit priest Father Diego Luis de San Vitores entered the Mariana Islands. When the Chamorros engaged the Spaniards and their muskets, Choco designed a movable shield to protect the Chamorros from the Spanish musket balls (García ([1683] 2004; Matsuda 2012: 118).[11]

The ancient specialists, who served as medicinal practitioners, shamans, diviners, and sorcerers, were known as a *makåhna* (*macana*, alternate spelling) or *kåkahna* (*kahuna*, in Polynesian). Both types of practitioners manipulated *kåhna* (spiritual energy or *mana*), possibly with the assistance of spirit-familiars or spirit-friends. *Kåhna* resides within everything and affects or animates all living and dead entities. The *makåhna* (witch) and *kåkahna* (sorcerer), who may have been male or female, could control the weather, especially the rain; bring or prevent storms; destroy the harvests or make them bountiful; and attract or drive away the fish. To some degree sanctioned by the community, the *makåhna*, who underwent a period of apprenticeship under a master, could employ their power intentionally to do harm. Conversely, the *kåkahna* (lit., 'one who possesses *kåhna*') inherited their power. A sorcerer would employ the skulls of deceased ancestors when enacting their spells, prophecy, and divination (*påhot*) (García [1683] 2004: 173–174).[12] García (ibid.: 226) relates how the skulls were appealed to in order to bring rain (*malåñan uchan*). After a corpse (*måtai*) had decomposed, the Chamorros would exhume it and remove the skull, which was kept in a woven basket in the deceased person's house (*guma'*). Ancient Chamorro religion centered upon ancestor veneration. Before people engaged in important activities such as warfare, travel, planting, harvesting, and fishing, offerings were made to their ancestors' skulls, in an attempt to receive the ancestors' permission, protection, and assistance. According to the accounts of San Vitores, the ancient Chamorros believed that an ancestor's spirit (*aniti* or *anite*) survived death (ibid.: 173–174, 226).

Drawing on the 'living' power of their ancestors, the ancient Chamorros were able to build confidence and courage. The skulls reminded them not only of their ancestors but more importantly of their ancestors' courage, skill, and battle techniques. The power, protection, and assistance of the ancestors were sought in war, and the Chamorros deployed their ancestors' skulls when they entered into battle (*mumu*). The skulls were used to instill fear in enemies by showing them that an ancestor accompanied every warrior on the battlefield.

García ([1683] 2004: 240, 243) recounts battle scenes in which skulls were deployed. One account relates how on 11 September 1671, two thousand Chamorros attacked 31 Spanish soldiers stationed in a church. For eight days and nights, the Chamorros showered the soldiers with sling stones (*acho' atupat*) with such force that the stones broke through the church's roof. Describing the clash, García adds: "They [the Chamorros] also dug earthworks to protect themselves from the sallies of our soldiers, who were not content to fight within their fortifications. But the barbarians, seeing that the Spaniards destroyed their work, took counsel with their *macanas* [*makåhna*] and commended their trenches to the devil in an explicit pact, placing in them the skulls of their deceased" (ibid.: 240). However, after the trenches were overrun and the skulls taken and destroyed, the Chamorros sued for peace: "Finally, on October 20 [1671], the enemy hurled himself at our enclosure. Our men made a sally with such courage that in the shortest interval they put the enemy to flight, destroyed the earthworks, cast the skulls on the ground, and trampled on them ... That terrified them to such a degree ... they came with great humility to beg forgiveness, peace, and mercy" (ibid.: 242–243).

Such was the power of the ancestors that if they allowed their position to be overrun, then the living accepted the defeat as inevitable. The Chamorros did not merely surrender to the Spanish; they surrendered to their ancestors. After San Vitores was killed, the Spanish moved the Chamorros who lived on the northern islands into camps on Guam, initiating a 30-year war from 1670–1700. As Hattori (2004: 91) points out, at the time of the post-conquest 1710 census conducted by the Freycinet expedition, only 3,539 Chamorros survived—1,867 males and 1,672 females—out of an original population estimated to number from a low of 40,000 to a high of 100,000 people. It would seem that the ancient Chamorro culture, along with the way of the *makåhna* and *kåkahna*, had come to an end. Nevertheless, the Spanish/Catholic plan to annihilate Chamorro culture was by no means entirely successful. Despite intermarriage with Spanish, Filipinos, and Mexicans, the language survived (Howells 1973: 247–248).

Based on the above accounts, it is clear that the ancient Chamorros did employ war magic in their domestic battles and in warfare against the Spanish. Likewise, across Micronesia people resorted to magic and war magic to obtain desired results. Moreover, the use of love potions has persisted into the present day (Caughey 1977; Young et al. 1997). The island of Yap was once seen as the seat of a great kingdom ruled by magical power (Lessa 1950). The Chuuk (Truk) specialist in combat tactics, the *itang*, employs magical charms and potions (actual poisons) to subdue an enemy (Caughey 1977). The medicine men and women of Pohnpei also employ magical formulas (Riesenberg 1948). In this regard, Micronesia offers many prospects for future studies of both ancient and contemporary uses of magic. On Guam, despite the apparent disappearance of the *makåhna* and *kåkahna* as such, enchanted Chamorro beliefs and practices persist. Indigenous medicine enjoys a popular following. Here the *suruhånu* and *suruhåna* (male and female herb doctors) attract local followers who appeal to them for remedies against mysterious illnesses that resist or baffle Western medical treatment.

Ancestral Ghosts: *Taotao Mo'na*

The Chamorro *taotao mo'na* (lit., 'people of before') are ubiquitous on Guam, prevalent in desolate places, remote beach areas, the limestone forest, the 'boonies',[13] graveyards, karst caves with water in them, and deserted houses (Jayne Flores 2005: 20). *Taotao mo'na* are regarded as the spirits of the ancestors and are perceived to be good or evil. Benign *taotao mo'na* may become the familiars or spirit-helpers (*ga'chong*) of the indigenous healers (Tenorio Rodriguez 2004). Malevolent *taotao mo'na* (*chátante*) are regarded as demons. Usually invisible to adults, *taotao mo'na* are more often seen by children. Strange and bizarre occurrences, hauntings, poltergeist activity, misfortune, bad luck, illness, and death may all be attributed to the presence of a *taotao mo'na*. Punishments may be exacted for moral infringements; for example, people must not enter the forest without first asking the spirits for permission (*gågao nina'siña*). Unexpected or inexplicable bruises and welts result from the victim being pinched (*dine'on*). On Guam, the *taotao mo'na* are believed to inhabit the banyan trees (*Ficus benghalensis*). Farmers and developers strip the land to the bare earth yet leave the banyan trees intact.[14] If a *taotao mo'na* haunts a family, a Catholic priest (*påle'*) may be called to the house in order to exorcise the spirit through a simple ceremony. The family forms a circle, holding hands, and prays together with the priest, who sprinkles holy water upon the premises.

On Guam it is sometimes suggested that the Spanish conquistadores introduced the legend of ancestral ghosts (originally encountered on their travels through Southeast Asia) in order to induce fear in the colonized peoples and inhibit their travel across the island—a tactic of psychological warfare that accorded with *reducción*, the Spanish policy of control.[15] In addition, the Chamorros were banned from taking to the sea in their fast skiffs (*såhyan*), which could easily outpace the Spanish craft on the open water. The local fear of *taotao mo'na*, however, is of indigenous origin and may derive from the notion that traveling upon the land of a different clan exposed the traveler to the ancestral spirits of that clan. In any case, the Catholic Church does not dismiss belief in the indigenous spirits; rather, it promotes them, if inadvertently, through its efforts to assist in their eradication or pacification by exorcism (*pugao anite*), using holy water, prayer, the Bible, sacred talismans, relics, and other means. The promotion of a heightened fear of the unseen is a strategic form of war magic and warrior religion commonly utilized by invading European colonialists.

Fear of the spirits is of course linked to the fear of death, whether from warfare, natural disasters, earthquakes, typhoons, or contagion (Hertz 1907). Introduced diseases, such as smallpox, to which the Chamorros had little immunity, could motivate people to seek protection from the power of Christ and His holy representatives, the priests. San Vitores, the 'master priest' (*må'gas påle'*), introduced Catholicism to Guam in 1668 (García [1683] 2004) and continued to proselytize until his murder in 1672.[16] In his missionary zeal to protect the wider community from the contaminants of sin and to help the sick, assist the dying, and save the damned, San Vitores found two methods especially useful to convert the heathens and idolaters. These ideological cleansing procedures—a tried and true Via Dolorosa, tested through centuries of conversion in Spain and Europe—were confession and procession.

San Vitores sought out and pursued sinners, infidels, and unbelievers, and to their amazement he uncannily "revealed to them their secret weaknesses. Who could have told him, they thought, save the holy angels, to whom he was so devoted?" (García [1683] 2004: 53). Alongside the priests' magnanimous efforts to learn the indigenous language, confession—the religious duty to make formal admission of sins privately to a priest in order to receive repentance and absolution—facilitated the priests' entry into the fabric of political, social, and sexual networks within the community. Through confession the priests surveyed a breadth and depth of personal information that modern social scientists would envy. While some anthropologists regard confession as the precursor to psychoanalysis, particular attention should be drawn to the fact that, as knowledge is power, the priests placed themselves in a supremely advantageous position over the 'flock' (Foucault 1980). Such was the power of the information machine that had been set in motion that the priests appeared to possess preternatural knowledge of people's problems, whether romantic, sexual, familial, or economic.[17] Elsewhere, Farrer (2009: 133-171) has discussed this type of phenomenon as the enchantment of performance.

Similarly, the Catholic confessional celebrated its performative component in the procession, which was linked to saints' days and fiestas and could be conducted on an impromptu basis as an occasion for proselytization. Taken to an extreme, the procession operated on the principle of ritualized mass hysteria whereby people collectively despaired of misfortune and death caused by sinful behavior and the work of the devil. Those Chamorros who did not convert and confess might be regarded as dangerous, potentially in league with the forces of evil, and were easily scapegoated for the woes of the community.

In short, late medieval Catholic fanatics were the self-proclaimed spiritual warriors of Christ, at war with the forces of Satan. Consciously or not, they employed confession as an insidious type of war magic to infiltrate and access the enemy's networks. Here, enchantment of performance refers to the means to acquire otherwise secret information regarding the machinations of the supposed evil-doers. During the procession, the priest would act out seemingly 'miraculous' foresight and insights into some individual's problems gained from another's confession, and thus offer spiritual advice and succor through the performance of enchantment in the form of reconciliation, absolution, and salvation (Farrer 2009: 87-131).

Chamorro Re-enchantment

Since 1998, Leonard Iriarte has led a Chamorro chant and dance cultural revival group, an indigenous "community arts organization" (Kihleng 2004: 22) known as I Fanlalai'an (The Place for Chant).[18] The group performs traditional chants for various formal, public ceremonies around the island, such as the inauguration of a Chamorro cultural center and meetings of the Guam Chamber of Commerce. Iriarte also represents Chamorro spiritualism for gatherings of the Interfaith Thanksgiving Service at the Fo Guang Shan Buddhist Temple. Other private chants are performed at *latte* sites, in caves, and for initiations to the group, as well as marriages and burials. The chants and dances are reconstructed from Guam's myths, legends, archaeological materials, and historical accounts, in association with signs given through dreams.[19] The group employs an archaic version of the Chamorro language (*fino' håya*), stripped of Spanish and other non-native loan words (fig. 6.1). This is to render the words spoken more familiar and attractive to the ancestors. As Iriarte explains about a chant that he sang in a Ritidian cave: "Almost all of the language would be understood [by contemporary Chamorros], but it's all allegory, symbolism. The ghosts would definitely understand that."

Iriarte himself is a youthful-looking, middle-aged charismatic figure with gray-flecked long black hair pinned at the back with a stick of carved white bone. For chants and performances, and sometimes for day-to-day attire, he wears a long black sarong (*såde'*) fixed with a black nylon belt. The name 'Iriarte' is of Basque origin; the family also claims a Kurdish forefather who settled on Guam and wed a Chamorita (i.e., female Chamorro). In addition, Iriarte has German relatives who visit on special occasions, related through a forefather who settled on Guam and married a Chamorita. Iriarte's group frowns upon the shaved-head look sometimes seen on Guam. They regard the head as sacred and deem long hair to be a source of power. According to the group's research, wearing the hair in a topknot was a post-contact innovation, and Chinese immigrants probably introduced the shaved-head style. Iriarte came to the conclusion that the ancient Chamorros used hair picks (*akeyo'*) made from the tailbone of a very large Pacific blue marlin (*båtu* or *båto'*). Such picks may double as weapons to slash or punch a hole in the flesh. Iriarte relates that the I Fanlalai'an group "found an artifact in Luta [Rota] that funnily enough had the same design."

One night in October 1987, Iriarte shot 10 bullets into the undercarriage of a B-52 aircraft, causing it to crash-land.[20] He used a Ruger Mini-14 semi-automatic rifle with a modified South African sight system, loaded with military 5.56 caliber rounds. The shooting occurred near Ritidian Point when he was on night guard duty with two other territorial conservation officers on the wildlife preserve near the Anderson Air Force Base. Convicted on a charge of attempted murder (since no one was injured), Iriarte served 30 months in a federal correctional institution located in Tucson, Arizona. On Guam it was held that the gun had gone off accidentally after the guards had smoked marijuana.

Years earlier in the 1970s, when Iriarte was a young man barely out of school, he camped near Gun Beach with two friends. In the rainforest on the way to the beach, they stumbled upon a set of *latte* stones. The other men hesitated, fearful to proceed through the space, as *latte* sites are also burial grounds for the ancient people. Iriarte called the men to help him lift the fallen capstones back onto the squat stone posts. Together, the three men heaved the massive blocks back into position. During the day they set up camp near the beach. The tide was in, and Iriarte set off waist-deep along the reef to go fishing, despite his companions' protests that this was the wrong time for fishing. He expected to catch only enough for dinner. Then, all of a sudden, a shoal of fish surrounded him. Iriarte thought that he would try to spear a single fish for dinner in the sure knowledge that, whether or not he was successful, the rest of the fish would immediately bolt in fright. To Iriarte's surprise, the fish did not disperse. Instead, they circled around him tighter and tighter, in

FIGURE 6.1 | Fanlalai'an, Solomon Islands FestPac, 2012

Photograph © Ron J. Castro

ever-greater numbers, as he caught one after another until he had filled a large net basket. For Iriarte, this superb unexpected catch demonstrated the blessings of the *taotao mo'na* for his respect of the *latte* site.

Decades later, Iriarte stood in the same place by the same beach, this time torch fishing (*sulo'*) at night and at low tide. He stood upon the exposed reef and peered into the water with a powerful headlamp, wondering where all the fish had gone. Suddenly, he sensed an ominous presence beneath the waves, only a foot away, that belonged to a black figure, which "looked like a really muscular guy wearing a skin-tight body suit." In an interview with a local magazine, Iriarte described what happened next: "I hit him right in the face with the light. He was shadow man, you could see depressions where the eyes should be—but no eyes, protrusions where a nose should be—but no nostrils, no lips, and like a protrusion on the sides of the head as if he had ears, but I couldn't see the detail of the ear [and then I thought] that's the *taotao mo'na*" (Jayne Flores 2005: 19). The fearsome black figure in the ocean reveals to Iriarte and his companions and followers the continued presence of the *taotao mo'na*, whose *latte* stones he had re-erected from the ground.

Such profound uncanny experiences prompt Iriarte to stand among the *latte* stones and chant his respects; they are the wellspring from which he draws artistic inspiration to create chants, dances, iconic symbols, and jewelry for his group of followers. Here I provide a section from one of Iriarte's chants, "Ini Na Latte."[21] During performances, Iriarte leads the chant in a fierce drawl with choral repetitions from male and female members of the group (cf. Safford [1905] 2009: 108). Hands slap hard upon big thighs to count out the beat.

INI NA LATTE
Ini na latte, i haligi,
Ini na latte, i haligi,
Mahetok i acho' gi gima' ulitao
I acho' tåno' i acho' tåsi
Acho' alutong i taotao-måmi,
Acho' alutong i taotao-måmi,
I taotao, i taotao-måmi,
Fanaiguihi, fanaiguihi,
Na' matatnga i mañe' lu-mu,
Hu!

THIS *LATTE*/HOUSEPOST
This *latte*, the house post,
This *latte*, the house post,
Hard is the stone of our men's house
The stone of the land, the stone of the sea,
Basalt stone are our people,
Basalt stone are our people,
The people, our people,
Become like that, become like that,
Encourage your brothers.
Hu!

The chant is a robust affirmation of Chamorro rights to occupy the land. The indigenous people of Guam are permanent like stone and remain on the island despite millennia of occupation, intermarriage, and invasion. Best performed at a *latte* site by the beach, this chant is meant to precede a fight against invaders. At the end, the lead chanter calls out a command, "Hu," to summon his brothers and sisters, the community, to fight. Iriarte explains that the house post is also recognized as "symbolizing the penis and something springing from it," that is, the people. Here, he points out, *latte* secretly means an "augmented strategy" (magic) that is behind what the singers do. "We come equipped with our knowledge and culture," he says, referring to the vocal connection to the ancestors, the *taotao mo'na*.

Pregnant women and children are susceptible to 'negative energy' and are easily harmed by malevolent spirits. Geckos (*guåli'ek*) sense the energy of people and chirp when they discern the manipulation of *kåhna*. Augmented strategic knowledge includes understanding the sounds that the geckos make at different times during the day: alarms sound the shifts of light toward the dangerous liminal periods accompanying dusk and dawn. The geckos' cries may also be interpreted as manifestations of *kåhna* (spiritual power) when an individual deliberately or unintentionally transmits thoughts across distances beyond the purview of normal speech. *Makanåyi* is a more sinister form of *kåhna* manipulation. Unlike a hex, which could be accidental, *makanåyi* is premeditated and intentional, at worst a death spell cast through ill intent. The idea, however, is that a person may be killed to heal the community. *Makanåyi* may therefore be employed for the common good against an individual who is disrupting the social equilibrium. Following Iriarte, Jayne Flores (2005: 22) presents an example of *makanåyi* in a less sinister form: a girl who had been warned earlier not to fool around with the chants lost her voice in the middle of her performance and was told to be careful not to *makanåyi* (bewitch) herself—presumably to avoid punitive action from the ancestors.

Conclusion

The ancient Chamorro culture had a cult of the dead. *Kåkahna* oiled ancestral skulls to control the weather and bring rain. Chamorro warriors took the skulls of their ancestors, along with those of their enemies, such as the slain Spanish, into battle. The cult of the skulls apparently ceased with the conversion of the Chamorros to Catholicism. This is not to say that the Chamorro 'deathscape' (Farrer 2006)—configured as a cultural, symbolic, practical, and performative way of understanding death—evaporated into the cosmic mist. Rather, the cult of the dead remained focused upon the *taotao mo'na*. The embodied practice of war magic has been attenuated into a fear of *taotao mo'na*, but this in itself inspires Iriarte and others like him toward a contemporary Chamorro re-enchantment based upon a veneration of, and respect for, the ancestors. War magic survives in the remnants of words that are recombined into chants, incantations, and spells with the purpose of manipulating *kåhna* to respect and appease the dead. Studies in Chamorro ethno-history and contemporary ethnography therefore show that the deathscape has shifted from skulls and sharpened leg bones to a respectful fear of spirits, ghosts, and *taotao mo'na*. Given that the Jesuit and evangelical Christian worldview is fundamentally itself a deathscape, the colonized people endured a collision of deathscapes during the transformation from ancient Chamorro beliefs and practices to contemporary Chamorro Catholicism (cf. Atienza de Frutos and Coello de la Rosa 2012).

Sorcery is regarded as the cajoling of spirits, whereas religion is understood as an appeal to divine powers. Defining sorcery via compulsion and religion via supplication, however, treads a fine line and begs a question of degree rather than kind. Given a strict definition of religion and sorcery, even the Jesuit priest San Vitores could be defined as a sorcerer: to join the Jesuits he lied, cajoled, and deceived his own father and the Holy Fathers of the Jesuits (García [1683] 2004). San Vitores knew that Chief Matå'pang had promised to kill him if he baptized the chief's child, but the priest chose to ignore this warning in his search for a 'noble death' (Diaz 2010; García [1683] 2004; Roberts and Saniotis 2006). Although he was beatified in 1985, the Catholic Church has been slow to elevate San Vitores, this "soldier of an alien god" (Rogers 1995: 41), to sainthood, partly due to his lack of a sympathetic following on Guam and more probably due to the fact that he brought about his own martyrdom.

Although the Spanish colonial forces converted the 'heathen' to Catholicism, covered their bodies, and killed off their dance, the Chamorro language—the rudimentary element of verbal art forms, incantation, and ritual chant—survived, passed down through centuries of matrilineal lineage. In the present day, I Fanlalai'an re-creates ritual context using arcane but vital indigenous words gleaned after years of carefully triangulated research inspired by mystical or uncanny experiences. The chant is a form of Chamorro artistic expression and performance that facilitates the respectful remembrance of the ancestors, both through the use of arcane language and through the action of chanting itself. Whether Iriarte's act of shooting down the Boeing B-52 Stratofortress can be considered an accident or a bold act of resistance, an example of war magic augmented by the *taotao mo'na*, remains open to question. What is clear is that the self-conscious revitalization of the Chamorro culture is a project essential to the indigenous people's cultural survival. In its effort to define and lead the continued reproduction of Chamorro culture, contemporary Chamorro spiritualism places the chant back into re-enchantment.

Acknowledgments

D. S. Farrer thanks the following: Leonard Iriarte and Jeremy Cepeda for acting as the key informants for this research; James Sellmann for lending me a free hand to reframe his philosophical treatise; Roxana Waterson, Margaret Chan, Ellis Finkelstein, and John Whalen-Bridge for reading the draft at various stages of its composition and making useful suggestions; and Victoria-Lola

Leon Guerrero, Kelly Taimanglo, James Oelke, and Anne Hattori for their useful comments. James Sellmann thanks Rich Olmo and Harley Manner for comments on his early draft

---

D. S. Farrer is Associate Professor of Anthropology at the University of Guam. He is the author of *Shadows of the Prophet: Martial Arts and Sufi Mysticism* (2009), and co-editor (with John Whalen-Bridge) of *Martial Arts as Embodied Knowledge: Asian Traditions in a Transnational World* (2011). His research interests include martial arts, performance, visual anthropology, and the anthropology of art with a regional focus toward Southeast Asia and the Pacific.

James D. Sellmann received a PhD in Chinese philosophy in 1990 and an MA in philosophy in 1983 from the University of Hawai'i. He is the Dean of the College of Liberal Arts and Social Sciences and a Professor of Philosophy and Micronesian Studies at the University of Guam. He has authored *Timing and Rulership in Master Lu's Spring and Autumn Annals* (2002) and over 60 academic articles, book chapters, and encyclopedia entries, having published in peer-reviewed journals, such as *Asian Philosophy* and *Philosophy East and West*.

Notes

1. For Weber (1946: 155), "the fate of our times is characterized by rationalization and intellectualization and [following Schiller], above all, by the 'disenchantment of the world'." Rationalization refers to institutionalization, systematization, and "the knowledge or belief ... that principally there are no mysterious incalculable forces that come into play, but rather that one can, in principle, master all things by calculation" (ibid.: 139). Disenchantment involves the stripping of magical elements from thought. As Gerth and Mills (1946: 51) point out: "The extent and direction of 'rationalization' is thus measured negatively in terms of the degree to which magical elements of thought are displaced, or positively by the extent to which ideas gain in systematic coherence and naturalistic consistency." See also Farrer (2009: 114).
2. The *lonat* or small circle over the 'å', as in Guåhan, means that the 'a' should be pronounced as the 'a' in 'are'. Chamorro is an Austronesian language containing many loan words derived from Spanish, Portuguese, Chinese, and other languages. The Chamorro definitions presented in this chapter should be regarded as tentative rather than absolute.
3. Cunningham's (1992) text was written and designed for high school students. Other historical and mythological collections published for children by the Department for Chamorro Affairs (DCA) include *Hestorian Taotao Tano': History of the Chamorro People* (DCA 1993) and *Hemplon Nåna Siha: A Collection of Chamorro Legends and Stories* (DCA 2001). Further materials disseminated for a general readership are available at Guampedia, an online encyclopedia project that focuses on Guam's culture, history, and contemporary issues (see http://guampedia.com).
4. This figure has been recently updated, based on additional research. For Ritidian, the oldest habitation is currently dated within the range of 3499–3309 radiocarbon

years before the present, which translates as 1550–1322 BCE (Carson 2012a), with yet earlier results anticipated for the Mariana Islands in future research (Carson 2013).
5. Following the historical accounts of Louis de Freycinet ([1819] 2003), Thompson (1969: 56) claimed that the ancient Chamorro class structure was divided between the "noble caste (*matua*)" (possibly *matao*), who were "deep-sea fishermen"; the "middle class (*atchaot*)" (possibly a mistranslation of 'a rival'), who assisted the nobility; and the "low caste (*mangatchang*)," who were "restricted to hunting river eels with wooden-tipped spears" and had to marry only within their caste. Russell (1998: 139–151), however, criticizes this tripartite account of the ancient Chamorro social structure as an overly hierarchical, Eurocentric perspective that was derived more than 100 years post-contact. He proposes instead that the social structure might be better understood as more egalitarian and less divided, with careful respect paid to elders. Furthermore, under a system of matrilineal kinship, women wielded considerable influence over property, inheritance, and family life (ibid.: 151; see also Souder-Jaffrey 1992).
6. Mike Carson, personal communication, 18 November 2010.
7. Farrer conducted interviews and fieldwork with Iriarte from 2009–2012. A version of this chapter was prepared for the ASA12 conference (see http://www.nomadit.co.uk/asa/asa2012/panels.php5?PanelID=1160). Chamorro chant groups have emerged since the 1990s as part of an increasingly self-conscious 'Chamorro revival'. Other revivalist groups focus more on dance, and their performances, which show much Hawaiian influence, are clearly geared toward tourist entertainment. See also Judy Flores (1999, 2004) and Flores's work on chant and dance at http://guampedia.com.
8. *Takmonyon* refers to 'one who is very capable of fighting', from the root word *mumu*, meaning 'fight' or 'war'.
9. Petersen (2009: 194–195) states that "[i]n most Micronesian societies these ghosts, spirits, and gods—there is not a clear distinction between entirely supernatural beings and the spirits of the deceased—are known by some variant of the term *eni* or *ani*."
10. While Alkire (1972) collected the pairs of opposites, he did not formulate their non-dual interaction.
11. See also http://guampedia.com.
12. Petersen (2009: 195) notes that "skulls of loved ones are preserved and revered" in a number of Micronesian societies, including those of the Kiribati, the Marianas, and the Chuuk.
13. 'Boonies' is presumably a borrowing from the Philippines (via Spanish or US colonizers), where 'boondocks' is the slang for wild or remote/backward places, derived from Tagalog *bundok* (mountain) (Roxana Waterson, pers. comm., 24 June 2011).
14. *Taotao mo'na* spirits, considered as vengeful forces of ancestral nature living in banyan trees, resemble the fearsome vampires (*pontianak*) ubiquitous in the Malay states of Southeast Asia (Farrer 2009: 258). Historically, such spirits may be linked to ancient cults engaged in the worship of trees (Frazer 1978: 58–64).
15. The term *reducción* refers to placing the indigenous people in concentration camps in order to restrict their movement, although not necessarily to reduce their number.
16. For more on San Vitores, see http://guampedia.com/father-diego-luis-de-san-vitores.
17. The attribution of sacred or mystical power to esoteric skill is a type of framing that Farrer dubs 'occulturation'. Occulturation occurs when an esoteric skill is framed as magic through ritual performance (Farrer 2009: 68, 249–250).
18. The chant group was previously called Guma' Pålu Li'e' (House of the Seeing Mast) (Jayne Flores 2005: 19).

19. Concerning the revival of Guam dance, see Judy Flores at http://guampedia.com/chamorro-dance.
20. See "Guam Officers Deny Shooting B-52 Bomber," *Los Angeles Times*, 12 February 1988, http://articles.latimes.com/1988-02-12/news/mn-28794_1.
21. This chant also appears on a cassette disc produced by Iriarte's group. A local reviewer had this to say about the disc: "*I Linalai Fino' Håya Siya*, a CD collection of Chamorro chants, is a welcome reminder that the indigenous culture of Guam and the Northern Marianas [sic] is very much alive, thank you. The chants are contemporary, based on oral history interviews, and developed on a Seventeenth Century model" (Kihleng 2004: 22).

References

Alkire, William H. 1972. "Concepts of Order in Southeast Asia and Micronesia." *Comparative Studies in Society and History* 14, no. 4: 484–493.
Atienza de Frutos, David, and Alexandre Coello de la Rosa. 2012. "Death Rituals and Identity in Contemporary Guam (Mariana Islands)." *Journal of Pacific History* 47, no. 4: 459–473.
Benjamin, Geoffrey. 1996. "Rationalisation and Re-enchantment in Malaysia: Temiar Religion, 1964–1995." Department of Sociology Working Paper No. 130, National University of Singapore.
Benjamin, Geoffrey. 2014. *Temiar Religion 1964–2012: Enchantment, Disenchantment and Re-enchantment in Malaysia's Uplands*. Singapore: NUS Press.
Carson, Mike. 2010. "Radiocarbon Chronology with Marine Reservoir Correction for the Ritidian Archaeological Site, Northern Guam." *Radiocarbon* 52, no. 4: 1627–1638.
Carson, Mike T. 2011. "Palaeohabitat of First Settlement Sites, 1500–1000 BC in Guam, Mariana Islands, Western Pacific." *Journal of Archaeological Science* 38, no. 9: 2207–2221.
Carson, Mike T. 2012a. "Evolution of an Austronesian Landscape: The Ritidian Site in Guam." *Journal of Austronesian Studies* 3, no. 1: 55–86.
Carson, Mike T. 2012b. "An Overview of *Latte* Period Archaeology." *Micronesica* 42: 1–79.
Carson, Mike T. 2013. *First Settlement in Remote Oceania: Earliest Sites in the Mariana Islands*. New York: Springer.
Carter, Lee D., William L. Wuerch, and Rosa Roberto Carter. 2005. *Guam History: Perspectives*. 2 vols. 2nd ed. Mangilao: University of Guam Richard F. Taitano Micronesian Area Research Center.
Caughey, John L. 1977. *Fa'a'nakkar Cultural Values in a Micronesian Society*. Philadelphia: University of Pennsylvania Publications in Anthropology.
Cunningham, Lawrence J. 1992. *Ancient Chamorro Society*. Honolulu: Bess Press.
de Freycinet, Louis C. [1819] 2003. *An Account of the Corvette L'Uraine's Sojourn at the Mariana Islands, 1819*. Trans. Glynn Barratt. Saipan: MARC and Commonwealth of the Northern Marianas Islands (CNMI) Division of Historic Preservation.
DCA (Department of Chamorro Affairs). 1993. *Hestorian Taotao Tano': History of the Chamorro People*. Hagåtña: Department of Chamorro Affairs.
DCA (Department of Chamorro Affairs). 2001. *Hemplon Nåna Siha: A Collection of Chamorro Legends and Stories*. Hagåtña: Department of Chamorro Affairs.

DeFant, David G. 2008. "Early Human Burials from the Nation Beach Site, Tumon Bay, Island of Guam, Mariana Islands." *Journal of Island and Coastal Archaeology* 3: 149–153.

Diaz, Vincente M. 2010. *Repositioning the Missionary: Rewriting the Histories of Colonialism, Native Catholicism, and Indigeneity on Guam.* Honolulu: University of Hawai'i Press.

Driver, Marjorie. 1993. *Fray Juan Pobre in the Marianas, 1602.* MARC Miscellaneous Series 8. Mangilao: University of Guam Richard F. Taitano Micronesian Area Research Center.

Elkins, James, and David Morgan, eds. 2009. *Re-Enchantment.* New York: Routledge.

Farrer, D. S. 2006. "'Deathscapes' of the Malay Martial Artist." *Social Analysis* 50, no. 1: 25–50.

Farrer, D. S. 2008. "The Healing Arts of the Malay Mystic." *Visual Anthropological Review* 24, no. 1: 29–46.

Farrer, D. S. 2009. *Shadows of the Prophet: Martial Arts and Sufi Mysticism.* Dordrecht: Springer.

Farrer, D. S. 2012. "The Performance of Enchantment and the Enchantment of Performance in Malay Singapore." *Moussons* 20, no. 2: 11–32.

Fischer, J. L. 1957. "Totemism on Truk and Ponape." *American Anthropologist* 59, no. 2: 250–265.

Flores, Jayne. 2005. "Interview with a Taotao Mo'na." *Guahan Magazine* 3, no. 3: 18–23.

Flores, Judy. 1999. "Art and Identity in the Mariana Islands: Issues of Reconstructing an Ancient Past." PhD diss., University of East Anglia.

Flores, Judy. 2004. "Artists and Activists in Cultural Identity Production in the Mariana Islands." Pp. 119–135 in *Shifting Images of Identity in the Pacific*, ed. Toon van Meijl and Jelle Miedema. Leiden: KITLV Press.

Foucault, Michel. 1980. *Power/Knowledge: Selected Interviews and Other Writings 1972–1977.* Ed. Colin Gordon. New York: Pantheon Books.

Frazer, James G. 1978. *The Illustrated Golden Bough.* Ed. Mary Douglas. London: Macmillian.

Fritz, Georg. [1904] 2001. *The Chamorro: A History and Ethnography of the Mariana Islands.* 3rd ed. Ed. Scott Russell; trans. Elfriede Craddock. Saipan: CNMI Division of Historic Preservation.

García, Francisco. [1683] 2004. *The Life and Martyrdom of the Venerable Father Diego Luis de San Vitores, S.J.* Ed. James A. McDonough. MARC Monograph Series No. 3. Mangilao: University of Guam Richard F. Taitano Micronesian Area Research Center.

Gell, Alfred. 1999. "The Technology of Enchantment and the Enchantment of Technology." Pp. 159–186 in Alfred Gell, *The Art of Anthropology: Essays and Diagrams*, ed. Eric Hirsch. Athlone Press: London. Originally published in 1992 in *Anthropology, Art, and Aesthetics*, ed. Jeremy Coote and Anthony Shelton. Oxford: Clarendon Press.

Gerth, H. H., and C. Wright Mills. 1946. "Introduction: The Man and His Work." Pp. 3–74 in Weber 1946.

Goodenough, Ward H. 1986. "Sky World and This World: The Place of Kachaw in Micronesian Cosmology." *American Anthropologist* 88, no. 3: 551–568.

Graham, Gordon. 2007. *The Re-enchantment of the World: Art versus Religion.* Oxford: Oxford University Press.

Hanlon, David, and Geoffrey M. White, eds. 2000. *Voyaging through the Contemporary Pacific.* Oxford: Rowman & Littlefield.

Hattori, Anne P. 2004. *Colonial Dis-ease: US Navy Health Policies and the Chamorros of Guam, 1898–1941.* Honolulu: University of Hawai'i Press.

Heathcote, Gary M. 2006. *Taotao Tagga': Glimpses of His Life History, Recorded in His Skeleton*. Non-technical Report Series. Mangilao: University of Guam Anthropology Resource and Research Center.

Hertz, Robert. 1907. "Contribution à une étude sur la représentation collective de la mort." *Année Sociologique* 10: 48–137. Also published in 1928 in *Sociologie religieuse et folklore*, and in English in 1960 as "A Contribution to the Study of the Collective Representation of Death" in *Death and the Right Hand*, trans. Rodney Needham and Claudia Needham. New York: Free Press.

Hezel, Francis X. 1995. "Introduction: Congeries of Spirits." Pp. 1–11 in Douglas Haynes and William L. Wuerch, *Micronesian Religion and Lore: A Guide to Sources, 1526–1990*. Westport, CT: Greenwood Press.

Horridge, Adrian. 1995. "The Austronesian Conquest of the Sea—Upwind." Pp. 143–160 in *The Austronesians: Historical and Comparative Perspectives*, ed. Peter Bellwood, James J. Fox, and Darrell Tryon. Canberra: Australian National University.

Howells, William. 1973. *The Pacific Islanders*. New York: Charles Scribner's Sons.

Keesing, Roger M. 2000. "Creating the Past: Custom and Identity in the Contemporary Pacific." Pp. 231–254 in Hanlon and White 2000.

Kihleng, Emelihter. 2004. "Chamorro Tradition." *Pacific Magazine* 29, no. 3: 22.

Lessa, William. A. 1950. "The Place of Ulithi in the Yap Empire." *Human Organization* 9 (Spring): 16–18.

Lessa, William. A. 1975. *Drake's Island of Thieves: Ethnological Sleuthing*. Honolulu: University of Hawai'i Press.

Matsuda, Matt K. 2012. *Pacific Worlds: A History of Seas, Peoples, and Cultures*. Cambridge: Cambridge University Press.

Matthews, Laura. 2010. "Resident: No Local Funds for Military Buildup Roads." *Pacific Daily News*, 20 October. http://www.guampdn.com/article/20101020/NEWS01/10200316/Resident-No-local-funds-for-military-buildup-roads.

Mauss, Marcel. 1979. *Sociology and Psychology: Essays*. Trans. Ben Brewster. London: Routledge & Kegan Paul.

Morgan, William N. 1988. *Prehistoric Architecture in Micronesia*. Austin: University of Texas Press.

Oliver, Douglas L. 1989. *Oceania: The Native Cultures of Australia and the Pacific Islands*. Honolulu: University of Hawai'i Press.

Petersen, Glenn. 2009. *Traditional Micronesian Societies: Adaptation, Integration and Political Organization*. Honolulu: University of Hawai'i Press.

Prince, Ruth, and David Riches. 2001. *The New Age in Glastonbury: The Construction of Religious Movements*. New York: Berghahn Books.

Riesenberg, Saul H. 1948. "Magic and Medicine in Ponape." *Southwestern Journal of Anthropology* 4, no. 4: 406–429.

Ritzer, George. 2005. *Enchanting a Disenchanted World: Revolutionizing the Means of Consumption*. 2nd ed. Thousand Oaks, CA: Pine Forge Press.

Roberts, Michael, and Arthur Saniotis. 2006. "Introduction: Empowering the Body and 'Noble Death.'" *Social Analysis* 50, no. 1: 7–24.

Rogers, Robert F. 1995. *Destiny's Landfall: A History of Guam*. Honolulu: University of Hawai'i Press.

Russell, Scott. 1998. *Tiempon I Manmofo'na: Ancient Chamorro Culture and History of the Northern Mariana Islands*. Micronesian Archaeological Survey, Report No. 32. CNMI Division of Historic Preservation.

Safford, William E. [1905] 2009. *The Useful Plants of the Island of Guam*. Agana Heights: Guamology Publishing. Facsimile reprint of the original book published in 1905 by the US Government Printing Office.

Scott, James C. 1990. *Domination and the Arts of Resistance: Hidden Transcripts.* New Haven, CT: Yale University Press.

Souder-Jaffrey, Laura M. T. 1992. *Daughters of the Island: Contemporary Chamorro Women Organizers on Guam.* 2nd ed. MARC Monograph Series No. 1. Mangilao: University of Guam Richard F. Taitano Micronesian Area Research Center; Lanham, MD: University Press of America.

Swain, Tony, and Garry Trompf. 1995. *The Religions of Oceania.* London: Routledge.

Tenorio Rodriguez, Fred C. 2004. *The Humble Man of God: One Man's Communion with God and Creation.* Berkeley, CA: Dominican School of Philosophy and Theology.

Thompson, Laura. 1969. *The Secret of Culture: Nine Community Studies.* New York: Random House.

Trask, Haunani-Kay. 2000. "Natives and Anthropologists: The Colonial Struggle." Pp. 255–263 in Hanlon and White 2000.

Underwood, Robert A. 1985. "Excursions into Inauthenticity: The Chamorros of Guam." Pp. 160–184 in *Mobility and Identity in the Island Pacific,* ed. Murray Chapman and Philip S. Morrison. Wellington: Victoria University Press. A special issue of *Pacific Viewpoint* 26, no. 1.

Vilar, Miguel G., Chim W. Chan, Dana R. Santos, Daniel Lynch, Rita Spathis, Ralph M. Garruto, and J. Koji Lum. 2013. "The Origins and Genetic Distinctiveness of the Chamorros of the Marianas Islands: An MtDNA Perspective." *American Journal of Human Biology* 25, no. 1: 116–122.

Waterson, Roxana. 1997. *The Living House: An Anthropology of Architecture in South-East Asia.* Reprint. Singapore: Thames and Hudson. Originally published in 1990 by Oxford University Press.

Weber, Max. 1946. *From Max Weber: Essays in Sociology.* Ed. and trans. H. H. Gerth and C. Wright Mills. London: Routledge & Kegan Paul.

Young, John A, Nancy R. Rosenberger, and Joe R. Harding. 1997. *Truk Ethnography: Ethnography of Truk, Micronesia.* Micronesian Endowment for Historic Preservation. San Francisco: United States National Park Service.

Chapter 7

WAR MAGIC AND JUST WAR IN INDIAN TANTRIC BUDDHISM

Iain Sinclair

Non-violence is by no means incidental to Buddhist identity. The regular observance of five precepts, beginning with the precept to avoid killing, is a prerequisite for belonging to any Buddhist community, either as a monk or as a layperson. This common constraint ought to preclude Buddhist involvement in warfare, as Lambert Schmithausen (1999: 45) points out in his seminal essay. Nevertheless, precepts can be ignored and principles abandoned. The commitment of Buddhist practitioners and institutions to non-violent behavior is increasingly coming into question as reports of majority Buddhist nation-states using military force become more frequent. In the introduction to his co-edited volume, *Buddhist Warfare*, Michael Jerryson (2010: 3) agrees with the popular understanding that "[v]iolence is found in all religious traditions, and Buddhism is no exception."

Nonetheless, because abstention from killing is so central to Buddhist identity, Buddhist pacifism is not a 'stereotype' (Jenkins 2010); it is axiomatic. Instances

References for this chapter begin on page 162.

of Buddhists waging war do not necessarily constitute what Jerryson (2010) calls 'Buddhist warfare', much less 'violent Buddhism' (Tikhonov and Brekke 2012), in the sense of doctrinally sanctioned activity. A common pattern or basis for acts of violence perpetrated by followers of disparate Buddhisms is indeed difficult to establish. The various sectarian and regional manifestations of Buddhism, such as East Asian Zen or Southeast Asian Theravāda, employ different and in some cases wholly discordant scriptural corpuses. Some traditional teaching discussed in connection with Buddhism and war carries no weight outside a sectarian domain and can be controversial even among its own adherents (Jenkins 2010; Pandita 2011). Contemporary Buddhist discourses on 'just war' likewise tend to rest upon weak scriptural support. The *Mahāvaṃsa*, for instance, often cited to justify Sri Lanka's Theravādin Buddhist wars against Tamils, is an extra-canonical tract of only parochial relevance (Bartholomeusz 2002: 53–64). When considering the connection between doctrine and violence, those elements that are shared across traditions and are most prominent in Buddhist life—the monastic and lay precepts against killing, in particular—cannot be casually ignored. The abhorrence of killing is a pervasive enough theme in Buddhist teachings that Buddhist involvement in war can never be routine or straightforward. It is doubtful that there is such thing as Buddhist warfare, if this means war waged in the name of a monolithic, universalist Buddhism and condoned by it unequivocally.

In order to minimize the problems of satisfactorily defining Buddhism, attention will be focused here on classical India, the uniquely authoritative wellspring of all Buddhist traditions. Buddhist India produced an abundance of war-related material, most of it conveyed in texts called tantras. These texts appeared and gained acceptance from the sixth to the twelfth centuries CE and were widely translated into Chinese, Tibetan, and other Asian languages. The teaching of the tantric 'vehicle', the Vajrayāna, focuses on the gaining of worldly power and enlightenment through techniques such as ritual, the recitation of mantras, visualization, and yoga. Although the Vajrayāna is rarely discussed in generalist treatments of Buddhism, it was anything but marginal in South Asia. Its doctrinal foundations are shared with the Mahāyāna Buddhist mainstream (Dasgupta 1950: 1–41), and it competed prominently with other tantric religions, such as Śaivism. Followers of tantric or 'esoteric' Buddhism were renowned for performing spectacular rites, often as a form of 'war magic' in order to protect the realm and support military campaigns. The fact that war was prevalent in the heyday of the Vajrayāna is reflected in the emergence of new religious and ritual forms adapted to it (Davidson 2002: 64–68). Numerous tantric manuals deal with the performance of war magic, here understood as the invocation of supra-mundane power for military purposes. The hundreds of spells, prescriptions, and procedures that have survived to the present day eclipse the piecemeal non-tantric Buddhist discourse on warfare. If we are to understand the ways in which Buddhists have confronted and conducted war, we must investigate the literature concerned most directly and fulsomely with violence—the tantric corpus. This is the task that I undertake in the present chapter.

The treatment of Buddhist war magic here is brief and selective, covering only a few key works. I have opted for examples—some of which are from sources that have not yet been studied or translated—that seem typical and that could form the basis of a typology. In order to expand the discourse on Buddhist principles and war, I also examine war-magical works that illuminate ethical concerns. The branch of war magic dealing with prognostication, divination, and so on will not be considered, as magical intelligence gathering techniques do not entail the breaking of Buddhist precepts. Nor will I focus on tales of war-magical players such as tantric gurus. Vivid though they may be, the historicity of these tales is often doubtful. Rather, I will draw upon widely disseminated works of tantric Buddhism extant in the original Sanskrit, supplemented with Indian material available in translation in the Chinese Tripiṭaka (hereafter referred to as *T*, the Taishō edition, Takakusu and Watanabe 1924–1932). This material will be discussed in approximately chronological order, with the earliest and less sophisticated works treated first.

While my remarks here concern the Sanskritic and tantric tradition of India's classical past, which ended in the thirteenth century, it is worth pointing out that this form of Buddhism has visible resonances in the present day. The Vajrayāna practiced in Nepal, Tibet, Mongolia, and Japan today is a continuation of an Indian inheritance, and this is most evident in the use of Sanskritic incantations and liturgy. Tantric ideas and practices of Indian pedigree, having been spread by the Tibetan diaspora, are increasingly visible throughout the Western world and in East Asia. War magic and just war thinking lies at the heart of one of the most prominent global vehicles of Tibetan Buddhism, namely, the system of the *Kālacakra-tantra*. Furthermore, the mantric techniques of the Vajrayāna have close connections with other magical milieux originating in Indian civilization, for instance, those of the Śaiva Tamils, Daoist mediums, and Indonesian shamans, which are discussed elsewhere in this book. More generally, the world of tantric Buddhism offers fresh material for debate on the relationship between magic, religion, and rationality. The evidence presented here supports some aspects of the theorization of magic, for example, Kapferer's (2002) claim that magic not only addresses a state of crisis, but also can be one of its products.

Harmlessness and War Magic in Early Tantric Buddhism

Early Buddhism, as practiced in the period from its first dissemination up to the beginning of the first millennium, emphasizes reclusion and private salvation. War, together with other occurrences of mass suffering, was regarded as an insoluble social problem to be shunned, not treated. Consequently, the early Buddhist corpus tends to refer to war as a defect to be remedied at the level of the individual: one becomes peaceful when one's inner defects are cleansed (Salomon 2007: 61). War is, however, a corporate undertaking in which individual action is constrained and decisions to inflict harm are depersonalized. Private withdrawal presents no practical solution to the massive and indiscriminate suffering that most warfare inflicts. In the centuries after it was first taught, Buddhist pacifism did not put an end to war, and since it did not advocate forced conversion, it had to accommodate other, less peaceful paths.

An Indian king could adopt Buddhism and uphold its precepts, but by convention he remained responsible for matters of state that included capital punishment and military affairs (Zimmermann 2006). Indeed, the ideal Buddhist emperor and global ruler, the *cakravartin*, in spite of his commitment to non-violent conquest (Schmithausen 1999: 55), was still characterized as a military supremo, a father to "heroic sons, virile ... destroyers of enemy armies (*parasainyapramardaka*)" (Lamotte 1976). The Buddha-to-be, Siddhārtha, was prophesied at his birth to be renowned as either a world renouncer or a world conqueror. It was out of the question that he could be both, for renunciation and rule were deemed incompatible. Since the ancient Buddhist teachings codified in the Sanskrit *āgamas* and the Pāli *sutta* canon were directed primarily at recluses, they offer little, if any, useful guidance on the declaration and waging of war. This lack of scripturally sanctioned pragmatism in early Buddhism leads Schmithausen (1999: 53) to characterize its war-waging ethos as unprincipled and "schizoid."

From the fourth century onward, Buddhists became more interested in harnessing India's age-old culture of mantric power, ritual, and magic (Nakamura 1987: 313ff.). The earliest compositions of magical character belong to the *dhāraṇī* genre, which originally comprised mnemonic summaries of long texts that became, by extension, incantations. Even in these early texts, war is an ever-present danger. Marauding armies and kings were ranked among the great hazards that might confront itinerant Buddhists. The fear of encountering armies and the like could, however, be averted through the recitation of a certain *dhāraṇī*, such as the *Sahasravarta-dhāraṇī* (T 20.1036: 24ff.). The association between (subjective) reassurance and (objective) safety in these texts likewise provided fertile grounds for quasi-magical thinking. Some *dhāraṇī* texts aimed to satisfy the military needs of kings, whose patronage was desirable since they could act as either protectors or destroyers of Buddhist institutions. One recension of the *Cintāmaṇidhāraṇī*, for example, recommends that medicine empowered by the *dhāraṇī* be distributed to the king's troops in order to defeat an opposing army (T 20.1080: 194c5).

Early formal processes of war magic appear in independently circulated ritual manuals, the *kriyātantras*. War-magical operations prescribed in these texts give directions for which mantras are to be recited, the number of repetitions, and the times and places for doing so. They detail the fabrication of liturgical devices such as magic circles (*maṇḍala*) or talismans (*yantra*). The usual aim is to invoke the protective powers of a spirit, bodhisattva, or other such Buddhist object of worship, summoning it into the constructed device. These figures were designated with generic terms of respect—*devatā* (Sanskrit), *yid dam* (Tibetan), *běnzūn* (Chinese), or *honzon* (Japanese) (Takahashi 1978)—terms that I will here uniformly translate as 'deity', although with the caveat that creation theism is not necessarily intended. Objects of Buddhist veneration may wield godlike powers, but their divinity does not encompass the whole of creation.

Several deities in the Buddhist pantheon are venerated specifically for their ability to intervene in war. Some, such as Vaiśravaṇa, ruler of the north, and the ferocious Āṭavaka, have received the military rank of Yakṣa commanders-in-chief (*mahāyakṣasenāpati*). These figures have left few traces in the Sanskritic world, but their cults, having been transmitted through East Asia from the seventh to ninth centuries, still have a presence in Japan's tantric Buddhism and its war-magical repertoire (Chandra 1980: 142ff.; Duquenne 1983). Others, such as the war goddess Mārīcī (Hall 1990) and the 'Great Black' protector Mahākāla (Stablein 1976), are still well-known in both the Sanskritic tradition and its present-day successors. Wherever their cults manifest, Buddhist war deities are required to be portrayed as overtly bellicose. Mahākāla is routinely shown with frightening attributes: squat with bared fangs and a hanging garland of severed heads, grinding a chopper in a skull. A common form of Mārīcī, whose sculptures survive in parts of Eastern India, has eight weapon-brandishing arms and is often depicted as standing in the reverse bow-drawing posture (*pratyālīḍhapadā*) upon a war chariot pulled by seven boars.

In spite of these war deities' combative iconography, the war magic associated with them can be remarkably non-violent. According to the *Mārīcī-kalpa*, the powers of Mārīcī can render the devotee unnoticeable to armies on the march (T 21.1257: 274aff.). Mārīcī is generally invoked for her power to make the devotee invisible to "evil people" (Hall 1990: 169). Insofar as such war-magical procedures are defensive and avoid killing, they remain compatible with basic Buddhist precepts.

Much war magic is duly directed at bypassing or nullifying a threat—usually specified as the 'opposing army' (*parasainya*) or 'opposing forces' (*parabala*)—rather than attacking it. One widespread kind of magic aims at the 'stunning' (*stambhana*) of the opposing army. Two large tantric digests, the *Amoghapāśa-kalparāja* and *Mañjuśrī-mūlakalpa*, current in the seventh and eighth centuries, respectively, set out techniques for the 'stopping' or 'freezing' of hostile armies. Procedures for bringing about *stambhana* or other battlefield effects could be simple or elaborate. Sometimes the desired effect could be achieved merely by reciting certain incantations. The *dhāraṇī* of the protectress Sitātapatrā (White Umbrella) has an army-stopping power effective at a range of "up to 12 to 50 leagues" (*pañcāśatyojanābhyantara*). In applying spells, the tantric practitioner might have to enchant some item by reciting the deity's mantra over it. The *Siddhaikavīra-tantra*, for example, requires paralyzing talismans (*yantra*) to be prepared with mantra repetitions and planted as close as possible to the camp of the enemy army.

The sword- and lasso-wielding Buddhist deity Acala (Unmovable) is more directly connected with immobilization procedures. A manual now surviving only in Chinese (T 21.1200: 11b25) describes how an opposing army may be stopped by painting Acala's form on banners hoisted at the front line. Immobilization is then to be brought about by visualizing the enemy bound with Acala's lasso. The mantra of Acala may also be used to induce bickering or surrender in the enemy camp.

Fanciful though it may be to conceive of an army magically frozen in its tracks, this is precisely the scenario imagined by some Indian writers. A scene in the *Uttara-rāmacarita* of Bhavabhūti, a play contemporaneous with the cults of the aforementioned deities, describes an immobilized army falling suddenly silent, "still as though painted in a picture (*atha likhitam ivaitat sainyaṃ spandam āste*)" (V.13c). In the ensuing drama, no harm comes to the army in its frozen state, and the antagonist goes on to employ this stunning technique as a peacemaking gesture.

War-magical procedures that do not aim at paralysis or immobilization of the enemy may invoke similarly harmless effects. Armies targeted by Buddhist war sorcery could be 'dispersed' or 'scattered' (*bhidyate*) or 'routed' (*bhagna*). Such operations could be compatible with Buddhist precepts of non-violence, but the possibility of harm is not excluded since the outcomes could entail injury and destruction. An immobilized or scattered army is an easy target, vulnerable to starvation, disease, and bad weather. The uniquely Himalayan case of an army said to have been frozen to death in a magically summoned blizzard is mentioned by Dalton (2011: 135). Magical means may have been wondrous, but they were not extraordinary enough to exempt the performer from the karmic consequences of those actions, at least in the early phases of the Vajrayāna.

A Paradigmatic Myth for the Deployment of War Magic

Conditions for the use of war magic are rarely specified explicitly. It is implied that magic is acceptable if it is used defensively against targets described as threatening or hostile. For example, if an enemy army is "causing incidents on the border" of a kingdom, one should invoke the furious deity Trailokyavijaya, reciting his mantra for three days (*T* 20.1116: 610aff.). A pre-emptive magical strike is permitted when armies are "poised to invade" (*T* 21.1272: 315a14).

An early paradigmatic case for the use of war magic is offered in a Buddhist retelling of the mythical war in heaven between the gods and the demonic asuras. A paraphrase of this ancient tale introduces a widely disseminated spell of war magic, the *Dhvajāgrakeyūrā-dhāraṇī*. The story begins with the troops of Vemacitra, the asura lord, ambushing the gods. The defeated gods then take human form and ask the Buddha for help. He responds by imparting a *dhāraṇī* that should be written on a ring hung from the tips of war standards (*dhvajāgra*) in order to defend the gods' territory. The *dhāraṇī* is said to have the power to induce internecine fighting in the enemy camp, scatter enemy troops, or prevent the enemy's outright victory.

The legend of the asuras' conquest of the gods carries readily recognizable associations. One form of it is established in Buddhist lore as ancient as the *Dhvajāgrasūtra* of the *āgamas* (Skilling 1997: 424–426). The asuras always embody armed aggression and unrighteous conduct. Kings who waged campaigns of extreme brutality were categorized as 'asuric' in the treatises on statecraft, the *arthaśāstras*. Kauṭalya's *arthaśāstra* distinguishes three kinds of conqueror: the righteous (*dharmavijayī*), the covetous (*lobhavijayī*), and the demonic or asuric (*asuravijayī*), the last identified by their plunder and murder of the "sons and wives" of the vanquished (XII.i.10–16). An asuric opponent attacks without regard for *dharma*, the rules of war. The asuras in the frame story of the *Dhvajāgrakeyūrā* therefore exemplify the type of (hostile, unlawful) opponent who can serve as a target for (defensive, *dharmic*) war magic.

The trope of the war between the gods and the asuras appeared in other war-magical works. In the *Nārāyaṇaparipṛcchā*, another defensive *dhāraṇī* is sought by a god—Nārāyaṇa, in this case—fighting off asuras. Here too Nārāyaṇa asks the Buddha for advice on defeating the asuras after they have wrought death and havoc upon the gods. Nārāyaṇa in turn receives a *dhāraṇī* to be written on the rims of the wheels of chariots on the front line. To apply the spell, the practitioner mounts one of these mantrified chariots, visualizing the mantric goddess Mahāvijayavāhinī devouring the enemy, while the king paints the *dhāraṇī* on the wheels of his own chariot. This *dhāraṇī* is also said to yield secondary benefits ranging from rebirth as a bodhisattva to the recollection of one's past lives (*jātismara*). It was not uncommon for *dhāraṇī* to be advertised as fulfilling goals that were conducive both to worldly success and to transcending the world. Such convergences of magical and religious aims become more prominent in later tantric Buddhism.

Frightful War Magic at the Front Lines

Some forms of war magic were deployed not only in the relative safety of the court or monastery, but on the field of battle itself. A number of battlefield magics are associated with the bodhisattva Mañjuśrī, who is often depicted as a boy-prince (*kumāra*) wielding a sword that is emblematic of his insight (*prajñākhaḍga*). Mañjuśrī's iconography is evocative of martial culture, as it bears more than a passing resemblance to the peacock-riding Śaiva war god Skanda, who is likewise called a *kumāra*. As chapter 28 of the *Mañjuśrī-mūlakalpa* instructs: "Fixing the visage of the Boy-Prince (*Kumārarūpa*) upon a golden peacock at the top of one's standard, one enters battle; the opposing forces will be routed just from the sight of it" (XXVIII: 245). According to this digest, a practitioner should also be on hand to infuse the swords, maces, and soldiers' armor with the mantras of Mañjuśrī before they enter the fray. A manual of comparable scope and antiquity, the *Amoghapāśa-kalparāja*, places the practitioner himself at the head of the battle formation, shouting mantras and twirling 'snake lassos' (*nāgapāśa*), making the enemy fear their venom (*T* 20.1092: 258a10).

It is remarkable that these Buddhist digests of magic envisage such close involvement in armed conflict, yet they rarely discuss the magically assisted combatants' culpability in the harm they may cause. This unusual obliviousness to bad karmic effects reflects the likelihood that soldiers were not expected to be observant Buddhists. Soldiering was the duty of the *kṣatriya* caste of Hindu society (Schmithausen 1999: 45). The view in these digests that magically assisted combat need not lead to casualties is likewise strikingly credulous. The mantra-infused mêlée in the *Mañjuśrī-mūlakalpa* anticipates that the assailant shall "scatter the enemy's army and protect his own," and in doing so, "no weapon shall touch him" (*śastrair na spṛśyate*). These scenarios do not detail the expected fate of the enemy.

The spell wielder's intimidating presence on the battlefield is a key element in some tantric procedures. Several such methods focused on the elephant-headed deity Vināyaka are put forward in one Buddhist text that claims the high pedigree of being "taught by Vajrasattva," now preserved only in Chinese translation (T 21.1272). Here it is said that a four-armed, three-eyed statue of Vināyaka, fashioned from human bone and hung from a pole, will stop an enemy elephant or horse running amok. Wrapped in a funeral shroud and a flayed human skin, the same image provokes "fear in the hearts of the enemy." As an alternative, the tantric master may ride naked on an elephant to the enemy encampment, holding a skull bowl "full of excreta, phlegm, and so on," which he imbibes and spits in their direction. This act is said to make the enemy soldiers (and their horses) faint in horror (T 21.1272: 315a27–316c22). The use of substances deemed highly polluting in Indian society situates these techniques in the transgressive tantric tradition. Nonetheless, the emphasis is still on repulsion rather than the inflicting of harm. These tantric practitioners can still roam the battlefield without breaching Buddhist precepts.

Enlightened Yogins Waging Enlightened Warfare

Whereas the sources discussed so far assume that a master of war magic need not engage in hand-to-hand combat, in some tantric traditions the goal is to kill. Much of this lethally oriented practice is taught in texts classified as *yoga-*, *mahāyoga-*, or *yoginī-tantra*s. This may then be called yogic war magic, as distinct from the invocatory war magic described above, which coaxes a powerful deity to intervene on the practitioner's behalf. The war magic of the yogin, by contrast, relies on direct personal identification with the deity. The effectuation (*sādhana*) of divine power is brought about through union (*yoga*) rather than solicitation. For later tantric Buddhists, the 'deity' (*devatā*) is nothing other than an entity (*sattva*) or image (*bimba*) that manifests the practitioner's own (*sva-*) gnosis (Takahashi 1978: 211).

In this higher class of tantras, war magic is but one of many possible applications (*prayoga*) of the mantric powers of a yogin. These yogins routinely recite mantras and engage in visionary meditation in order to cultivate a sense of unity with their chosen deity. A follower of the *Guhyasamāja-tantra*, a seminal work classified in India as a *mahāyoga-tantra*, uses his mantras for purposes ranging from the healing of illness to the stopping or slaying of an enemy (*śatru*). He may enter the meditation called "Stunning All Armies," visualizing mountain-sized forms dropped upon the enemy's heads. As such meditation "stops even an army of Buddhas, without a doubt, [the enemy] dies," according to *Guhyasamāja* (XIII.67–68). Directives of this kind differ from the previously discussed invocatory techniques not only in their lethality, but also in dispensing with most, if not all, outer paraphernalia. The possibility of killing with a thought reflects the emphasis of these tantras on the primacy of the mind, personified as the Buddha Akṣobhya.

In the *yoginī-tantra* class of tantric works, which follow the *yoga-tantras* and which mostly have Akṣobhya as their chief Buddha, some war magic continues to require liturgical substances and implements. The *Herukābhidhāna* (or *Laghusamvara-tantra*), one of the earliest tantras of this type, puts at the yogin's disposal war magic techniques of great deadliness. Engines and mounts of war may be stopped with no more than "an utterance" (XLV.26–27). By earnestly reciting the mantra of Heruka, a manifestation of Akṣobhya, the yogin can even destroy the enemy (XLVI.4). But in order to bring a ruler and his army directly under control, a yogin must resort to the performance of *homa*, that is, burnt offerings (XL.4). The war-magical chalk ritual (*khaṭikasādhana*) of the *Hevajra-tantra* likewise operates with the aid of ritual paraphernalia. Having prepared chalk paste with millions of mantra repetitions (*pūrvasevā*), the yogin smears the paste around the neck of an earthenware water pot. He then breaks the neck of the pot, thereby decapitating an entire army (I.ii.22).

These tantras and their traditional commentators rarely dwell on the question of how it is permissible for Buddhists to practice murderous war magic. Rituals aimed at magically causing death are merely one instance of the transgressions commended in these texts. Basic Buddhist precepts—the well-known injunctions against killing, stealing, lying, and so on (Broido 1988)—are inverted in the higher tantric tradition. To attempt to reconcile the Buddhist precepts with their tantric opposites is to enter a hermeneutical minefield, one "in which problems of interpretation stand to the fore in a way almost unheard of" in other religious milieux (Wedemeyer 2007). In South Asia, access to a commentarial tradition was regarded as indispensable for learned tantric practitioners (Sferra 2009: 457, 462). Understandings of the tantras were also constrained by initiatory secrecy, opaque brevity, non-standard or allusive language, and competing schools of exegesis. Those who study the tantras today must also attempt to overcome barriers of cultural and historical differences, as well as chronic problems of textual transmission.

While the difficult question of what higher tantric teaching 'really' means cannot be answered with easy confidence, it is at least possible to identify key factors in interpretation. One important consideration is that magical slaying, along with other transgressive acts enjoined in the higher tantras, can be sanctioned insofar as it is a manifestation of transcendence (Dalton 2011: 33–34, 81). A yogin who attains a transcendent state—defined as overcoming dualities such as existence/non-existence (Dasgupta 1950: 43)—is elevated beyond conventional norms. The ethical regime followed by ordinary practitioners no longer applies. Yogic transcendence confers higher judgment and at least partly nullifies the negative karmic effects that would trouble less accomplished persons.

Some Buddhist communities recognized that a high level of transcendence could indeed be achieved through the tantras. The lofty heights at which yogins operate are mirrored in hyperbolic discourse, as seen in another war-magical meditation of the *Guhyasamāja*: "[I]f [this meditation] terminates even an army of Buddhas, ferocious ones, there is no doubt that it will crush [a foe (*ripu*)]" (XIII.71). But if it seems that these higher tantras excuse licentiousness, it is important to point out that transcendence is valued greatly and taken seriously. Attitudes toward transcendence may be permissive, but only insofar as transcendence has actually been achieved. Transgressive conduct is acceptable for those whose accomplishments are genuine, but not for anyone else. Some degree of transcendent attainment was presupposed in order to be able to comment on the tantras at all (Sferra 2009: 457).

Underlying yogic war magic is the common tantric principle that inner accomplishment yields outer mastery. To control subjective experience is also to control objective reality: the overcoming of dualist distinction is the wellspring of the yogin's magical power. This inner-outer homology, which informs so much thinking in the Buddhist tantras, helps to explain why worldly and world-transcending practices are juxtaposed in tantric texts. There is a clear self-awareness of these juxtapositions in the *Hevajra-tantra*. Its introduction states that "black magic for paralyzing armies," together with other shady magic, is part of the tantra's "manifold common purpose" (I.i.8). This purpose is soteriological, being, "first of all, the only way of evoking Heruka ... in order for there to be liberation" (I.i.11).

War's Inevitability According to the *Kālacakra-tantra*

Indian tantric Buddhist thinking about war culminates in one of its final creations, the *Kālacakra-tantra*, which is customarily read together with its commentary by Puṇḍarīka, the *Vimalaprabhā*. Just war considerations are much more prominent in the Kālacakra system than in the earlier Buddhist scripture discussed by Jenkins (2010). The Kālacakra literature deserves special attention—certainly more than the single-sentence treatment of Schmithausen (1999: 58)—due to its sophistication, its self-consciously Buddhist pedigree (unlike other tantras, it is said to have been taught by the historical Buddha), and its significance for the mature Buddhist tradition, especially the present-day Tibetan diaspora.

The Kālacakra system situates its revelation in the utopian enclave of Sambhala (also spelled 'Shambhala'), a Buddhist kingdom where Brahmanical Hinduism and other religions also flourish. Sambhala serves as the system's paradigmatic case, the ideal site for the implementation of its soteriology, in which many strands of tantric Buddhist thought are incorporated. The tantric notion that transcendent yoga facilitates mastery over both the body and the mundane, war-torn world reaches its apex in the Kālacakra literature. A defining event in Sambhala's prophesied future is the invasion by an enemy of asura-like aggressors and its repulsion by Sambhala's Buddhist king. This prophecy exemplifies the position that even a pacifist religion must fight to survive. The stressful historical circumstances surrounding the Kālacakra's revelation no doubt influenced this position. By the turn of the eleventh century, when the earliest texts of the system had appeared (Cicuzza and Sferra 1997), Indian Buddhists endured real invasions and faced the prospect that all Buddhist institutions in South Asia would be wiped out, together with the civilization that allowed them to flourish.

In the Kālacakra literature, the aggressors are the 'barbarians' (mleccha), foreigners from beyond the boundaries of the classical Indian world. The vividness with which the mlecchas are described shows that they were real people whose habits were closely observed (Newman 1998: 331). Military campaigns of the period that resulted in the forced conversion or extinction of entire Buddhist communities are recorded in non-Buddhist accounts; the Buddhist use of war magic is also reported in these sources (Ahmed 2008: 148). The Kālacakra literature defines the mlecchas primarily by their ideology, depicting them as followers of a 'barbaric religion' (mlecchadharma). Although the mlecchas were sometimes also identified by an imprecise ethnonym (tāyin, or Tājik), they are most closely identified with their religion, a monotheism presented as the 'absolute antithesis' (atyantādharma) of Buddhism (Newman 1998: 323ff.). An irreconcilable difference between the bauddha (Buddhist) and mleccha religions is perceived in their different attitudes toward the use of force: "Religion [for Buddhists] is non-violence, and [for others religion] is violence" (Kālacakra II.99d).

This incompatibility between Buddhism and other major religions underpins the Kālacakra-tantra's vision of inevitable conflict. A line is drawn between non-violent Buddhists and two violence-accepting groups: asuric 'barbarians' and Hindus. According to the Vimalaprabhā, commenting on Kālacakra II.98, the non-violent character of Buddhism derives from its practitioners' experience of emptiness and compassion. Buddhists are inclined to act in a non-harmful (ahiṃsā) manner because their compassion is directed toward all sentient beings. Barbarians, on the other hand, are said to adhere to 'fantasized' (kalpanā) beliefs that are inherently violent because they mandate, for example, the killing of animals. Hindus, for their part, follow 'mingled' doctrines (miśradharma) of violence and non-violence. Their violence is in part a fulfillment of the obligations of Vedic sacrifice and so on (yāgādyartha) and is in compliance with the edicts of charismatic teachers (guruniyama), but it is also in part habitual warmongering (cf. Kālacakra II.100, 178b). Hindus are, however, said to share with Buddhists a belief in the karmic consequences of violence, which differentiates them from the mlecchadharma. These comparisons led the revealers of the Kālacakra literature to the position that non-violent resistance is unsustainable in the face of religiously entrenched violence. Civilizations separated by opposing attitudes toward violence will clash.

Just War Doctrine in the *Kālacakra-tantra*

The notion that Buddhist pacifism will be compelled to face its antithesis is formulated in the *Kālacakra-tantra* as a prophecy of coming war (Newman 1995, 1998). The prophecy states, in brief, that the kingdom of Sambhala will ultimately be invaded by a *mleccha* army (*Kālacakra* I.157–160). At that time, the future *cakravartin* ruler of Sambhala, Rudra Cakrin, will engage in battle, assisted by Hindu gods, and will lead his army to conquer the *mlecchas*. Rudra Cakrin's victory will usher in a new age in which the Vajrayāna safely prospers

(*Kālacakra* I.160–165). This scenario, although particularized and mythologized, serves as a general model for a legitimate Buddhist war: it defines a just cause (the preconditions for the use of force), the manner in which war should be waged, and the conditions under which hostilities are to end.

That the Sambhala mythology is intended to guide real-world action is demonstrated by two expositions of military technology. The war magic and weaponry specified in the Kālacakra are to be employed only when stated conditions are met. The first exposition on astrologically synchronized yoga (*svarodaya*) aims at both divining and altering the outcome of a battle (I.94–127). The second exposition consists of plans for constructing war machines such as catapults, traps, ships, siege towers, and so on (I.128–148). As these devices are unquestionably put to work to inflict death and carnage, strict constraints are imposed upon their use: "Do all of this [military preparation] for the sake of protecting your own territory, not out of enmity or greed (*dveṣa-lobhaiḥ*)" (I.149d).

Here, finally, are clear Buddhist rules for going to war. They allude to the ancient three grades of morality in conquest—righteous, greedy, and asuric—enumerated in the above-mentioned *arthaśāstra* on warfare. Tantric Buddhist war must be defensive, undertaken "for the sake of protecting one's territory." Wars motivated by enmity (*dveṣa*) toward an opponent or by the desire to plunder an enemy's wealth are forbidden, these acts being typical of barbarians and their *dharma* of violence (Newman 1998: 344). Defensive wars, by contrast, are conditionally acceptable. The rules of engagement (*niyama*) are binding for practitioners of this ideal tantric Buddhist system, namely, "those who are well-versed in the Kālacakra" (*Kālacakraparijñāninām*).

Even a defensive war is, of course, a violent undertaking. However, an adherent of non-violent Buddhism may engage in justifiable violence by means of the correspondence between the outer and inner worlds—the distinctive yoga of the later Vajrayāna. In the Kālacakra system, a yogin's campaign against his inner mental defilements is simultaneously a battle against the outer *mleccha-asuradharma* armies (Newman 1998: 329n41). Correspondences between the wars within the body (*dehe*) and the outer world are delineated in a dedicated section of the *Kālacakra-tantra* (II.48–50). The tantric practitioner is the Buddhist warrior-king in the outer world (*cakrin*). The Hindu gods who are his allies correspond to aspects of a liberating process, namely, the abolition of the 12 branches of dependent origination (*dvādaśāṅgā niruddhāḥ*). The four divisions of the army are the four boundless qualities of the practitioner's enlightened personality. On the opposing side, the barbarian leader is a practitioner's wrongdoing (*pāpa*), following a sinful path that causes personal suffering; the barbarian general symbolizes ignorance (*avidyā*). The conquest of such enemies opens up the way to liberation (*mokṣamārga*). But not just any worldly war can be the counterpart of a private crusade for enlightenment. The tantra adds: "So [as these correspondences make clear] the war against the barbarian leader is inevitable for living beings within the body; the war with the barbarians externally … is an illusion, not [a real] war" (II.50cd). The commentary on this verse in the *Vimalaprabhā* offers another revelation about the nature of the final battle. During the Buddhist king's encounter with the *mlecchas*, "[h]e shall wreak devastation on their religion, not sacrifice their lives" (*Vimalaprabhā* V.5 on *Kālacakra-tantra* I.127). The preservation of life in war is therefore regarded as paramount, even—especially—in a last-ditch battle to preserve non-violent Buddhist ideals. Life matters; violent religion, on the other hand, is expendable.

In spite of the fact that religion is targeted in the defensive warfare advocated in the *Kālacakra-tantra*, this could not be unproblematically described as a holy war, a 'Buddhist war'. It is insisted that war in the real world, to the extent that it can be considered real at all, must refrain from using lethal force. War is a last resort and must not be used as a pretext for furthering hateful ethnic, religious, or other agendas. The enemy is identified with antagonistic ideology, not with a particular racial or social group. It is also made clear that the war of the Sambhala myth is not waged exclusively in defense of Buddhism; it is also intended to preserve a cultural complex that includes the Hindu caste system and the societies of other non-Buddhists such as tribals (*śabara*). A defensible civilization is defined, then, by its adherence to varied expressions of the ideology of non-violence. This emphasis on the principled refusal to condone killing must be distinguished on a fundamental level from the sanctioning of 'holy war' or war waged in the name of an ephemeral or supernatural entity.

Concluding Remarks

Attitudes toward war conveyed in Vajrayāna texts do not represent a departure from Buddhist principles of non-violence; instead, they signify new thinking about how those principles apply under duress. Magic provided a means for Buddhists to wage war without engaging in hand-to-hand combat, which was out of the question for the monastic class and most laypeople. Nevertheless, Buddhist magicians would still feel the karmic effects of their own and others' hostile magic even if they did not get blood on their hands. Magic was also needed to enhance real warfare, and some tantric experts would work at the front lines. Prescriptions for participation in warfare, scattered throughout early tantric texts, are therefore compatible with Buddhist ethics when they endorse harmless techniques for the suspension, ending, or avoidance of battle. Either war magic is applied so that no bodily harm is the consequence, or it is used by adepts whose exceptional spiritual attainments exempt them from conventional moral considerations. It was also envisaged that war magic would be used to fight a recognizably hostile, asuric enemy. The eventual consolidation of these disparate trends in the Kālacakra system finally produced a clear definition of a just war—one that was defensive, unavoidable, dispassionate, and minimally harmful, waged against a systemically violent opponent. In Buddhism's final days in India, the desire to prevent the annihilation of its pacifism became so acute that military action was elevated to a soteriology: the skirmish in the outer world and the battle within were now one and the same.

Acknowledgments

Earlier versions of this chapter were read at the Indology Graduate Seminar, University of Hamburg, and at the United Nations Day of Vesak, Hanoi. Several improvements were kindly suggested by Douglas Farrer, Harunaga Isaacson, Ian Mabbett, Alexander von Rospatt, Péter-Dániel Szántó, David Templeman, and John Whalen-Bridge.

Iain Sinclair is a PhD Candidate at the School of Philosophical, Historical and International Studies, Monash University, Australia. His dissertation focuses on the formation of the Newar Buddhism of Nepal during the eleventh to fourteenth centuries. More generally, his research investigates the history of ideas in Sanskritic civilization, particularly as expressed in non-theist religion. He lived and worked in Nepal and Southeast Asia for several years and conducted research at the University of Hamburg.

References

Primary Sources (in Sanskrit alphabetical order)

Amoghapāśa-kalparāja
  Mikkyō Seiten Kenkyūkai. 1998–2000. "Transcribed Sanskrit Text of the Amoghapāśakalparāja (I)." *Annual of the Institute of Comprehensive Studies of Buddhism, Taishō University* 20 (part 2: ibid., 21, 1999; part 3: ibid., 22, 2000). Chinese translation: *T* 1092.

Guhyasamāja-tantra
  Matsunaga, Yūkei. 1978. *The Guhyasamāja Tantra*. Osaka: Tōhō Shuppan.

Dhvajāgrakeyūrā-dhāraṇī
  Giunta, Paolo. 2008. "The *Āryadhvajāgrakeyūrā nāma dhāriṇī*: Diplomatic Edition of MS Tucci 3.2.16." Pp. 187–194 in *Sanskrit Texts from Giuseppe Tucci's Collection Part I*, ed. Francesco Sferra. Manuscripta Buddhica No. 1. Rome: IsIAO. Chinese translation by Dānapāla (Shihu), *T* 943.

Nārāyaṇa-paripṛcchā
  Banerjee, Anukul Chandra. 1941. *Nārāyaṇaparipṛcchā: Sanskrit and Tibetan Texts*. Calcutta: University of Calcutta.

Mañjuśrī-mūlakalpa (aka *Mañjuśriyāmūlakalpa*)
  Śāstrī, Gaṇapati, Taruvāgrahāram, ed. 1920–1925. *Āryamañjuśrīmūlakalpaḥ*. Anantaśayanasaṃskṛtagranthāvali Nos. 70, 76, 84. Anantaśayana: Rājakīyamudraṇa-yantrālaye. Reprint. Delhi: Sri Satguru Publications, 1989, *Bibliotheca Indo-Buddhica* Nos. 57–59, 3 vols. Chinese translation: *T* 1191.

Sitātapatrā-dhāraṇī
  Anonymous. 2004. *Dhīḥ: Journal of Rare Buddhist Texts* 33: 147–154. Chinese translation: *T* 945.

Siddhaikavīra-tantra
  Pāṇḍey, Janārdan, ed. 1998. *Siddhaikavīramahātantram*. Rare Buddhist Text Series No. 20. Sārnāth: Central Institute of Higher Tibetan Studies.

Herukābhidhāna (aka *Laghusamvara-tantra*)
Pandey, Janardan, ed. 2002. *Śrīherukābhidhānam Cakrasaṃvaratantram with the Vivṛti Commentary of Bhavabhaṭṭa*. Rare Buddhist Text Series No. 26. 2 vols. Sārnāth: Central Institute of Higher Tibetan Studies.
Hevajra-tantra
Snellgrove, David, ed. [1959] 1980. *The Hevajra Tantra: A Critical Study*. 2 vols. London Oriental Series Vol. 6. London: Oxford University Press. Chinese translation: *T* 892.
Kauṭalya. *Arthaśāstra*.
Kangle, R. P., ed. 1969. *The Kauṭilīya Arthaśāstra*. Part 1: *A Critical Edition with a Glossary*. 2nd ed. Bombay: University of Bombay.
Bhavabhūti. *Uttara-rāmacarita*.
Kale, Moreshvar Ramchandra, ed. [1934] 2006. *The Uttararāmacharita of Bhavabhūti. Edited with the Commentary of Viraraghava, Various Readings, Introduction, a Literal English Translation, Exhaustive Notes and Appendices by M. R. Kale*. Delhi: Motilal Banarsidass.
Śrī Yaśas. *Kālacakra-tantra* and Śrī Puṇḍarīka. *Vimalaprabhā*.
Upādhyāya, Jagannāth, ed. 1986-1994. *Vimalaprabhāṭīkā of Kalki Śrī Puṇḍarīka on Śrī LaghuKālacakratantrarāja by Śrī Mañjuśrīyaśa*. 3 vols. Sārnāth: Central Institute of Higher Tibetan Studies.

Secondary Sources

Ahmed, Manan. 2008. "The Many Histories of Muhammad B. Qasim: Narrating the Muslim Conquest of Sindh." PhD diss., University of Chicago.
Bartholomeusz, Tessa J. 2002. *In Defense of Dharma: Just-War Ideology in Buddhist Sri Lanka*. London: RoutledgeCurzon.
Broido, Michael. 1988. "Killing, Lying, Stealing, and Adultery: A Problem of Interpretation in the Tantras." Pp. 71–118 in *Buddhist Hermeneutics*, ed. Donald S. Lopez, Jr. Studies in East Asian Buddhism No. 6. Honolulu: University of Hawai'i Press.
Chandra, Lokesh. 1980. "Vaiśravaṇa/Kuvera in the Sino-Japanese Tradition." Pp. 137–147 in *Studies in Indo-Asian Art and Culture*, vol. 6, ed. Lokesh Chandra. New Delhi: International Academy of Indian Culture.
Cicuzza, Claudio, and Francesco Sferra. 1997. "Brief Notes on the Beginning of the Kālacakra Literature." *Dhīḥ* 23: 113–126.
Dalton, Jacob P. 2011. *The Taming of the Demons: Violence and Liberation in Tibetan Buddhism*. New Haven, CT: Yale University Press.
Dasgupta, Shashi Bhusan. 1950. *An Introduction to Tāntric Buddhism*. Calcutta: University of Calcutta Press.
Davidson, Ronald M. 2002. *Indian Esoteric Buddhism: A Social History of the Tantric Movement*. New York: Columbia University Press.
Duquenne, Robert. 1983. "Daigensui (Ātavaka)." *Hōbōgirin* 6: 610–640.
Hall, David A. 1990. "Marishiten: Buddhism and the Warrior Goddess." PhD diss., University of California, Berkeley.
Jenkins, Stephen. 2010. "Making Merit through Warfare According to the *Ārya-Bodhisattva-gocara-upāyaviṣaya-vikurvaṇa-nirdeśa Sūtra*." Pp. 59–75 in Jerryson and Juergensmeyer 2010.
Jerryson, Michael. 2010. "Introduction." Pp. 3–16 in Jerryson and Juergensmeyer 2010.
Jerryson, Michael, and Mark Juergensmeyer, eds. 2010. *Buddhist Warfare*. New York: Oxford University Press.

Kapferer, Bruce. 2002. "Introduction: Outside All Reason: Magic, Sorcery and Epistemology in Anthropology." *Social Analysis* 46, no. 3: 1–30.

Lamotte, Étienne. 1976. *Le traité de la grande vertu de sagesse de Nāgārjuna: (Mahāprajñāpāramitāśāstra)*. Vol. 4. Trans. Gelongma Karma Migme Chodron. Louvain: Institut Orientaliste.

Nakamura, Hajime. 1987. *Indian Buddhism: A Survey with Bibliographical Notes*. Delhi: Motilal Banarsidass. Reprint of 1980 1st ed., published in Tokyo.

Newman, John. 1995. "Eschatology in the Wheel of Time Tantra." Pp. 284–289 in *Buddhism in Practice*, ed. Donald S. Lopez, Jr. Princeton, NJ: Princeton University Press.

Newman, John. 1998. "Islam in the *Kālacakratantra*." *Journal of the International Association of Buddhist Studies* 21, no. 2: 311–371.

Pandita, Ven. 2011. "The Buddha and the Māgadha-Vajjī War." *Journal of Buddhist Ethics* 18: 125–144.

Salomon, Richard. 2007. "Ancient India: Peace Within and War Without." Pp. 53–65 in *War and Peace in the Ancient World*, ed. Kurt A. Raaflaub. Oxford: Blackwell.

Schmithausen, Lambert L. 1999. "Aspects of the Buddhist Attitude towards War." Pp. 45–67 in *Violence Denied: Violence, Non-violence and the Rationalization of Violence in South Asian Cultural History*, ed. Jan E. M. Houben and Karel R. van Kooij. Leiden: Brill.

Sferra, Francesco. 2009. "*The Laud of the Chosen Deity*, the First Chapter of the *Hevajratantrapiṇḍārthaṭīkā* by Vajragarbha." Pp. 435–468 in *Genesis and Development of Tantrism*, ed. Shingo Einoo. Tokyo: University of Tokyo, Institute of Oriental Culture.

Skilling, Peter. 1997. *Mahāsūtras: Great Discourses of the Buddha*. Vol. 2. Sacred Books of the Buddhists No. 46. Oxford: Pali Text Society.

Stablein, William G. 1976. "The Mahākālatantra: A Theory of Ritual Blessings and Tantric Medicine." PhD diss., Columbia University.

Takahashi, Hisao. 1978. "Honzon no gengo wo megutte: Mikkyō kyōten wo chūshin to shite." [On the Sanskrit Equivalents of 'Honzon'.] *Journal of the Graduate School, Taisho University* 2: 201–212.

Takakusu, J., and K. Watanabe, eds. 1924–1932. *Taishō Shinshū Daizōkyō* [Taishō Revised Tripiṭaka]. 85 vols. Tokyo: Taishō Issaikyō Kankōkai.

Tikhonov, Vladimir, and Torkel Brekke, eds. 2012. *Buddhism and Violence: Militarism and Buddhism in Modern Asia*. New York: Routledge.

Wedemeyer, Christian K. 2007. "Beef, Dog, and Other Mythologies: Connotative Semiotics in Mahāyoga Tantra Ritual and Scripture." *Journal of the American Academy of Religion* 75, no. 2: 1–35.

Zimmermann, Michael. 2006. "Only a Fool Becomes a King: Buddhist Stances on Punishment." Pp. 213–242 in *Buddhism and Violence*, ed. Michael Zimmermann. Nepal: Lumbini International Research Institute.

INDEX

Afghanistan, 7
agency, 8, 9, 10, 12, 26, 67, 99, 100, 116, 128
Ahmad Sayudi, 61
aji, 15, 49–51, 53–58, 61, 62
al-Qaeda, 2
amulets, 5, 17, 88–90, 93, 99
anthropology, 2–3, 7, 10–12, 14, 68, 98, 108, 128
anti-colonialism, 15, 20, 62
anxiety, 5, 90
archery, 8, 32
Arjuna, 58
assault sorcery, 1–2, 20, 107, 122–123
attitudes, 5, 8, 31, 63, 158–159, 161
Azande, 108. *See also* Zande

Bali, 47; and Balinese manuscripts, 64n2
Banten, 57, 60, 64n14
battles, 19, 74; battlefield, 89, 102n8; against evil, 34; for human souls, 18; of ideas, 1; magical formations, 18; psychological preparation for, 8
becoming-animal, 13
beguilement, 17, 99
Bei Ji Shangdi, 34–35
Bierce, Ambrose, 13
birth, 3; conceptions of, 47; and rebirth, 42–47, 112–114, 155; rituals of, 5, 49, 59, 60; of Siddhārtha, 152
black magic, 2, 3, 14, 15, 19, 67, 71, 80, 84n2. *See also* magic; sorcery

blood, 4, 7, 19, 94, 161; bloodshed, 1; disease of, 89; in feces, 119; and *tangki*s, 14, 25, 33, 38–40
body, 3, 12, 14, 19, 30, 31, 38, 40, 42, 58, 64n4, 74, 91, 102n16, 116, 117–118, 119, 140, 160; body fault, 17, 120; body intruder, 120–121; cosmic body, 112–114; dead body politics, 95; disembodiment, 17, 94, 112–114; mind-body dualism, 20; self-mortification, 36, 40; techniques of, 48, 62, 128; vital points of, 56. *See also* embodiment; possession
British Army, 4
Buddhism, 2, 14, 19, 30, 40, 42, 89–91, 134, 137, 149–162; Mahayana, 43; Tantric, 14, 17, 19, 58, 89–91, 93, 149–153, 156–161; Theravada, 42
bureaucracy, 81

cannibalism, 18, 112, 121
Catholic Church, 4, 136, 142
Catholicism, 128, 136, 141–142
celebration, 9, 40, 78, 96, 103n21, 137
Chagnon, Napoleon, 108–109
Chamorro, 3, 14, 18–19, 127–1
chant, 11, 18, 26, 95, 118, 127–128, 130, 137–138, 140–142, 144n7, 144n18, 145n21
charisma, 9; charismatic leadership, 8, 20, 138
child abuse, 5; ritual of paedophagy, 109

Chinese medicine, 31–31, 33, 38
Christianity, 5, 7, 10, 14, 49, 63, 89, 96, 123, 142
cognitive dissonance, 4
colonialism, 2, 3, 8, 11, 12, 17, 18, 20, 67, 108, 127–142; American, 131; Dutch, 48–49, 69; Spanish, 19, 130. *See also* occupation
Comte, Auguste, 4
conversion, 4, 10, 18, 136–137, 141, 151, 159
Copeman, Jacob, 89
cricket, 11, 48, 89
crisis, 9, 123, 151
cults, 10, 47, 55, 61, 144n14, 153; subaltern, 49

damned, the, 33, 136
dance, 10, 11, 13, 18, 20, 25, 29, 36, 38, 40, 74–75, 102n15, 114, 130, 137, 140, 142, 144n7, 145n19
death, 2, 3, 5, 8, 11–13, 17, 50, 78, 79, 88, 94, 95, 100, 109, 112, 117–123, 131, 133–134, 136–137, 141, 155, 160; magical, 1, 2, 15, 19, 108–109, 110, 113–114, 154, 157; rituals of, 5, 60; spells, 3, 33
deathscape, 18, 141–142
Deleuze, Gilles, and Félix Guattari, 13
demons, 1, 10, 14, 26, 28, 29, 30–35, 38, 43, 91, 100, 136, 154; attacks, 40; demonic forces, 4, 8; demon-killing, 14; and demonology, 28, 31–32; and tales, 3. *See also* exorcists; possession
destruction, 2, 5, 7, 15, 118, 123, 154
devil, the, 135, 137; *iblis*, 77. *See also* Satan
discipline, 5, 10, 11, 92, 95, 102n15
disease, 5, 14, 38, 72, 78, 89, 93, 118, 123, 136, 154
disenchantment, 4, 128, 132, 143n1. *See also* enchantment; re-enchantment
diviner, 10, 134
divination, 134, 151
druids, 3–4, 10
Durkheim, Emile, 4

education, 5, 16, 47, 82; educated, the, 31, 32
Elias, Norbert, 48
Ellen, Roy, 26

embodiment, 3, 20, 49, 63, 94. *See also* body
enchantment, 17, 99–100, 128; of performance, 128, 137; performance of, 128, 137; technology of, 99–100, 128. *See also* disenchantment; re-enchantment
England, 5
epistemology, 2, 11, 26, 91
espionage, 4; and intelligence, 2, 4; magical, 151
ethics, 7, 8, 10, 13, 49, 151, 157, 161
ethnography, 1, 2, 10, 12, 14, 15, 17–19, 90, 92, 95, 98, 99, 103n29, 107–108, 110, 115, 127, 142; colonial, 11; film, 11
Eurocentrism, 8, 144n5
Evans-Pritchard, E. E., 2, 9, 12, 68, 84n1, 108. *See also* witch; witchcraft
execution, 4, 119, 128
exorcism, 20, 26, 28–31, 33, 40, 136
exorcist, 3, 14, 25, 27, 29–31, 44n5
experience, 3, 9, 11, 17, 60, 71, 82, 113, 114, 117, 118, 120, 121, 123, 140, 159; subjective, 158; transcendental, 27; uncanny, 142

faith, 5, 51
familiars, 10, 134, 136
family, 5, 81, 92, 117, 132, 136, 138, 144n5
fasting, 50, 51, 53, 56, 58
fin-de-siècle, 9
Frazer, Sir James, 4, 67, 144n14

Geertz, Clifford, 7
Gell, Alfred, 99, 128
genocide, 5
ghosts, 10, 15, 18, 28–35, 44n2, 55, 76, 94, 100, 135–136, 138, 142, 144n9
gods/goddess: Çiva, king of the gods, 56; Durga, 97; God/Allah, 1, 2, 5, 10, 18, 27, 30, 33, 37, 55, 58, 64n15, 77, 80, 82, 91, 94, 100, 132, 142, 144n9; godheads, 36; godman, 89; Hindu, 99, 102n20, 103n25, 103n29, 159–160; Kala, 56; Kali, 97; Mahāvijayavāhinī, 155; Mārīcī, 153; Monkey, 30; Morrighan, 3; Nārāyaṇa, 155; Rama, 27; Skanda, 155; warrior gods, 14, 26, 28
Gondo Sudiro, 60
guru, 10, 50, 52–53, 58–59, 151; *guruniyama*, 159

haddith, 8
Hamengkubuwono IX, 61, 62, 64n17
Hamengkubuwono VII, 60
healer, 4, 28, 43, 88, 136
healing, 9, 10, 15, 17, 28, 28, 31–33, 43, 50, 52, 58, 64n7, 72, 76, 80, 99, 107, 109, 114, 120–121, 156
hekura, 17–18, 108–114, 116–123
hell, Chinese, 33
Hindu-Buddhist period, 62
Hinduism, 17, 27, 30, 55, 88–91, 93–96, 99, 102n20, 103n25, 155, 158–161
Hokkien, 14, 25, 28, 44n5
hunting, 10, 13; headhunting, 47; hunters, 77, 78, 144n5

I Fanlalai'an, 18–19, 127–128, 130, 137–139, 142
ilmu kebal, 72–74, 76, 78
incantation, 11, 12, 19, 33, 38, 141, 142, 151–153
insurgency, 16, 91, 98
insurrection, 16, 98
Interfaith Thanksgiving Service, 137
invisibility, 15, 56
invulnerability, 5, 12, 15, 20, 37, 43, 47, 50–51, 56–58, 60, 61, 72, 74. *See also* magic
IPSI (Pencak Silat Association of Indonesia), 48
Irariwë, 18, 122
irrationality, 16, 68, 82–83. *See also* rationality
Islam, 2, 8–10, 11, 14–16, 47–49, 61–63, 71, 77, 80–83, 84n5; modernist, 16; radical, 63. *See also* Muslims

Jambi, 15–16, 68–69, 71–72, 74, 77, 79–83
Java, 3, 13–16, 46–64
jealousy, 17, 80, 122
Jesus, 4, 89; crucified, 18
Jung, Carl, 9

kákahna, 134–135, 141
Kali Yuga, 4
kanaimà, 13, 122
kanuragan, 15, 47–50, 54, 56–57, 60–63. *See also* rituals
Kapferer, Bruce, 2, 9, 13, 26–28, 98, 151
karma, 40, 42, 43

kebatinan, 54, 64n1, 64n10, 71
keris, 74, 53. *See also* power objects
Khaldun, Ibn, 8
killing, 15, 15, 19, 72, 99, 109, 119–122, 149–150, 153–154, 156–157, 159, 161; killers, 81, 102, 122. *See also* murder
kuppi, 16, 91–93, 95, 99–100

legal process, 3, 10; *adat*, 79; unlawful, 155
Leiden School, 48, 54–55
Levtzion, Nehemi, 8
Lichtenberg figures, 38
liminality, 1, 3–4, 13, 98; liminal ritual, 128, 141. *See also* rituals
LTTE (Liberation Tigers of Tamil Eelam), 16, 91–93, 95–103

magic, 1–20, 25–28, 35, 40, 49, 67–68, 71–72, 79–83, 90–91, 98, 109, 116, 118, 123, 127–128, 131, 133, 135, 141, 144n17, 151–152, 154–155, 161; analogue, 93; Daoist, 33, 38; defensive, 12, 19, 72, 155; ghostly, 33; invocatory, 19, 36, 38, 50, 54, 90; love, 128; and magico-primitivism, 2; thunder, 38; yogic, 19, 156–159. *See also* black magic; invulnerability; sorcery; spiritual protection; war magic
Majapahit, 60
makåhna, 134–135
Malaysia, 8, 27
malice, 5
Malinowski, Bronislaw, 11–12, 68
mantra, 15, 19, 50, 54, 57–58, 61, 64n11, 76–77, 80, 91, 93, 150, 152–157
martial arts, 8, 11, 13; karate, 62; kung fu, 62; *silat*, 13, 48, 74; taekwondo, 62
Mataram dynasty, 60
medicine, 16, 43, 80, 89, 91, 152; Chinese, 31–32; folk, 33;
mental illness, 5, 30
Micronesia, 128, 129, 131–133, 135, 144n9, 144n12
military, 5, 7, 18, 19, 40, 61, 62, 64n17, 81, 98–100, 103n26, 127, 131, 138, 149–150, 152–153, 159–161
misfortune, 3, 5, 10, 12, 114, 118, 136–137; Kala Bendu, 55
Morris, Brian, 7
Muhammad, the Prophet, 8, 82

murder, 9-10, 20, 136, 138, 154, 157. *See also* killing
Muslims, 8, 48-49, 61-83, 71, 80. *See also* Islam
mysticism, 2, 9, 12, 15, 16, 55, 58-59, 64n1, 67, 84n5, 88-89, 128, 142, 144n17

Nazis, 4
necromancer, 10
New Age, 4, 17, 130
non-violence, 149, 154, 159, 161. *See also* violence
numinous, the, 7

occult, the, 4, 7, 10, 19-21, 31, 68, 81, 84n1; economies, 4
occulturation, 144n17
occupation, 18, 20, 101n3, 132, 141. *See also* colonialism
oracles, 14
organization, 5, 7-8, 20, 48, 61-62, 98, 137; factory, 5
or leng, 34-36
Orientalism, 8, 10
Otto, Rudolph, 7, 9

Papua New Guinea, 3, 12
Patriot Act, 7
peace, 15, 40, 43, 55, 101n3, 135, 151, 154
performance, 1-3, 9-11, 14, 20-21, 25, 27, 29, 31, 36-38, 40, 43, 81, 101n7, 128, 137, 138, 140-142, 144n7, 144n17, 150, 157
permission, 134, 136
pharmakon, 9
phenomenology, 2, 7, 68, 83
plague, 33
poison, 9, 10, 13, 15, 17, 20, 59, 77, 118, 135
politics, 3, 5, 10, 12-16, 20, 48, 60-63, 68-69, 71, 77, 83, 95, 127, 137
Polynesia, 3, 130, 134
Ponorogo, 61
possession, 4, 10, 14, 16, 27, 30, 40, 50, 51, 62, 78, 90, 121, 127; spirit-possession, 14, 16, 26, 51, 74, 78. *See also* body; trance
postmodernism, 9, 68
power objects, 10, 16, 18-19, 34, 38, 40, 90, 93, 99-100, 133-134, 152-153;

relics, 136; skulls, 18, 19, 132, 134-135, 141-142, 144n12, 153, 156; spirit-power, 14, 34-35, 37-38, 132. *See also keris*
prayer, 26, 56, 58-59, 99, 127-128, 136; *dunga*, 50; Hindu, 94; in Islam, 8, 11, 52
prejudice, 4, 90, 107
prestige, 17, 122. *See also* status
priests, 5, 18, 134, 136-137, 142; Jesuit, 134; priest-chief, 3, 136; warrior, 10
protection, 11, 12, 16, 62, 72, 90, 93, 136; against animals, 15, 58-59, 72; and rites of, 16-17, 93, 100; spiritual, 5, 134; votive, 2, 88. *See also* magic, defensive; spiritual protection
Protestant attitudes, 8
psychology, 17; depth, 9; of instrumental rationality, 17, 99

rasa, 50-51, 54
rationality, 4, 20, 99, 151; enchanted, 133; instrumental, 17, 99-100; of Islam, 8; scientific, 67-68. *See also* irrationality
re-enchantment, 3-4, 18, 98, 128, 130, 137, 141-142. *See also* enchantment; disenchantment
Reid, Anthony, 3
religion, 1-5, 7-14, 18, 20, 31, 49, 63, 96, 101n5, 127, 131, 142, 151, 158-159, 161; ancient Chamorro, 132, 134; Chinese popular, 40; Micronesian, 128, 132; 'primitive', 9-10, 15; tantric, 150; transcendental, 88-89, 91. *See also* warrior religion
remedy, 9, 20
revolution, 7
rituals, 2, 5, 7; 9-14, 15, 18, 20, 26-27, 30, 33, 48, 58-62, 64n14, 76, 78, 90, 93-98, 117-119, 121-122, 128, 142, 150, 152-157; initiation, 33, 47, 49, 52-53, 56-57; Islamic, 8; *nuo*, 29; ordeals, 13, theater, 14-15, 26-28, 31, 40, 43. *See also kanuragan*; liminality
ruwatan, 56-57, 60

sacrifice, 31, 40, 42-43, 91-92, 94-95, 98, 122, 159, 161
Satan, 10, 77, 80, 108, 137. *See also* devil, the
savage, 4, 9, 11, 108; mind, 20

scarification, 10, 13
scriptures, 7, 19, 150, 152, 158
secrecy, 15, 38, 47–49, 63, 74, 95, 99, 101n3, 122, 136–137, 141, 157
secret societies, 10, 12, 14
secularism, 5, 15, 32, 48–49, 62–63, 100; materialism, 16
semiotics, 2
sex, 51, 88, 137
shamanism, 3, 2, 10–14, 16, 17, 21n2, 21n4, 32–33, 107–110, 113–124, 134, 151; dark, 2–3; duality of, 72; *dukun*, 74; female, 32, *shapori*, 17–18, 109–110, 112–114, 116–123
sickness, 1, 3, 10, 15, 17, 32, 42, 52, 116–120, 123, 136
Singapore, 3, 14, 25, 28–30, 36, 39–43
slametan, 59
sociology, 3, 9; of religion, 2
soldiers, 11, 15, 19, 33, 61–62, 74, 99–100, 103n26, 103n28, 133–134, 142, 155–156; spirit-soldiers, 33, 38
sorcery, 2–5, 8–13, 15–17, 26, 32, 63, 67, 84, 107–109, 122–123, 127–128, 134, 142, 154; assault, 1–2, 20, 107, 123; Ōka sorcery, 17, 116, 118, 122–123; sorcerer-physicians, 31, 33; sorcery-witchcraft, 10. *See also* magic
souls, 18, 31, 108; *batin*, 59; mastery of, 2, 12; multiple, 117; soul-eating, 109, 121; theft of, 118–119
Southeast Asia, 3, 11–12, 14, 25, 69, 131, 136, 144n14, 150
Spanish, the, 18, 129–131, 134–136, 138, 141–144
spells, 1, 3, 11, 32, 33, 38, 50, 52, 54, 72, 77, 80, 89, 118, 122, 127–128, 134, 141, 150, 153–156, 158; death, 3, 141
Spencer, Herbert, 4
spirit-medium, 14, 21n2, 25–27, 29–30, 33
spirits, 2, 10, 14–15, 18, 29–33, 35, 38, 44n2, 49, 54–55, 61, 64n2, 74, 76–81, 89, 93, 102n15, 108–110, 113–114, 121–122, 132, 135–136, 141–142, 144n9, 144n14
spiritual protection, 5. *See also* magic, defensive; protection
Spiro, Melford, 7
Sri Lanka, 3, 14, 16, 90, 92–93, 95–96, 98, 100, 103n23, 150
St. Leonard's Parish Church, 5, 6

stage magic, 4
status, 10, 114; existential, 117. *See also* prestige
stress, 5, 158
structuralist, 7
subjectivity, 3, 9, 12, 37, 152, 158; intersubjective, 3, 114
Sufism, 8–10, 12, 15, 48, 51, 55, 57, 59, 61–63, 84n5
Suharto, 15, 62–64
suicide attacks, 2, 99–100; suicide bombers, 3
Sumatra, 3, 14–15, 67–70, 80, 84n2, 121
summoning, 10, 13, 19, 33, 38, 114, 119, 141, 152, 154
supernatural, the, 1, 7–8, 10–12, 15–18, 20, 21n3, 26, 32, 67, 71–72, 74, 76, 78–81, 83–84, 91, 100, 121, 128, 144n9, 161
supplication, 8, 10, 103n27, 142
syukuran, 59

talisman, 1, 19, 35, 38–39, 92, 136, 152–153
Tambiah, Stanley J., 7
Tamil Tigers, 16, 88–103
tangki, 3, 15, 25–31, 33–34, 36–43
taotao mo'na, 18, 132–133, 135–136, 140–142, 144n14
tattoo, 10, 13
terror, 2, 13–14, 16
terrorism, 3, 5, 7, 14, 16
theater, 14, 15, 26, 31, 40, 43, 96
thunder, 34–35; magic, 38; Yaru, 112
Tiangong, 33
Tjindéamoh Tjindekémbar, 60
torture, 4, 92, 99
tradition, 3–4, 7–8, 15, 26–29, 31, 33, 38, 48–49, 57, 62, 68–69, 74, 77, 80–81, 83, 90, 98, 123, 130, 137, 149–151, 153, 156–158
trance, 10, 13–14, 18, 20, 25, 29–30, 57, 64n14, 75, 78, 90, 97, 114, 120–121. *See also* possession
transmission, 15, 49–51, 57–58, 76, 157
trickster, 4
Trobriands, 11, 48, 99
Trotsky, Leon, 7
Turner, Bryan, 8
Turner, Edith, 21n4
Tylor, Sir Edward, 4, 67

values, 30, 37, 48–49, 62, 92, 96
VE Day, 5, 6
vengeance, 17, 109, 121–122
victim, 9, 12–13, 17, 20, 29, 57, 116, 118–122, 136
victory, 5, 6, 154, 159
violence, 1–3, 5, 9, 11, 14, 17, 19, 33, 48, 90, 107–108, 131, 150, 159–160; self-inflicted, 37. See also non-violence

Wagner, Roy, 112
war, 1–2, 13–14, 17, 19, 34, 49, 55, 61–62, 64n17, 98–99, 118, 131; Buddhist, 19, 159, 161; definitions of, 2, 5, 7; Indonesian anti-colonial (1945–1949), 15, 48; just, 19, 150–151, 158, 161; LTTE, 92; of maneuver, 7; permanent, 7; Spanish-Chamorro, 18, 133–137, 144n8, 150–152, 154; on terror, 5; virtual, 26
warfare, 1, 3, 5, 7, 11, 13, 15, 18, 48, 50, 55, 60–62, 64n1, 108, 123, 134, 136, 149, 151, 160–161; Buddhist, 150; ancient Chamorro, 133, 135; defensive, 161; enlightened, 156; intra-shamanic, 114; psychological, 136; spirit, 14, 25; supernatural, 17, 121; virtual, 2; Yanomami, 122

war magic, 1–5, 7, 9–15, 17–20, 25–29, 31, 33, 37, 40, 43, 45, 48, 49, 63, 100, 116, 118, 127–128, 133, 135–137, 141–142, 149–161. See also magic
war magician, 2, 10; Kanukubusi, 11
warrior religion, 1–3, 5, 8–12, 15, 18, 20, 49, 63, 127–128, 136
war sorcery, 5, 12, 118, 15
Whitehead, Neil L., 2, 9, 13, 122
witch, 10, 12. See also Evans-Pritchard
witchcraft, 4–5, 10, 11–12, 17, 24, 33, 67, 84n1, 108–108, 110, 120, 123. See also Evans-Pritchard
wizard, 10, 31
World War I, 5, 7
World War II, 4, 5, 7

Yanomami, 3, 14, 17–18, 108–113, 115–118, 120–124
Yellow Emperor, 32

Zande, 12. See also Azande

www.ingramcontent.com/pod-product-compliance
Lightning Source LLC
Chambersburg PA
CBHW072157100526
44589CB00015B/2261